MORNING GLORY

MORNING GLORY

A History of
British Breakfast Television

by IAN JONES

with illustrations

by GRAHAM KIBBLE-WHITE

KELLY PUBLICATIONS
2004

First published by
KELLY PUBLICATIONS
6 Redlands, Tiverton, Devon EX16 4DH UK
2004

ISBN 1 903053 20 X

Contents

Acknowledgements

Heartfelt thanks are due to all those who consented to be interviewed for this book: Michael Atwell, Carol Barnes, Greg Dyke, Ed Forsdick, Paddy Haycocks, Mike Hollingsworth, Lis Howell, David Lloyd, Peter McHugh, Ron Neil, Nick Owen, Richard Porter, Nick Ross, John Stapleton, Nicholas Witchell and Ruth Wrigley.

For their continued interest and kind words I'd also like to extend my gratitude to Andrew Collins, Len and Lynda Kelly, Jane Redfern and Ian Tomkinson. My mum, dad, and sister Becky deserve praise for their sustained patience and enthusiasm.

Above all, I'd like to thank four people without whom not one word of this text would have been possible to write: Chris Hughes, Steve Williams, Jack Kibble-White and Graham Kibble-White. Both Steve and Chris contributed innumerable anecdotes and recollections that were remarkable in their detail, besides casting an eye over the finished manuscript and offering up a host of thoughtful suggestions. Jack proved a vital source of motivation throughout the book's various stages, and then combed through the final work with a masterful thoroughness. Graham was responsible for commissioning the original on-line version of MORNING GLORY that appeared on *www.offthetelly.co.uk*, and has watched over this project from start to end with unwavering benevolence. I'm indebted to him for his warmth, assistance, and especially for the wonderful cover design and the series of fluent, witty illustrations he drew to accompany the text.

All four of these people displayed tireless and inspirational encouragement right from day one, and their advice and support have been vast and unceasing. This book is dedicated to them.

ONE

"The last new thing in television"

"This is BBC1. In a few moments it'll be...*Breakfast Time*."

As the familiar image of the swirling BBC globe faded, along with the voice of the continuity announcer, the TV screen filled with a shot of the sun rising slowly over London's Tower Bridge. A pleasant, chiming tune began to ring out, and early morning traffic could be glimpsed making its way across the River Thames. After a minute or so, the music swelled, the picture faded and a brightly segmented motif appeared confirming that this was indeed the start of the BBC's new breakfast programme.

But what came next was a complete surprise. Cameras revealed that the traditionally rather staid current affairs complex at the BBC's Lime Grove studios had been transformed into a lush ensemble of deep red leather sofas, lattice-work wall panelling and calm colour schemes. There wasn't a desk in sight; instead, small tables boasted tea- and coffee-making facilities. Nothing like this had ever been seen on British TV before.

A familiar face loomed into view. "It's 6.30am, Monday 17 January 1983," he began. Decked out in an fetching pair of slacks and cosy pullover, Frank Bough was undertaking the awesome task of introducing viewers to the unknown and eerie world of breakfast television. "You're watching the first edition of BBC Television's *Breakfast Time*," he continued, "Britain's first ever regular early morning television programme. A very good morning to you all."

Almost in an instant, the shock of the new was replaced with the allure of the safe and the reassuring. A relaxed and inviting atmosphere was conjured up through Bough's wise salutation, and it was echoed in the faces of the two younger personalities, Selina Scott and Nick Ross, sitting alongside him. They made it seem perfectly natural to have your television set switched on first thing in the morning. Watching at home, you felt this was a place you were happy to be.

Then, two weeks later, a rival breakfast service began. Against a maelstrom of hype and high promises, ITV's own early morning programme TV-am took to the air on Tuesday 1 February at 6am. It had already established itself in the public consciousness through relentless promotion of its star presenters and its famous eggcup motif. Now it heralded its debut broadcast with a stunning title sequence involving the crew of HMS Hermes and thousands of volunteers on Bristol Downs spelling out the words 'Good Morning Britain'.

A dapper David Frost ponderously extols a bleary nation to join him for a spot of breakfast

The cameras came up on a set comprising a collection of paisley sofas, armchairs, wicker tables and a hefty jug of orange juice. An immaculately turned out David Frost greeted viewers with the immortal words, "Hello, good morning and welcome to a new studio, a new news network and a new national network!" Perched alongside him were fellow small screen luminaries Michael Parkinson, Anna Ford and Angela Rippon. From within this rarefied tableau, Frost and co declared their intention to bring elucidation to the country now that they had, "at last, what we always wanted: you".

Robert Kee, the last remaining presenter making up what the press had dubbed breakfast TV's 'Famous Five', reminded viewers, "In case you haven't noticed, and I don't really see how you could help it, television history is being made at this very moment." Angela Rippon was even more effusive: "We do hope that you're going to stay tuned to us, not just for this morning's programmes, but every morning, every day of the week, at least for the next eight years. Good morning Britain!"

Here were two competing breakfast programmes, two very contrasting styles and approaches, and two very risky and unique experiments in television innovation. Yet, the arrival of breakfast TV in Britain approached the status of a national event. Across the country, people reportedly stayed at home in order to watch the first editions of both *Breakfast Time* and TV-am to their ends, and witness the moment when their TV landscape changed forever.

In the words of Ron Neil, the creator of *Breakfast Time*: "It's the last new thing in television. There's nowhere else; from now on, it's downhill."

British breakfast television was always going to be a gamble. No one knew what would work and what people would watch. But it was also a very public gamble. In a country where TV screens had always been empty first thing in the morning, the arrival of something as new and out of the ordinary as breakfast television was never going to be a dull affair. A population, long domesticated into eating toast and cereal in the sole company of their radio sets, was now to be faced with the rude intrusion of pictures as well. It was unlikely that such a conspicuous and alien presence would be granted a permanent place at the nation's breakfast table without some sort of struggle.

Yet, at the start of the 1980s, breakfast television was the one issue that obsessed the UK TV industry. From the highest echelons of management, through to programme-makers and presenters, no part of the business seemed untouched by speculation and curiosity about this strange new kind of broadcasting. It was a level of interest all the more remarkable for having emerged almost overnight after decades of scepticism towards the whole idea of running any kind of TV first thing in the morning.

Since television was first launched in Britain in 1936, few within the media establishment had ever seriously countenanced the idea of breakfast programmes. For a start, it was too costly – only a fool would throw money away transmitting at such an anti-social hour. It was considered too problematic: a host of awkward union negotiations and staffing issues were bound to be involved, which would invariably take forever to settle. Cultural snobbery was a third factor: breakfast TV was thought simply too down-market for the discerning British viewer. Above all, it was a genre with roots in the United States, which meant – to those reared on fiercely homegrown and patriotic sentiments, of which there were many – it was simply out of the question.

Breakfast TV had existed in the US since 14 January 1952, when the NBC network launched its groundbreaking *Today* programme, the world's first real breakfast show. Though essentially a straight news service, *Today* had engineered a celebrated mix of authority and eccentricity by balancing heavyweight reportage with elaborate gimmicks that quickly became national obsessions. In its early years, the sometimes-portentous features would be interspersed by appearances from one of the *'Today* Girls'. This roster of glamorous females initially did little other than take it in turns to sit in the studio and pout at the camera. Later, however, some of them were able to shake off the beauty queen tag and graduate to the rank of official co-host. There was also the famous in-house performing chimpanzee J. Fred Muggs, an utterly bizarre but hugely popular idea that developed out of a desire to attract younger viewers and family audiences.

Neither the 'Girls' nor J. Fred survived on-screen long into the 1960s, but *Today*'s legacy and influence was so great that it was able to monopolise breakfast television for 23 years, seeing off a number of short-lived services from the rival CBS network, and making stars of people like Dave Garroway, Barbara Walters and Hugh Downs.

However, its dominance came to an abrupt end in 1975, when ABC launched *Good Morning America*. This programme was a major departure, being produced, not within a news division, as was tradition, but in an entertainment department. It swapped the usual formal studio set of desks and chairs for sofas and the feel of a living room, and indulged in shameless show biz and celebrity antics alongside the usual news and features. *Good Morning America* turned breakfast TV conventions upside down, and though ratings were low to begin with, it soon capitalised on its notoriety to evolve into a very striking and surprisingly energetic service. Come the start of the early 1980s, its ballooning popularity meant that NBC's *Today* had, for the first time, fallen behind in the ratings.

All of this had prompted mild interest and a great deal of bemusement amongst the elder statesmen of British television who, by and large, continued to peer down their noses at what they saw as the ultimate embodiment of trashy, offensive broadcasting. But even they had not been able to keep early morning TV screens in the UK entirely blank. Back in April and May 1977, Yorkshire Television had mounted an experimental breakfast service, solely for viewers in their own region, entitled *Good Morning Calendar*. It was a decidedly shoestring effort, lasting nine weeks, running between just 8.30 and 9.30am, and offering only a short news bulletin, cheap cartoons and the US drama *Peyton Place*.

Unsurprisingly, given Yorkshire TV's cautious expenditure and resolutely low expectations, barely anyone tuned in. The uninspiring line-up of programmes and curious transmission time (it hit the air when most people were already out at work or school) seemed only to confirm the majority view that breakfast TV was indeed a folly. The subject was off the agenda once again.

Just a few years later, however, breakfast television mania was rampant, thanks to a most unlikely source: the otherwise uninspiring and charmless business of the ITV franchise round. This was a ritual that all the broadcasting companies making up the ITV network had to go through every so often, where each had to appear before the Independent Broadcasting Authority (IBA) to argue for their contracts to be extended.

By tradition, this was a cumbersome rubberstamping exercise, though it did give the IBA the chance to throw out companies who, in its view, clearly hadn't been delivering, and so it was never completely predictable. But not even the most open-minded of individuals expected the announcement that came on 24 January 1980. To pretty much universal disbelief, the IBA revealed that the next time all the individual ITV regional franchises came up for renewal, a new breakfast franchise would also be up for grabs.

This was big news. General opinion within the industry had been that nothing new would be on offer: the IBA was not famed for its innovatory credentials. Now, from being the stuff of the occasional pipe dream, breakfast TV suddenly seemed about to become a reality.

This reversal of decades of anti-breakfast television feeling had come about astonishingly quickly. In April 1979, a trio of Thames Television staff, comprising presenter Jonathan Dimbleby and producers David Elstein and Martin Smith, had begun lobbying the IBA to consider the introduction of breakfast TV in Britain. They proposed launching an early morning service, not as an extension of an existing ITV company, but in the form of an entirely new, stand-alone franchise. As identified by writer Michael Leapman in his account of the birth of independent breakfast television, *Treachery: The Power Struggle At TV-am*, their principal motive was to create an opportunity for experienced hands like themselves to explore new ways of packaging news and current affairs while working outside the ITV network.

The IBA's chairwoman, Lady Plowden, wasn't particularly taken with their radical scheme, but other members of the Authority felt differently. As time went on, the prospect of spicing up the normally grim process of franchise renewal with a new, exciting project became increasingly appealing. It would certainly attract publicity. It would show the IBA to be a dynamic, modern organisation, unafraid of change. Plus, if the example of America was anything to go by, it could well draw the attention of some high-class personalities.

Such arguments were voiced strongly by one IBA member in particular: the businessman, Christopher Bland. Realising the benefits of pepping up the routine of reallocation with something unexpected and undoubtedly novel, he lobbied earnestly for the breakfast franchise to be offered, helping to swing round other wavering elements on the Authority.

Ultimately, Lady Plowden gave in, but not without reservations. In that landmark announcement of January 24, she chose her words carefully. On several occasions her text included the phrase, "If a breakfast contract was awarded" – so as to cover the IBA if no suitable bidders came forward. Deliberate weight was also laid on the kind of breakfast service the Authority was looking for. It would run seven days a week, but with the emphasis on news, information and current affairs. Entertainment was definitely not a priority. Applicants were only given until Friday 9 May, a period of less than four months, to send in their proposals.

The peculiar process of the ITV franchise round historically attracted a delicate marriage of highflying accountants and glamorous celebrities. The lure of not only appearing on but also owning a part of a real TV company almost necessitated the formation of some curious alliances. So it was that, largely thanks to the enormous flurry of publicity whipped up by the IBA's January proclamation, the breakfast television franchise caught the separate attentions of David Frost and Peter Jay.

Frost, already a TV host of almost two decades standing, was a veteran at playing the franchise game. In 1967, he had bid and won the right to broadcast the ITV London weekend service with his company, London Weekend Television (LWT). When the organisation almost collapsed, thanks to its lofty programming ideals and lack of money, Frost had jumped ship. Now he was keen to get back in the business of making, as well as presenting, television.

Peter Jay had a different agenda. An ex-Economics editor of the *Times*, former US ambassador and erstwhile presenter of LWT's heavyweight current affairs slot *Weekend World*, he wasn't swayed by visions of bright lights and fame. His ideals were of what he considered an altogether more highbrow stock. In 1975, Jay and *Weekend World* editor John Birt had written a series of articles for the *Times* complaining of what they branded a "bias against understanding" within news and current affairs reporting on British television. Stories were chosen for their visual punch, they contested, with deeper significances and analysis ignored. This fatally undervalued the medium of television, while simultaneously demeaning the profession of newscasting.

Jay and Birt's theories had been quickly lampooned as cerebral nonsense and a recipe for driving viewers away from news programmes, and TV companies out of business. Unbowed, Peter Jay now realised that the breakfast franchise was the ideal opportunity to put his theories to the test. He even coined a neat soundbite to sum up his beliefs: a "mission to explain". But in truth, it was Jay's august contacts and institutional prestige, rather than his earnest proselytising, which most convinced David Frost to approach him to front a joint bid for the breakfast ITV licence. Together, Frost reasoned, his own star status combined with Jay's authority and gravitas would make for a compelling mix.

There wasn't much time. The pair hastily set about wooing both the business community and celebrity circles to come up with a package they believed the IBA could not refuse. Jay's dry expositions were contrasted by Frost's eager promotion of "sexual chemistry", and soon a dazzling line-up of prospective presenters was formed. They managed to convince ITN newsreader, Anna Ford; BBC newsreader, Angela Rippon; experienced broadcaster, Michael Parkinson; investigative journalist Robert Kee; and BBC presenter, Esther Rantzen to all sign up. This was a glittering ensemble indeed and, unusually for British television, it was decided that all these stars would also own considerable shares in the company.

Others joined the team on the management side, including noted LWT executive Nick Elliott, and a dash of politics came in the shape of former government minister turned business consultant, Dick Marsh. Michael Deakin, Frost's long-time associate, helped secure the money, including a huge loan from Barclays Merchant Bank. This was combined with stock from various investors, chief of whom were Conservative MP Jonathan Aitken, whom Deakin knew from past association with Yorkshire TV, and his businessman cousin, Timothy Aitken, who ended up with the largest stake in the company. Not all of these names were disclosed to the press as many were still employed by rival broadcasters. The final piece of the jigsaw fell into place when the consortium agreed to adopt the name of TV-am.

Despite the tight deadline, they weren't alone in bidding for the breakfast licence – quite the opposite. Just as the novelty and potential of the contract had appealed to Frost and Jay, so others had rushed to throw their hats into the ring. In all, eight groups ended up applying for the franchise, and hours had clearly gone into dreaming up imaginative, memorable names.

Lining up alongside TV-am were AM-TV, AMT, Daybreak TV, Daytime TV, Morning TV and Good Morning TV. Proposals ranged from the hugely ambitious to the downright far-fetched. Daybreak TV seemed a strong contender, thanks to having both existing ITV company ATV and the *Express* Newspapers as backers. Good Morning TV pitched a Saturday show recorded in front of a studio audience presented "by an exuberant character emphasising the richness of life", reflecting, some argued, the presence of entertainment figures Ned Sherrin and Tim Rice on the company's board. Morning Television boasted influential BBC presenter David Dimbleby as a prospective host, while AMT proposed a 'good news' spot and 'humour columnists', plus a 'School Report' feature where children would be invited to send in write-ups of their own classrooms.

Completing the list of bidders was ITV's existing news provider, ITN, who promised the decidedly futuristic sounding 'computerized news'. In the end, however, thanks mostly to a carefully rehearsed performance and self-conscious display of swagger at the IBA interview on 11 December 1980 (tutored by John Birt), the TV-am consortium won the contract. Their success was made public on Sunday 28 December 1980, as was the somewhat less exciting news that they wouldn't actually be allowed on air until 1983, so as not to overshadow the start of Channel 4 in November 1982. Regardless, Frost and his team commemorated their achievement in lavish style, toasting what they were certain would be a profitable, invincible future.

Their celebrations were short-lived. A mere 24 hours later, the battle was joined as, from out of nowhere, the BBC announced that it, too, intended to launch its own breakfast programme. Astonishment engulfed the television industry. Was this the same BBC who had spent much of the previous 12 months, and for that matter the past decade, moaning about its impoverished condition? How could it possibly afford, let alone justify, an extra three hours of broadcasting each morning?

It was behaviour that took many, including the IBA, completely by surprise. Breakfast TV was the sort of thing that was all very well for the commercial network to get involved in – but a public service broadcaster, paid for by the viewers themselves? Even the then Conservative Home Secretary, William Whitelaw, was moved to warn BBC Chairman George Howard, "Your enemies will use it against you."

But Howard remained resolute and his competitive spirit was matched by that of other BBC management supremos, such as Aubrey Singer, Director of Radio. Their argument was that the BBC would be utterly foolish to ignore the prospect of such a major expansion in commercial television. After all, the Corporation had fatally underestimated the appeal of ITV when it launched in 1955. Faced with an equally substantial challenge, it shouldn't be left behind a second time.

There was much unease, however, over what form the service should take, and opinion was divided right up to Director-General Ian Trethowan. Should their breakfast television be openly highbrow and sober, like BBC Radio 4's acclaimed *Today* programme – or an overtly light-hearted, entertaining package, perhaps emulating the style recently pioneered by *Good Morning America*? The BBC also had an experiment, of sorts, to draw upon. This was the fleeting 'Radiovision' service, tried for a short period in 1980. Radio Scotland's *Good Morning Scotland* programme was simulcasted on BBC TV Scotland by putting cameras in the radio studio. Yet, just had been the case with their rivals ITV, it was not deemed a success, appearing dull and lifeless and hampered by technical problems.

The then Managing Director of Television, Alasdair Milne, recalled, "We had a number of options – should we leave it to [ITV], should we compete, or should we find some halfway house? There was no extra money and no question of suggesting to the government a supplement to the licence fee... I was sure myself that the morning hours were going to be very important to us in the future, particularly from the news point of view... If we left ITV a free start in the morning, it seemed possible that, in due course, people would automatically start with the commercial channel for their morning news and stay with it for the rest of the day."

Ultimately, the Corporation hierarchy decided to commit themselves, but rather than rush into doing anything they'd come to regret, they left the exact composition and structure of the new programme to be settled at a later time. They also made a point of waiting for the launch date of TV-am to be confirmed, and then began planning to ensure that their own service would take to the air first. Simple and sneaky to be sure, but such a calculated move would turn out to be a masterstroke.

A reshuffle elevated Alasdair Milne to the post of BBC Director-General, and Aubrey Singer to Managing Director of Television. Both believed strongly in making breakfast TV a critical and commercial success, and were helped in their early stages of planning by Michael Checkland, Director of Resources, who made a number of organisational savings to ensure the new service had a viable budget. Their most important collective act, however, was to bring in Ron Neil to oversee the launch of the programme. It's not an overstatement to claim that his appointment on 11 May 1982 marked the true birth of British breakfast television.

Neil, a Scottish current affairs producer, masterminded everything that came together to create the programme that would eventually be named *Breakfast Time*. "It was very much the context that if ITV was going to be there with a breakfast programme, the BBC must," he recalls today. "You couldn't have ITV screens lit up in the morning and the BBC not. So, I was left in no doubt that I had to get *Breakfast Time* on the air, and I was also left in no doubt that I had to get it on the air *first*. Looking back on it now, it was amazing – and obviously people more senior than me had quite strong ideas about who should present it and what it should be like, but, bless them, they gave me a completely free hand."

The first thing Neil oversaw was the conversion of the BBC current affairs studios at Lime Grove in West London into a topical programmes unit that would house not just *Breakfast Time* but existing programmes *Nationwide* and *Newsnight*. "Through the summer [I sat] in a strange room in Lime Grove, which was cordoned off with desks and things. There wasn't any proper production centre, we had to build one," he continues. "Then we just started the process of recruiting people, sitting round and brainstorming as to what a breakfast television programme might look like." Neil endorsed the installation of a hi-tech newsroom computer and software packages. He also mapped out an effective production schedule and plotted how, once on air, each programme would be carefully prepared round the clock, from 9pm the previous evening through to transmission time at 6.30am.

Above all, Ron Neil was responsible for constructing a workable and enduring breakfast television programme format. With hindsight, his decision appears beautifully straightforward: to go for an approachable, light-hearted template rather than one that was haughty and intense – or, as he described it, the *Mirror* over the *Guardian* or the *Times*.

"I'd worked for many years on [the early evening magazine programme] *Nationwide*," he explains, "and *Nationwide* had taught me an awful lot about what an audience wants and what an audience likes, so I think I had an understanding of what made popular current affairs television. And I was pretty certain that at that time in the morning people did not want to be machine-gunned with non-stop news and information. News should play a very important part of it, but the popular feature content should have a high part to play as well." American breakfast TV also had a crucial influence. "Our partners at that time were NBC," Neil continues, "so we went and spent some time watching their *Today* programme. We took all that into our thinking."

Neil assembled a team of experienced staff to turn his plans into reality, headed up by three insightful senior producers: Tim Orchard, Colin Stanbridge, and Mike Hollingsworth. Hollingsworth, formerly News and Current Affairs editor at Central TV, had already approached David Frost with a view to becoming involved in TV-am, but found his views on reporting and journalism at odds with Peter Jay. Now he joined his new BBC colleagues in the eager preparation of what he chooses to remember today as the "new frontier of television".

Over at TV-am, Peter Jay responded to the looming BBC opposition by deliberately ignoring the example of US breakfast telly and sticking doggedly to his faith in hard news. Yet, almost immediately, his efforts to get his fledgling station off the ground ran into problems.

Firstly, there was the huge cost of building the company's HQ and studios. Initially these were to be at Wandsworth, based at an existing complex owned by businessman Keith Ewart, but this idea was dropped after a failure to resolve differences over who would actually own the new properties. Instead, a site overlooking Regent's Canal at Camden Lock in north London was chosen.

To develop the location, a starting budget of just under £5m was allocated – twice what would have been needed to convert Ewart's property. The amount quickly rose, however, as the eye-catching and controversial design by architect Terry Farrell took shape. Interior walkways and huge tropical plants created a sense of the surreal, while the building's grounds boasted a luxury canal boat to be used for meetings, plus a proper two-storey house for visiting guests. Comical giant eggcups were added to the roof. Finally, mammoth glass walls were constructed to allow everyone to see what everyone else was doing. This was supposed to break down psychological barriers between the various levels of TV-am management – but, in reality, it rid the offices of any privacy and began to foster creeping paranoia.

To offset this opulence, corners were cut on the technological side. All the station's editing machines were put in one room, making for disorganized, noisy compiling of reports. Jay suffered a loss of personnel when both Esther Rantzen and Nick Elliott dropped out. Ironically, this didn't help resolve another thorny problem: the exact delegation of responsibilities within the company. There was perpetual confusion over how Michael Deakin, appointed Director of Programmes, should and could interpret Jay's "mission to explain". This wasn't helped by a bewildering chain of command that unravelled beneath Jay, involving Managing Editor Clive Jones, News editor Bob Hunter, Editor-in-chief Hilary Lawson, Features editor Kevin Sim, plus Deakin. Who was in charge of whom? Nobody was surprised when competition over how resources should be divvied up between news or features lead to rivalry between Hunter and Deakin – and Hunter quit just before the station went on air.

Meanwhile the remaining presenters, the so-called Famous Five, were doing their best to nurture a public face for TV-am. They had just one office between them and were forced to share three desks, though Michael Parkinson had been sure to commandeer one solely for himself, leaving the others to squabble over who doubled up with whom.

Parkinson, at least, already had experience of breakfast TV in the shape of *Good Morning Australia*, which he and wife Mary had fronted for a period on Australia's Channel 10. All the same, a TV-am promotional video compiled in 1981 was careful to parade the hosts *en masse* in a chorus of praise. Anna Ford cooed, "TV-am attracted me because it had so many professional television journalists who were used to working in live television," whereas Angela Rippon declared, "So, the audience is quite definitely there. But will they watch us? Why should they, in fact?" Quite so.

None of the problems Jay and his colleagues faced in the run-up to launch were insoluble or terminal. But the seeds of TV-am's traumatic on-screen birth were sown amidst Jay's perception and handling of these crises –

ones which *Breakfast Time*, being an in-house BBC production, never had to confront.

Time and money were being taken up with issues concerning technical matters rather than the all-important programme content. For example, it had been decided that the commercial breaks during TV-am's output would be portioned out to each ITV region rather than co-ordinated nationally. This, it was hoped, would bring more money into the company.

The trouble was that no technology existed at that time to allow a national station to transmit selectively to different regions. Accordingly, a new computer called Protel had to be hurriedly designed and built by GEC-Marconi at great expense to carry out just such a task. But when it came to test the machine in practice, it simply failed to work. More money had to be spent to hire out temporary equipment, and, in the end, Protel would not actually be ready until TV-am had been on screen for several months.

On top of this, a prolonged dispute between the acting union, Equity, and the Institute of Practitioners in Advertising (IPA) had begun. The IPA wanted to pay Equity members less for their work in advertisements on both Channel 4 and TV-am, reasoning that they'd be seen by smaller audiences compared to mainstream ITV. In response, Equity went on strike, limiting the number of adverts available for TV-am to use, and meaning those they could run were largely peopled by anonymous boring businessmen in suits.

It all added up to a very gloomy scenario, and one that increasingly led TV-am's shareholders to question Peter Jay's competence. Jay had retained the roles of both Chairman and Chief Executive of the company, despite previous assurances to the IBA that he would rescind the latter within months of receiving the franchise. From this unusual state of affairs stemmed unceasing confusion and the contagious impression that TV-am was taking to the air in spite of, rather than because of, its creator.

It was up to Jay, for instance, to resolve persistent problems with ITN over who was to be supplying TV-am with its news bulletins. This situation was not made any easier by the fact that TV-am had beaten ITN to win the breakfast franchise, which had left a lot of ill feeling between both organisations. Negotiations were duly held under Jay's instruction, but they repeatedly broke down, and it was only in late 1982 that a rather ragged agreement was reached for TV-am to access material through UPITN, the agency that sold ITN's material abroad. The upshot was a further weakening of Jay's reputation, and TV-am's news reports being amateurishly assembled from various sources rather than one single service.

As the launch date of 1 February 1983 neared, pent-up tensions repeatedly came to the fore. The first live test for the new studio and its equipment was on 31 December 1982 when David Frost hosted a special New Year's Eve programme for Channel 4. Though this passed off relatively smoothly, a month of pilot transmissions in January 1983 were disastrous, culminating in a memorable mid-show walkout by Michael Parkinson.

"The early dummy runs were frightening because it was shambolic," recalls Nick Owen, a Central TV presenter hired to read the sports news. "Apart from the top echelons, there seemed a lot of people with little idea of making TV programmes. A number of people gave up on it even before we went on air." As a joke, one of the pilot editions of the feature *Through The Keyhole* explored the interiors of Michael Deakin's house. When Angela Rippon witnessed the quiz's host, Loyd Grossman, deliberately lampooning her colleague's tastes, she was so appalled that she vowed never to introduce the slot again, either in rehearsal or on air.

Nonetheless, TV-am's front line managed to maintain a confident outward face. A brazen Peter Jay declared of the service: "Put aside any preconceptions and think of it as your popular morning newspaper – on television. The only truly amazing thing is that we got to 1983 without it." Anna Ford claimed, "Breakfast TV will certainly get its morning's worth from me. I'll work extremely hard." Angela Rippon was careful to maintain other engagements alongside her presenting responsibilities, including supervising her Angela Rippon Collection of bed linen. She was also more guarded than her associates. "All the presenters have some say in the running of the company, but we have a highly experienced staff who mesh together like cogs, so you don't stick your spanner in often," she observed. "Only if things went wrong, you might say, Why? And why did I have to be out there when it did?"

That was as close as any of the Famous Five would come to conceding doubts, as breakfast television finally prepared to make its debut on British screens.

TWO

"People just write to say, 'You make me feel so happy'"

After months of meticulous preparation and debates over formats, presenters and even studio furniture, the most crucial factor in the launch of British breakfast television proved to be the simple matter of timing. It might not have been that imaginative, or particularly gentlemanly, but the fact that *Breakfast Time* stole on air two weeks ahead of TV-am was devastatingly significant. It gave the BBC a vital fortnight in which it completely dictated the breakfast television agenda. It meant that *Breakfast Time* won the bulk of the headlines and became a national talking point. Most important of all, those 14 days grace gave the Corporation a chance to iron out any flaws within its own programme to ensure that *Breakfast Time* was at the peak of its game when the opposition arrived. TV-am was reduced to entering the world of breakfast telly, not on its own terms, but on someone else's.

The laid-back ambience that greeted viewers tuning into *Breakfast Time*'s first edition on 17 January 1983 was something the programme's editor, Ron Neil, had deployed to promote a very specific way of reporting the news. "There is a television technique where the presenter tells us that reporter Fred Bloggs has all the details on a story," he explained at the time, "and, in the minute he's allowed, Fred tries to get across all the facts he possibly can, so that they whistle past our ears like bullets with very few actually penetrating the brain. But if you sit down and say, 'You've been following the story, Fred; tell me about it,' it comes across as a relaxed conversation."

To support this, Neil was careful to emphasise that *Breakfast Time*'s look, feel and running order was far from set in stone. "I think it would be very arrogant at this stage to say that we know what people want to watch. For the first six months, frankly, we will be experimenting, until we find out from the response exactly what viewers do want, and adjust accordingly."

In fact, Neil and his team hit upon a neat, workable, popular format right from the start. Rather than tie each day's schedule to fixed times, items were publicised as being within blocks of 15 minutes. This was an idea borrowed from US breakfast TV, and allowed some flexibility should interviews over-run or important news stories break. Each *Breakfast Time* was carved up into these quarter-hour chunks, separated by news bulletins on the hour and half-hour read by former BBC documentary researcher Debbie Rix, plus regional news updates 15 minutes past and to the hour.

The rest of the line-up was a deliberate mix of the lightweight and the substantial. Fitness expert Diana Moran was hired to front 'Getting Britain Fit', an exercise slot scheduled between 6.45 and 7am. Her trademark lurid green leotard won her the tacky but catchy label, 'The Green Goddess', and her workouts turned out to be immensely popular with early risers. As a gimmick, Diana hosted her first week of sessions from a variety of outdoor locations, and the spectacle of slightly bemused but enthusiastic commuters committing themselves to energetic routines was an instant hit.

Back in the studio, Francis Wilson fronted half-hourly weather forecasts in front of his specially designed 'Weather Window'. This giant computer screen used new hi-tech images to render the elements in 3-D colour, in contrast to the rather amateurish quality of the BBC's standard magnetised maps. A trained meteorologist, Wilson had to get up at 3am each morning to call at the Imperial College for his information after the Met Office, feeling snubbed that the BBC weren't using one of its established forecasters, barred him from their premises.

But he wasn't there just to be a weatherman. Another key component of Ron Neil's thinking was that all his presenting team, from Frank Bough and Selina Scott through to secondary faces like Diana Moran and Wilson, should make a point of cultivating rounded, three-dimensional personalities on screen. In particular, they should try to appear approachable and homely, and go against people's preconceptions of news and current affairs being a remote, formal profession. In turn, this would help establish a better rapport with viewers, and a sense of the programme being part of the family.

Wilson was one who particularly seemed to relish this instruction. Right from day one, he took to appearing on air sporting a variety of colourful patterned sweaters or open necked chequered shirts. He also developed a somewhat suave, cheeky, debonair image for himself, and won legions of fans as a result. Wilson's 'Weather Window' even became the site for a few in-jokes, with humorous messages or images displayed at the end of each forecast. When *Breakfast Time* dovetailed into children's holiday programmes, Wilson occasionally introduced them himself, and cartoons such as *Battle Of The Planets* actually began on the 'Window' behind him.

Equally adept at exploiting the programme's relationship with viewers was astrologer Russell Grant. The BBC Director-General, Alasdair Milne, and many of the BBC Governors viewed his horoscope run-down disapprovingly, and, up to the last minute, Ron Neil remained under pressure to replace Grant's slot with a religious 'Thought For The Day'.

Yet, Grant and his voluminous rainbow coloured woolly jumpers – and even woollier predictions – turned out to be another quick success.

"I was dismayed when Ron Neil told me that serious news would be blended with not just show biz but cooking demonstrations and, worst of all, astrology," confides another of the *Breakfast Time* team, Nick Ross. "I was sceptical about how we could move seamlessly from unemployment figures to fashion or from bomb-blast to soufflé – and was downright cynical about some of the New Age stuff. As it happens, Russell Grant was one of the people I liked most when we got going." The general public agreed: within a few weeks, Grant was attracting bumper correspondence. "I get letters by the sackful," he claimed. "Two and a half to three thousand a week. People just write to say, 'You make me feel so happy.'"

Amongst other features greeting viewers during *Breakfast Time*'s first week on air were farming news from Norwich, gardening tips from Plymouth, a daily TV preview and a regular society 'gossip' slot with *Daily Express* columnist Chris Wilson. Special guests were brought in to review the papers, *Grandstand* reporter David Icke presented regular sports news, and an imaginative cookery spot was hosted by trained chef Glynn Christian.

A rotating selection of special correspondents and studio experts were also enlisted to dispense regular advice and opinion. "Almost everyone Ron Neil brought in turned out to be at least competent and often perfectly attuned to the task," recalls Nick Ross. In a slot entitled 'This Is America', Bob Friend, former BBC radio correspondent in New York, presented daily dispatches from the US while sitting in front of a large photograph of the Manhattan skyline at night. Radio One DJ Mike Smith introduced pop music news on Wednesdays, and there were regular appearances from personal finance specialist Alison Mitchell and practicing GP Dr Richard Smith. Both tackled queries sent in by viewers, and provided on-the-spot help through weekly phone-ins.

Behind the scenes, a highly organised and imaginative overhaul had revitalised the entire Lime Grove building to give *Breakfast Time* a sound, solid foundation. A mood of experimentation had been encouraged. "Any new suggestion was examined," Ross remembers. "I think I inspired the idea of an on-screen clock and lobbied hard for us to find a way to make it work. But no doubt others will say they had the notion first – whatever the truth of that, Ron Neil was game to try it."

At the heart of operations was an advanced newsroom computer, purposely installed to collate stories overnight. Neil had handed his colleague, Tam Fry, responsibility for choosing technology most suited to complement *Breakfast Time*'s image on-screen. Fry had applied for and won a government grant of £25,000 to purchase various equipment and software from the manufacturers Hewlett Packard, which in turn had enabled BBC Television Computer Services to develop its inaugural computerised newsroom system.

Fry also deployed Britain's first ever Paintbox electronic graphics package. "Paintbox was the first leap into graphics that wasn't a pencil and a crayon and a bit of paper," explains Neil. "We got it delivered in time for the first show. It was the first time electronic graphics had been used in Britain. It allowed us to do things like [the 'Weather Window'] with Francis that had not been done before. It was a revolution."

Holding everything together, regardless of guests, gizmos and on-screen paraphernalia, were *Breakfast Time*'s three main hosts: long time BBC face Frank Bough (formerly of *Nationwide* and *Grandstand*), Selina Scott (an ex-ITN newsreader) and established BBC presenter Nick Ross. This was an inspired mix of cosiness, glamour and familiarity that operated extraordinarily well from the off.

Bough had known Ron Neil for years and had worked closely with him when he was an editor on *Nationwide*. "He has always had that gift," Bough later wrote, "that only a few of the very best football managers have – that of getting you to play for him and his team." After reportedly considering and rejecting several high-profile candidates including Terry Wogan, Jimmy Young, Noel Edmonds and Russell Harty, Neil sent Bough a speculative letter in August 1982. It took its inspiration from the last meal the pair had enjoyed together, during which Bough had semi-humorously chided his colleague over the fact he'd yet to be offered the job of *Breakfast Time* host. The letter read, in its entirety, "Last time we had dinner. Can we now have lunch? To talk about breakfast."

"Frank was very very popular. In those days he was an 'Uncle Frank' figure to audiences," remembers Neil, "and he was used to presenting three hours of live television every week on *Grandstand*. I wanted to have that expertise. I didn't want somebody who'd only ever done a ten-minute news bulletin suddenly to be confronted with conducting a three-hour live programme. In front of the camera, I felt it was important to have somebody who could drive and motor for three hours. Selina hadn't that experience of course, but I just thought that Frank and Selina would be a good combination."

In retrospect, Bough and Scott made for an unlikely couple. The unusually large age difference between them sometimes left the former looking like a sort of over-protective father towards his younger, naïve starlet. But on the wall of the pair's *Breakfast Time* office a poster read, "Today is the tomorrow that worried you yesterday – and all's well," and a similar plucky spirit infected their relationship on camera.

After arriving for one rehearsal sporting an informal pullover, Ron Neil had insisted Bough adopt the look as a permanent on-screen image. This inspired suggestion later, allegedly, drew ire from Michael Parkinson about not dressing properly for an audience, but summed up the entire ethos of *Breakfast Time*, neatly emphasising its differences from traditional BBC news presentation.

Bough was also the absolute fulcrum of the entire operation. In Nick Ross's opinion, he was the, "on-screen lynchpin. None of us had remotely the experience of long, unscripted slabs of live TV that Frank had from his sports broadcasting. He brought a sense of serenity and reassurance. His unruffled composure made us feel this had all been done before, and on the first morning, as the last minutes ticked down to our opening transmission, when hearts were thumping and nerves were jangling, he clapped his hands and – addressing the producers and the technicians as much as Selina or me – gently and firmly said, 'Calm down.' We did."

"Ron's choice of Selina Scott was superb," Ross continues. "She was a huge attraction, the one member of our team who had the glamour to rival the celebs of TV-am, and, although she was never a consummate broadcaster who could stir the nation's heart like Jill Dando later did, she could stir the nation's loins and thrill the fashion writers and the gossip columnists. She was that rare commodity: a star."

In fact, Selina Scott wasn't the BBC's first preference. That honour went to another young female journalist named Anne Diamond, who was pencilled in for a place on the red sofas until the BBC posted her to *Nationwide* instead. "The strength of the programme was the relationship between Frank and Selina," affirms *Breakfast Time* producer Mike Hollingsworth today. "Selina was very down to earth. In the viewers' eyes she was girl-next-door fresh. And there was Uncle Frank who was very avuncular and comfortable, and a safe pair of hands."

"I had a background in news and current affairs," adds Nick Ross, "and was then doing a good deal of live broadcasting, chairing *Man Alive* debates on BBC2 and just starting *Crimewatch* on BBC1. Ron Neil presumably saw me as a young counterweight to Frank Bough."

Neil had been determined that *Breakfast Time*'s debut would make a strong impact, and sure enough, guests included leader of the Labour Party, Michael Foot, veteran entertainer Harry Secombe and US breakfast TV legend Barbara Walters. In the dying minutes of the programme, the entire team gathered around the sofas to celebrate with a huge bottle of champagne. The sight of Frank Bough, kitted out in shirt, tie and inoffensive brown jumper, struggling to pour from a gigantic vessel of bubbly into tiny BBC glasses, remains an iconic image of 1980s television.

All the same, initial press response was sceptical. The *Sunday Express* had warned of "The end of civilised life as we know it. The top of the morning, that most private time of day, is now to be invaded." A week into

*Frank Bough wields the BBC champagne
to toast a fine victory – a very fine victory*

the programme's existence the *Observer* had concluded, "*Breakfast Time*
is cheerful, light and professional. It may well turn out to be the least
worst breakfast TV in the world." The *Daily Telegraph* remained
particularly outspoken: "The most fatuous, mind-eroding, nerve-jangling
and, above all, the most completely superfluous and unwanted innovation
television has inflicted on the people of this country so far... What on
earth can anybody who is still in his right mind do to stem this menticidal
deluge and save people from themselves?"

Opinions expressed in *Radio Times* were even more mixed. One
correspondent noted: "Surely the sales of daily papers will be down from
now on. It's such a relaxed, informative show; the evening chat shows on
television will have to have a rethink." Another railed, in reference to
Russell Grant's horoscopes: "I was horrified and dismayed to see that
Breakfast Time has a slot for the occult. This puts BBC-tv on the level of
the sensationalist press; much worse, it is bringing the powers of
darkness at the start of the day right into people's living rooms, instead
of the 'light of the world'."

As far as the *Breakfast Time* team was concerned, such comments paled when set against the jubilant sense of having finally got their programme up and running. Unbeknown to viewers, it had only just made it onto air in time. The trademark sofas only arrived custom-built from Switzerland two days before the first programme. "We'd also had very tricky negotiations with the trade unions," outlines Ron Neil, "because it was the first time we were asking people to work through the night. Negotiations went on right into December. There were points when we'd been doing rehearsals without cameras, because we hadn't got the union agreement to man them. We were rehearsing in a studio where the set hadn't arrived and we couldn't use cameras. It was quite hairy."

Despite only having two weeks to rehearse everything on set, plus an eight-hour emergency Sunday session spent practicing the junctions between the various quarter-hour slots, the months of intensive planning had paid off. Slick co-ordination between presenters and the production team kept mistakes to a minimum and a cosy and inclusive atmosphere was in place from the word go.

Most important of all, at least as far as BBC executives were concerned, was *Breakfast Time*'s performance with audiences. Viewing figures for the 'peak quarter-hour' of 8 to 8.15am (a measurement introduced especially to record ratings for breakfast telly) reached two million during the first week: a commendable achievement. The consensus around the BBC was that the Corporation had scored a memorable and historic victory.

This outcome, recalls Nick Ross, could be "summed up in two words: Ron Neil. The BBC's show was being written off before it started. Everyone knew that TV-am had the most glittering presenters who would draw in the best talent and the key interviewees and a glitzy new, dedicated television centre in Camden Town, and the BBC operation was little more than a spoiler. It's hard to exaggerate just how routinely, in the weeks leading up to transmission, those of us preparing the *Breakfast Time* show felt patronised by the media. But Ron was having none of it. His was a classic flanking operation. He was far more daring – just look at the set, just consider Russell Grant – copying the best elements from chat shows and making TV feel as though it really lived naturally in the kitchen as much as the living room, let alone the library."

"I have to say we studied the market quite well, too," continues Mike Hollingsworth. "We knew that it would be a brash audience, an audience that was waiting to see exciting things happen but not in any length. I think it was just that we didn't take ourselves too seriously."

As for Frank Bough, he described the first few weeks of *Breakfast Time* as, "Like having jet lag without going anywhere... [but] it's not half as tiring when you are winning. Ron Neil has scored a 'bull's-eye'. This is a very happy lot of people."

A fortnight later saw a stream of Fleet Street reporters and illustrious celebrities congregating at London's Camden Lock for the launch of TV-am.

The station's weekday schedule was fixed to run from 6 to 9.15am and began its first day, 1 February 1983, as it meant to go on, with *Daybreak*, an hour of in-depth news and commentary fronted by Robert Kee and junior newsreaders Lynda Berry and Gavin Scott. The programme also included specialist bulletins screened in association with various worthy publications: farming news, read by Barry Wilson, was a joint initiative with *Farmers Weekly*; sports news was read by Nick Owen and Mike Morris in association with *The Sporting Life*; and the loftily entitled 'City Page' was a partnership with the resolutely highbrow journal, *The Economist*.

Intended to be a textbook illustration of Peter Jay's "mission to explain", *Daybreak*'s concern was with facts and information, and nothing else. But the mood changed come 7am when *Good Morning Britain*, which was intended to be the nub of TV-am, began. Here the full Famous Five made their first proper appearance, led by an exuberant if slightly peaky David Frost. The screen oozed power and money, and the cameras struggled, literally, to fit all of the dazzling assembly into one shot. Guests came and went, judgement was passed on events of a topical nature, and everyone made great play of what a privilege it was for viewers to be experiencing such a moment of history.

Unlike *Breakfast Time*, TV-am was a seven days a week operation. Its weekend output was structured a little differently, with transmission time (shorter on Sundays, from just 7 to 9.15am) divided on both days between *Good Morning Britain* hosted by Michael and Mary Parkinson, and the children's programmes *Data Run* and *Rub-A-Dub-Tub*. While the Parkinsons' Saturday show was more self-consciously lightweight than its weekday equivalent, the Sunday version purported to be slightly more analytical, including a review of the papers, arts and book news.

Data Run was a prerecorded show, designed to appeal to 8-14 year olds, hosted by Edwina Laurie (Lulu's younger sister) and a pretend computer called Edwin. Each programme was themed around lists of historical events, keep-fit work-outs, fashions, facts and dates; and its ethos was to be educational but fun – traditionally a somewhat perilous mix. Finally, there was the early morning Sunday show, *Rub-A-Dub-Tub*. This was for 4-8 year olds, presented by Charmaine Evans, and comprised cartoons, young children doing exercises and some songs.

Such was the theory and design of Chairman Peter Jay's TV-am; now it was to be tested in practice. To those at the company, the station's first week on screen appeared to pass off moderately well. Apart from an overlong 17-minute interview between Frost and Conservative MP Norman Tebbit, and a rather tasteless joke from Frost about pouring a boiling kettle over the heads of striking water workers, things seemed to progress without incident.

For all the panic beforehand, the simple fact that TV-am was finally on the air appeared to offset many lingering doubts. Besides, the response from the press to the station's first few days was impressive, with the *Daily Mirror* proclaiming, "TV-am Looks A Winner" and the *Daily Express* singing, "It's The Top Of The Morning Show".

"TV-am's marketing and David Frost's contacts had been so well managed that, although we had a very successful launch with *Breakfast Time*, the press said, don't worry, you ain't seen nothing yet," recalls Mike Hollingsworth. "Then, when TV-am's launch came, the press went wild. But of course the fact was that all the press people who'd covered the opening had watched very little of what was going out – they'd all been in David Frost's office quaffing large amounts of champagne and orange juice."

For those who had been watching, it only took a few days sampling to notice a striking difference between what was being written about the station and what it was actually showing on screen. Firstly, the promised "sexual chemistry" seemed in severely short supply. Two different members from the station's phalanx of presenters were to take turns as the chief hosts. David Frost and Anna Ford had been assigned the first month on the *Good Morning Britain* sofa, but had almost immediately appeared a mismatched couple who rarely gelled, and who bristled at each other's attempts at jokes.

Secondly, there was scant evidence of the "mission to explain". News reports were patchy and the analysis indifferent or just incomprehensible. Then there was the simple matter of trying to navigate your way as a viewer around the daily line-up of items. When he was promoting the station, Peter Jay had been at pains to point out how reliable the schedules would be: "Those items that are regular will be very regular; if you make sure of catching your train by leaving home 30 seconds after the weather forecast, you won't thank us for running the news a minute late." Yet, before the first week was out, it was clear that TV-am was always running late. Features were chopped and changed: overrunning, disappearing and reappearing all over the place. Even the news would turn up a few minutes late if one of the presenters, usually Frost, decided on a whim to continue an interview if he felt it deserved a bit more time.

The biggest problem was the combination of flawed presentation and decidedly unconvincing content. An unnecessarily complex and earnest array of items peppered the programme in a manner that rendered the relative merits and drawbacks of the different approaches adopted by *Breakfast Time* and TV-am crystal clear.

At the BBC, Ron Neil organized popular celebrities to come in to humorously review the morning papers, enlisting everybody from pop singers Paul Weller and Elvis Costello to the head of the Metropolitan Police Force and the Bishop of Liverpool. Conversely, TV-am had 'Press File', where a group of professional journalists gathered earnestly to analyse the content of the dailies. In itself, there was nothing particularly wrong with the concept; it was just that it felt more suited to a late night Radio 4 analysis programme than to mainstream breakfast television.

Other TV-am features had ungainly and garbled titles. 'Topical Comment And Update', 'On The Track' and 'Topical Follow-Up' turned out to be virtually identical segments of the show where the day's news was discussed in depth. Journalist Lynn Faulds Wood presented a 'Consumer News' spot in the vein of *Breakfast Time*'s regular phone-ins, but it was sold to the public as concerning items and products that "urgently need legislative control".

Coverage of arts and music was limited to 'The Critics', a review of contemporary films, plays and musicals, and offered performers and directors their right to reply. Elsewhere, the schedules included: 'Just What I've Always Wanted', a review of the "loonier products" on the market; 'A Day In The Life', a profile of an individual facing an important change in their life; and a slot simply entitled 'Food'.

In between these unpromising offerings, a retired Naval Commander named David Philpott shouted weather reports from in front of cheap maps. Philpott had written to TV-am in response to a job advert in the *Guardian*, but was somewhat under-resourced (compared to Francis Wilson and his hi-tech satellite forecasting). A system in which people stationed round the country were personally to ring Philpott and confirm weather reports had been ditched as it cost too much. Instead, TV-am's amateur meteorologist was left simply to call up his wife in Plymouth and ask her to look out of the window.

What with all of this, a faintly bizarre camp soap opera called *The Secret World Of Melanie Parker* set in the fictional community of Woodstone-Green, and other occasional features such as 'Hello/Goodbye' more suited to the Oxford Union Debating Society, TV-am threatened to buckle under the strain of its rambling, incoherent and poorly-sequenced constituent parts. Even the adverts were lack-lustre. Thanks to the on-running Equity dispute, the very first commercial screened on TV-am was a desultory affair featuring Ian Melrose, Marketing and Sales Director of

Wall's, appearing in person to joylessly try to persuade viewers to buy his sausages. Hardly attention-grabbing stuff, nor particularly remunerative for the cash-strapped breakfast company.

The consequence of this jumbled, unpalatable potpourri was that quietly and calmly, people began to switch off. To begin with, the press were none the wiser and the company remained oblivious – until the first set of ratings was published, and all hell broke loose. It showed that just 800,000 had tuned into TV-am's first week on air, compared to *Breakfast Time's* average of 1.6m.

This was a devastating shock. Nobody had been expecting TV-am to do so badly, not even the most cynical members of the print media. It had been thought likely that *Breakfast Time* would probably have the nose, thanks to its head start, but twice as many viewers as its opposition – and in the week of TV-am's glitzy high-profile launch?

800,000 was the absolute minimum number of viewers TV-am needed to attract to break even with anticipated income from advertisers. Any lower and revenue would start to dry up, and a decline into bankruptcy would become inevitable. If that was difficult to stomach, however, what happened next set alarm bells ringing across the entire British broadcasting industry.

Ratings didn't just continue to fall, but positively slumped into a downward spiral of dizzying proportions. The number fell to 500,000 in TV-am's second week against the BBC's 1.8m, and then to 300,000 by week four. Admittedly, these did mask wild variations in TV-am's viewing figures, which were at their highest at 9am after *Breakfast Time* finished. But they were often down to just 100,000 during the first hour of transmission: a figure too low to officially register anything other than zero ratings.

"TV-am's hype was brilliant," reflects Ron Neil. "I was pretty convinced at the back of my mind that we were going to get beaten into the ground, and that the audience would go for the Famous Five. I was guilty of being influenced by their hype. But why did it work for us, and not for them? I'm absolutely convinced it was because so many of our production team had had daily production experience in television on *Nationwide* or on radio on *The World At One* and the *Today* programme. Our people understood daily production, so we were able to get up and running more easily."

"There was just *such* a dire feeling about TV-am," adds Mike Hollingsworth. "There was no sense of how the audience wanted to be woken up in that gradual, bright, breezy style that eventually became the hallmark of breakfast TV. Its presenters thought people would watch at 6.30am what they'd watch 6.30 at night, which was of course totally wrong. They conducted interviews of 20 minute length and believed people would sit through them, whereas we realised that everything had to be in bite-sized chunks."

In Nick Owen's words, TV-am resembled nothing less than, "A cake with plenty of icing and little sponge. High profile, experienced names at the top – but a huge gulf underneath. I also felt the content was far too highbrow, with very little of the common touch. I had quite a run in with the programme editor because he didn't want to give overnight football results; he just wanted natty little film pieces about curling or grouse shooting."

Facing acute pressure from TV-am board members (in particular, Jonathan and Timothy Aitken), Peter Jay and his peers set about giving the station an immediate overhaul. In TV-am's fifth week on air, *Daybreak* was halved and *Good Morning Britain*'s start time brought forward to 6.30am. A news-clip competition entitled 'Run It Again' was introduced to liven up *Daybreak* a little, and a daily pop music video was aired at 6.50am.

Before the revamp could progress any further, however, events off-screen began to dominate those in front of the camera. Anna Ford and Angela Rippon had been scheduled to take on *Good Morning Britain* presenting duties from week five onwards, but Anna Ford only managed one day before falling ill with flu. David Frost stepped in to cover the day after, and then Michael Parkinson deputised for the rest of the week. His pairing with Angela Rippon proved to be something of a surprise hit, and, at the end of the week, Michael Deakin, Director of Programmes, voiced a wish to keep Parkinson on weekdays, even if Anna Ford recovered. Jay, however, refused to allow this, believing it went against the company's foundational policy of placing presenters on a par in authority with management. Anna Ford herself was certainly not happy at having her duties usurped and her ability questioned in such a fashion.

The impasse that followed prompted Deakin to write an impassioned letter to Jonathan Aitken on Sunday 6 March, setting out his grievances, not just over this matter, but everything else he believed was wrong with TV-am. His actions, albeit unwittingly, led to the groundswell of unhappiness and frustration at the way Peter Jay had run the company from day one, reaching critical mass.

Events moved quickly and within days, Deakin's letter had convinced both the Aitkens of the need to oust Jay. At a fiercely charged board meeting on Friday 11 March, called without the knowledge of most of the company's employees, arguments were put for and against Jay's immediate dismissal. The Aitkens battled hard, but they hadn't counted for some steely opposition led by Lord Camoys, Chairman of Barclays Merchant Bank, and the financier, Jacob Rothschild.

Realising they still had more work to do, the Aitkens withdrew to regroup. A second board meeting had been called for the following Monday, but they managed to get it postponed in order to shore up support. Jay also used the extra time to strengthen his defences, including a last-ditch attempt to talk Deakin into enlisting accomplished broadcast journalist Mike Townson as a new programme editor. This backfired, however, when Jay was unable to mask the reality that any such appointment would strip Deakin of all editorial responsibilities.

On Thursday 17 March, the axe finally fell. Jay was summoned to a special meeting at Barclays' headquarters at 2.30pm with Lord Camoys and Vice Chairman Dick Marsh. Camoys had been the prime target of the Aitkens' campaigning, and had now been persuaded of the need to call a halt to all the factionalism within the company. If this meant asking for Jay's resignation, then so be it.

The sheer helplessness of Jay's position was ruthlessly hammered home. On being presented with the board's request, he lapsed into a stunned near-silence, before apparently being "offered a small room with a telephone, with the opportunity to make two calls." Camoys reeled off a long list of company directors who would apparently be willing to vote for Jay's removal. It didn't include Barclays, or the individual shareholdings of Dick Marsh or Michael Deakin, but it still added up to 46.6% – a pretty damning vote of no confidence. For Jay, the matter was now indisputable. For the sake of TV-am, the station he had spent over three years of his life battling to get on the air, and which was supposed to represent the sum of his entire personal philosophy, he agreed to go.

The manner in which this judgement was first served and then accepted was not only profoundly ruthless but also strangely calm. The entire exchange was quite out of character for a company already festooned with a reputation for very public melodrama and emotional fireworks. There were no histrionics, valiant last-minute protests, or threats of revenge. Instead, Peter Jay's behaviour was a virtuoso display of sobriety and dignity. But it was all too late. The fact that he had never been able to inject those very same qualities into TV-am's on-screen persona rendered his downfall all the more potent.

His behaviour would not come to be remembered as that of a martyr falling onto his own sword out of desperation to ensure that his creation survived. Jay had got it wrong about breakfast television, and had done so in a spectacularly high-profile fashion. His exit marked the first of many turning points in TV-am's history, but no amount of courteous conduct could gloss over his track record of blunders and misjudgements. In the long run, there would be just as little residual sympathy for him as there remained for his pet theories.

Within hours of Jay's departure, Dick Marsh took over as company Chairman and Jonathan Aitken as Chief Executive. When rumours surrounding this sequence of events began to spread, many inside TV-am were incensed. Anna Ford led the charge, announcing to waiting press outside the studios the morning after Jay agreed to resign that, "There's been a great deal of treachery in the company and unfortunately, because of the bounds of our contracts, we're not allowed to talk about it. We would love to. I think history will expose those who have been most treacherous."

She then continued her campaign on air, with Angela Rippon as a ready accomplice. At one point during that day's programme, she announced, "With decision day in the Darlington by-election less than a week away, and other decisions going on here behind our backs...", and later, "There's an awful lot the papers aren't saying about TV-am at the moment. We'd love to tell you, but I'm afraid we're honour bound not to. Perhaps later we shall reveal all."

After the show was over, the pair, plus other staff, posed outside the offices, thumbs-up, with "JAY MUST STAY" slogans. But, in reality, Anna and Angela only knew what the press knew, which was that Jay was about to be asked to resign. They had no idea that he had already jumped. When that news became public, the station was tipped into utter tumult. At a press conference later that day, Jonathan Aitken drawled, "I hope that the emotions of the last few hours will cool and that rational and quiet decisions will be made by all concerned." In reality, his confirmation of what had taken place was the signal for the press to begin a field day, trumpeting that the station was in crisis; presenters rebelling, ratings in freefall, and meltdown imminent.

Ignoring all the voices of opposition, the Aitkens proceeded to take complete control. As a sitting MP, Jonathan Aitken wasn't officially allowed to run a TV company, so he quickly stepped down in favour of – unsurprisingly – Timothy. The new Chief Executive promptly sacked both Angela Rippon and Anna Ford for speaking out in support of Jay and therefore breaching their contracts.

The Famous Five began to disintegrate. When David Frost later sent Anna a pot plant as a gesture of sympathy, she reportedly threw the gift against her garden wall, shattering the pot. Some time later, she found that the plant had stubbornly and highly symbolically taken root where it fell. The feuding escalated further at a party on Tuesday 14 June, when Anna threw a glass of wine over Jonathan Aitken, and continued to simmer violently until October when she settled her compensation claim against dismissal from TV-am for £43,000. Angela Rippon would settle for £70,000 in January 1984.

Nobody seemed safe from the Aitkens' axe. Next on the list was Michael Parkinson, who had spoken out against the disposal of Anna Ford and Angela Rippon, claiming they had "been shabbily treated. It's a disgrace...I found it thoroughly nasty...It's a rotten bloody shame". He, too, seemed about to face the chop, before Timothy Aitken judiciously realised that Parkinson was the most popular presenter at the station and held fire.

To complete the round of front line changes, Nick Owen was promoted to replace David Frost as a weekday presenter. From the position of being sports reporter, Owen now found himself entrusted with the daunting task of helming the entire station. He recalls this procession of hirings and firings as rendering TV-am akin to "Piccadilly Circus. People coming and going all the time in front of and behind the cameras. It was quite remarkable." The turnover in staff was also taking a terrible toll on morale. "It was extremely unsettling," Owen continues, "because you never knew if you would be next. When they moved David Frost off the main programme, they wanted a big name like Aspel or Wogan, but there was no cash, so they went for me to hold the fort!"

Initially, Owen co-hosted the show with Angela Rippon, but when she went, he was joined on the sofa by Lynda Berry, another existing 'junior' member of the team now handed a swift promotion. Other remnants of the Jay era were either fired or encouraged to leave. The Aitkens' final act was to appoint a completely new Editor-in-chief, Greg Dyke, who was promised a salary of £40,000 a year, rising to £60,000 if he could get TV-am's ratings to top one million.

Less than three months into its life on air, the founding fathers of TV-am had been purged. The pace of the coup was severe. So, too, was the task now facing the survivors: nothing less than the creation of a new model breakfast station, in full public view, while still carrying on broadcasting. And they had to do it before the last remaining viewers followed the lead of everyone else and switched off.

THREE

"Who wants to watch Yehudi Menuhin at breakfast time?"

"I've always believed that you don't want to take over successful places," Greg Dyke stresses today. "I turned up at TV-am at the start of May 1983 with a commitment that I would relaunch the station three weeks later. Such was the confidence of youth it never crossed my mind that it could never be done, or that it wasn't achievable."

Dyke arrived at TV-am already a beguiling and charismatic figure in the TV industry. He had made his name as the founding editor of LWT's *The Six O'Clock Show*, successfully mixing light-hearted topical features with informative reports and interviews to make a widely regarded regional magazine programme. Launched in January 1982, the show boasted a swaggering self-confidence and flair, which disguised the fact that Dyke had less than half a dozen years experience in the business.

Its success had quickly brought Dyke to the attention of Michael Deakin, TV-am Director of Programmes, who initially tried to woo him to take up a post alongside Peter Jay. Dyke had passed on this unappealing offer, but when he was approached again several months later, TV-am had become a very different proposition. Relishing the challenge of solving the station's near-laughable predicament, he readily accepted the post of Editor-in-chief. "I gave [Jonathan Aitken] roughly an outline of what I thought was wrong with the place," Dyke continues, "and roughly what needed to be done."

Dyke's qualities were utterly opposed to those of Peter Jay: a talent for self-publicity, a keen sense of populism, and a healthy belief in pragmatism. Dyke also had one overriding touchstone: his own mother. He cited her as representing a key constituency of viewers that the TV industry often overlooked. The benchmark question, "What would it mean to my mother?" went not a little way in helping Dyke secure his programming strategy at TV-am and, later, at fellow ITV companies TVS and LWT.

Limited changes to TV-am's output had begun back in April 1983 when the Aitkens completed their takeover. The fatuous soap opera *The Secret World Of Melanie Parker* had been dropped, Lynn Faulds Wood's slots had been increased, and some much-needed order was added to the regular features. It was Dyke, though, who masterminded the station's complete overhaul, which he began planning as soon as he arrived.

"They'd appointed Clive Jones as my deputy before I got there," Dyke remembers, "and Clive and I more or less set up a partnership to run the thing. We found there was nothing there. There were no plans and everyone was struggling. Half the staff worked overnight, which was a complete waste of time because not much happens overnight. There was virtually no forward planning, which is what these things are all about – forward planning and good ideas. It was a lot of people who'd worked their butt off, and failed. Therefore, they were terribly emotional, and terribly upset about everything. Half the staff used to keep coming into my office and crying. And then there's me, walking in, wearing a pair of jeans and a dirty old sweater, smiling at the world. I just got on with building up a new show."

Dyke's chief concern was to rescue the ratings. As he himself cannily noted at the time, they were now so low that "if two old ladies had turned off, that'd be it – gone". Dyke drew up a raft of reforms that embraced every part of TV-am's output, and timed them all to come into effect the week beginning Monday 23 May. First, *Daybreak* was scrapped entirely. TV-am was now to comprise *Good Morning Britain* only, and to run from 6.25am all the way through to 9.30am.

Secondly, Wincey Willis was introduced as a new weather forecaster. "We just invented things, Clive and I," admits Dyke. "He said, 'Have you seen this weathergirl on Tyne Tees [Television]?' and I said, 'Well, no, but let's have a look.' We looked at her and said, 'OK, phone her up and get her.'" Sparky and vivacious, Wincey's demeanour was a world away from that of Commander Philpott, who was now shunted onto weekends. One morning, on air, she revealed that she owned an incredible 82 pets. Sniffing a hit, Dyke quickly invented another new slot: 'Wincey And Friends', which featured the eponymous star sharing some of her enormous menagerie with TV viewers.

"The real thing was just to have some ideas," Dyke emphasises today, "to get some organisation into it, and make sure you'd got a show." Together with Jones, he introduced a host of items that banished all traces of the 'Topical Comment And Update' forever. Regular competitions gave audiences the chance to win modest prizes, and you could get your hands on a customised TV-am eggcup if you had your birthday read out by the presenters.

Lizzie Webb was a former comprehensive teacher turned professional dancer. Recommended to Dyke by his PA, Jane Tatnall, she took over the daily exercise slot and adopted the title 'Mad Lizzie'. She was just the sort of incredibly popular and exuberant, immediate 'face' with which Dyke was intent on peopling TV-am. Elsewhere, the pop video was moved to a more primetime slot – 7.50am – and Jeremy Beadle, one of the hosts of LWT's award-winning show *Game For A Laugh,* was recruited to front an 'on this day in history' nostalgia package.

Dyke also oversaw the expansion of an otherwise innocuous feature involving a selection of cartoons introduced by a talking rodent named Roland Rat. This character ostensibly broadcast from his house, a dingy hut on the roof of the TV-am Camden Lock studios, where he hosted his *Spectacular Shedvision Show* with hapless sidekick Kevin The Gerbil. Born in a sewer under platform three of Kings Cross Station, Roland was a cocky, fast-talking cynical upstart who lusted after fame, seizing any moment to grab the limelight while insulting Kevin and the other characters who quickly joined his gang. These included Errol The Hamster, a jittery Welsh leek-carrying videotape editor; and Roland's girlfriend, Glenis The Guinea Pig, forever trapped in a cage in the Harrods' pets department.

The resulting amateurish mayhem was totally unlike anything else on British television, but its sheer élan and excitement was infectious. Behind it all was puppeteer David Claridge, who'd taken his concept to TV-am before Dyke had arrived and been given airtime thanks to the perceptive eye of Anne Wood, Head of Children's Output. It was Dyke, however, who realised Roland's potential and awarded him more permanent and better-publicised slots.

From that point on, Roland and his cronies quickly became one of the first things people began specifically tuning into TV-am to watch. Moreover, thanks to the attention they drew towards the station as a whole, and combined with the rest of the changes Dyke and Jones had implemented, viewing figures began to rise. "The average rating had been 200,000 in the peak quarter-hour," Dyke recalls. "In the first week of the relaunched show we got to 300,000, so I was already 'magical man' because I'd increased it by 50%."

Nonetheless, there was still a long, long way to go, so throughout the rest of May and into June, the revamp continued. Football pundit Jimmy Greaves became a daily TV correspondent. Timmy Mallett, a local radio DJ, began a weekly music news feature entitled 'Pop On Tuesday', and newspaper columnist Nigel Dempster was added to the team for a regular 'Diary' feature. Forget experts: the emphasis was now on getting anyone mildly famous with a bit of character and who was willing to get up early to come on and review virtually anything. 'Celebrity' became the new motto. Features were introduced that involved guessing the identity of a famous person from their baby photos, from their horoscope readings, and from a psychic's predictions. Celebrities were invited to realize their personal fantasies, to recall dramatic turning points in their lives and to revisit childhood haunts.

Next, Dyke brought in a colleague from his days working in newspapers, Peter McHugh, to rescue news output from the strictures of the Jay regime. "Peter Jay and the rest really did believe there was a bias against understanding," recalls McHugh; "that journalism was spoilt by journalists who became too set in their ways, who played down to the lowest possible denominator. In fact they didn't." He set to work trying to inject more topicality, energy and above all brevity to the station's reporting. It was a far from easy ride. "There was a very hostile relationship with ITN," he continues. "We were seen as a pipsqueak force, who claimed we were doing news – which we did. And then we claimed people were watching – which they were. But we didn't have any sacred cows."

Dyke was happy to leave some aspects of the station almost alone. *Data Run*, for instance, continued much as before, including items as diverse as visits from David Essex, the results of an 'If I Were Prime Minister' competition, and Roger McGough reading special breakfast-themed poetry. But when Michael Parkinson left the station for an allotted six-month break, Dyke enlisted another *Game For A Laugh* presenter to take his place as anchorman on the weekend shows: the urbane Henry Kelly. Robert Kee was quietly let go; Radio 1 DJ Paul Gambaccini began turning up to introduce music and film news; and even Dyke's old mate from *The Six O'Clock Show*, Danny Baker, was hired for a couple of weeks to front some suitably eclectic and random features.

The revolution was almost complete when, on Monday 13 June, Anne Diamond took her place on the sofa for the first time. An unassuming and diligent erstwhile regional news reporter, she had ended up treading water at the BBC, passed over for the job of *Breakfast Time* host. "We pinched Anne off *Nationwide*," underlines Dyke. "She wasn't doing much there; the BBC didn't rate her." When she made the jump to TV-am to replace Lynda Berry, who returned to reading the news bulletins, Anne Diamond was just 28. Yet there was something in her character that convinced Dyke that she was immeasurably suited for the environment of breakfast television. It would not be long before his judgement was proved right. The formation of Anne Diamond's on-screen partnership with Nick Owen marked the end of TV-am's transition from the now wholly redundant Peter Jay era. Soon the new pair began greeting audiences with an uneasy recitation of the day's tabloid bingo numbers – tacky and obvious, maybe, but it delivered viewers by the thousand, and that was all that mattered.

Back at the BBC, *Breakfast Time* editor Ron Neil and his team had watched with glee as chaos and confusion enveloped their rivals. "We had a three, four month run when it was frankly embarrassing looking at the other side," recalls Neil, "and we were terribly pleased with ourselves that we'd won." "The pressure at first was simply to look competent," adds Nick Ross. "At best we hoped to be a first-class alternative to TV-am, and certainly I do not recall any exhortations from Ron or higher management to beat TV-am in the ratings. However, after our first week, we were elated at how well the show had come together and were keen to see what tricks our rivals must have up their sleeves to beat us. Only after their first week on air did it dawn on us that we, the outsiders, were now in with a fighting chance of beating them, and only after a month did it become clear that we could thoroughly trounce them."

"The BBC came in and did something it wouldn't dare do today," argues Greg Dyke. "It came in and decided to do breakfast television because the opposition was doing it, and went two weeks early with a very popular show – a very good show, well made. I thought Frank and Selina did a really good job. I was always a big Selina Scott fan; she had a mystique that was special. Of course, when we overtook them, they then accused us of being crude and populist, but it wasn't crude and populist when *they* did it."

There was little love lost between the rival services. As Nick Owen concedes, "In the early days, competition was fierce. [The *Breakfast Time* team] were stuffing us and we suffered terribly both from their own barbed comments and those of others in speeches and the papers. People cracked gags about us on stage." "TV-am needed to triumph for commercial reasons," adds Nick Ross. "We just wanted to create the best we could. It was unfair, inasmuch as we didn't suffer the same business pressures as they did, but we were in no mood to feel sorry for them. They had crowed too loudly about how they would sweep the morning audiences away from us. Even though they were colleagues – and, in one or two cases, old friends – we didn't shed a tear."

Certainly, compared to TV-am, there was minimal upheaval in *Breakfast Time*'s line-up during its first few months. Frank Bough, Selina Scott and Nick Ross continued to alternate as presenters right through to the final week of July when their respective holidays began. But here, Ron Neil made a highly uncharacteristic mistake. He assumed that early morning audiences would fall off during the summer, thanks to better weather and holidays. Consequently, no attempt was made to introduce special features or recruit notable substitute presenters on *Breakfast Time* throughout July, August or early September. When Frank Bough went on holiday, one of the programme's deputy newsreaders, Andrew Harvey, was simply promoted to the rank of co-host. When Selina Scott took a break, fellow BBC presenter Sue Cook was hired for a few weeks to take her place. Sometimes, even newsreader Debbie Rix took a turn at presenting.

In contrast, Greg Dyke astutely reasoned that summer breakfast TV audiences did not taper away but were boosted by kids who didn't have to get ready to go to school. So, he kept his main team of presenters fronting the show right through the holidays, and introduced major new features designed for an anticipated audience of children and their families. Sure enough, with an increased number of youngsters switching on the TV for

*Greg Dyke – with help from Roland Rat – brings
sand castles, scorecards and sanity to TV-am*

something to do, this was the moment that TV-am's greatest asset found
his hour had come.

Summer 1983 was the summer of Roland Rat. The rodent was given a
special slot, *Rat On The Road*, which was screened daily from Monday 25
July. Roland and his pink Ratmobile Ford Anglia travelled to a different
city each week, insulting bewildered locals and dispensing 'Rat Bags' of
goodies while busy refining his cult status in the process. As he made his
way through Cardiff, London, Edinburgh, Oxford, Newcastle and York,
Roland and co managed to whip up considerable interest among children
eager for a glimpse of the Ratmobile and its increasingly famous
occupants. In a matter of months Roland's name seemed to be familiar
across the country and spoken about as if he were minor royalty.

Dyke further exploited the seasonal mood by hiring former kids' show
Tiswas presenter Chris Tarrant to host a daily live outside broadcast
from seaside resorts. "We invented a thing called 'By The Seaside'," Dyke
explains, "which was Chris Tarrant being very funny, very clever, and
quite innovative." Also starting the week beginning 25 July, 'By The

Seaside' utilised an old OB van (that was supposedly never paid for) and revelled in sand castle competitions, quests to find the 'Worst Landlady In Britain' and donkey rides at 6.45 in the morning. In Dyke's words it was, "mad, completely bonkers, but interesting," and it drew the crowds as Tarrant trundled relentlessly through Blackpool, Great Yarmouth, Scarborough, Brighton, the Isle Of Wight and Rhyl.

"Remember, these were the days when no-one else was playing children's breakfast programming in the summer holidays," Dyke adds. "We got the parents with 'By The Seaside', and the kids with Roland." Thanks to Dyke's canny scheduling – plus his willingness to hype Roland Rat up to such an incredible level – in the last week of July TV-am's ratings hit one million for the first time. Then came the moment of truth. "I went on holiday to Florida and got a phone call saying we'd passed the BBC!" Dyke continues. By mid-August, TV-am's viewing figures were occasionally peaking at an amazing 1.75m while *Breakfast Time* would sometimes dip as low as 1.2m.

Once again, there was to be no resting on laurels, and the changes continued to come. *Data Run* was replaced with *Summer Run*, essentially the same format as before, only less education-orientated and much more about shameless fun. Diana Dors made her debut on the station to launch her special 'X-cel' diet programme. "People relate to me," she cooed. "They thought [the diet] was a marvellous idea because so many women in this country are overweight." Viewers were invited to follow the progress of 12 lucky participants as they attempted to shed dozens of pounds. This was not exactly a rapid process, of course, and, rather helpfully for the station, meant that Diana continued to turn up on TV-am right through to the end of the year. She even found time to branch out into playing the role of agony aunt in a separate spot called, unsurprisingly, 'Open Dors'.

Other experiments with the format saw an unlikely eight-week pairing of Toni Arthur and John Noakes as hosts for the Saturday *Good Morning Britain*, while David Frost settled himself on the main Sunday programme. This was now, and would continue to be, his only show on TV-am, but soon became a rather illustrious appointment, attracting well-respected guests and heavyweight contributors. The fact that Sunday was, for some, a religious day was also acknowledged with the start of a regular 'Thought For A Sunday' slot, even if one week it was Diana Dors doing the preaching.

As word spread about the limited ratings revival, so a more buoyant mood seemed to take root at Camden Lock. Dyke's influence was felt, not just on-screen, but behind the camera as well, and at long last, morale within TV-am's HQ rallied. A brisk and brutal round of redundancies, it must be said, had also had an effect.

"The morale had been ridiculous," Dyke recalls, "it was so poor. We got rid of a lot of those people. Clive Jones and I drew up a list of, I think, 60 people who we thought ought to go. We got rid of them all in three months. Remember, they'd worked themselves to death, and failed. But some of them were quite good people. You had to lift their spirits, but once you start winning, it helps a lot." "It was very much you against the world," adds Peter McHugh. "You were held in contempt by your professional colleagues, in the same way as you are when you work in Fleet Street and you work on a popular newspaper."

Still, for all the good omens, costs remained tight, and absolutely no money was being made. This led to some all too obvious cutbacks, such as airing the same David Bowie video in the pop slot for three weeks running. The quality of the occasional OB special was also questionable. "Lack of funds meant we couldn't call on the facilities we needed to get out and about as much as we would have liked," remembers Nick Owen. A shambolic link-up from Epsom for the Derby on 1 June was matched in ineptitude by live coverage of 'Operation Sky Quest' on 6 August. This was an attempt by famed adventurers Per Lindstrand and Mike Kendrick to break the world record for the highest ascent by a hot air balloon. Audiences waited, agog, for live pictures of the balloon's epic journey, only to find their screens left blank once the travellers had sailed up beyond cloud level.

"When the summer finished and Roland finished, the ratings came back down again," concedes Dyke, "but they stayed at a million and we began to work up from there." New features carried on being introduced right through the autumn. Frankie Howerd was recruited to host a weekly slot called 'Voice Of The People'. This involved the veteran comic going out on the streets, accosting passers-by and telling them jokes while asking them about some burning issue of the day. Other innovations included a daily *Popeye* cartoon, video reviews from the waspish writer Gyles Brandreth, and the 'Monday Moan' where a special guest sounded off about a personal grudge. Roland Rat was also given a continuing presence on TV-am every Saturday in the shape of a new 10-minute slot entitled *Rat Rapping*.

This assortment of wit and whimsy might have been making TV-am a much more entertaining service to watch, but was all far removed from the careful stipulations laid down within the broadcasting licence that the company had originally been awarded. Ever since Greg Dyke had begun his radical overhaul, talk had been of not *if* but *when* the IBA would step in, demand changes, or possibly remove the franchise altogether. In order to postpone such drastic action, Dyke looked around for someone to help further boost the station's news credentials. "We needed someone who could do serious stuff," he confirms. He settled on respected BBC journalist and reporter John Stapleton.

"Greg asked me to join as a presenter," Stapleton remembers, "concentrating on the hard news element of the programme, and to inject some current affairs into it. I went straight there from the BBC – quite a cultural leap actually, going from *Newsnight* to reading the bingo numbers." Stapleton's exact role turned out to be twofold. "I did a thing called *Spotlight*, which was a daily feature where every day we put someone in the spotlight, a figure at the centre of the news, and did what was supposed to be a hard-hitting interview with them. Plus, a couple of days a week, I presented the whole show."

He was under no illusion as to the parlous condition of the company: his wife was TV-am consumer presenter Lynn Faulds Wood. Nonetheless, Stapleton was happy to join Dyke's squad: "The team were a lovely bunch, a very very talented group of young people, who'd been completely misdirected by the previous management who could not have got it more wrong."

John Stapleton's appointment compounded Dyke's line-up of core TV-am personnel, besides adding an important element to the mix: rigorous but accessible investigative journalism. "I think, previous to Greg's arrival, there'd been this rather pompous attitude from the presenters that 'whatever we think is interesting, the public will think the same'," argues Stapleton. "There were terribly long, tedious interviews that, quite frankly, didn't interest people at breakfast time. What Greg introduced was popular journalism, popular current affairs, and a much more snappy, reactive programme. Items lasted three minutes rather than 25."

By this point, late autumn 1983, faint alarm bells were finally starting to ring at the BBC. The Corporation certainly wasn't facing problems anywhere near the scale of those at TV-am – aside from one morning when a hiccup in the power supply meant the distinctive on-screen *Breakfast Time* clock started moving from one side of the picture to the other (because Frank Bough was interviewing Kenny Everett at the time, the BBC Press Office was able to explain the occurrence as in keeping with their guest's famed wackiness).

Instead, concern was expressed at TV-am's potential to start setting the agenda of British breakfast television, rather than merely following the BBC's lead. In response, Ron Neil began to slip some new features into the familiar *Breakfast Time* menu, but always with subtlety and without drama. Claire Rayner was appointed in-house agony aunt, and Mike Smith's role was enlarged to provide film news and items for younger viewers. A couple of new faces also joined the team: newsreaders Guy Mitchelmore and Fern Britton. Both quickly ended up fulfilling stints on the presenting sofa when Nick Ross temporarily left the programme on Friday 23 September to front *Sixty Minutes*, the BBC's replacement for *Nationwide*.

The biggest overhaul, however, took place the week after Ross's departure. A slight reworking of the timetable shifted the programme's regular sports news, paper review and TV preview to more clearly defined slots, while a new twice-weekly phone-in was introduced entitled 'Slim And Shine'. Here, elderly viewers were given a chance to have their dieting and fitness questions answered by health expert Audrey Eyton, while in a separate feature Diana Moran, the 'Green Goddess', invited celebrities to share their advice on good living in 'Star Tips'.

This greater emphasis on lifestyle issues was best typified by the addition of Esther Rantzen to the line-up. She appeared in a new regular slot each Wednesday called the *That's Life! File*, either repeating or following up notable cases from past and present series of *That's Life!* Its host had originally been a member of the TV-am consortium, only to drop out on becoming pregnant. Here she was, two years on, with her youngest child just over 16 months old – a fixture on the opposition.

Breakfast Time spent most of 1983 basking in a constancy that was a tribute to the foresight of its creators and to the well-crafted nature of its format. Yet, by the end of the year, its much-lamented rival had apparently begun to make serious incursions into the BBC's dominance. That TV-am was able to rally and mount such a challenge, however, had only proved possible thanks to the abandonment of everything it had been set up to do. The chief lesson that Dyke and his colleagues had taken on board and been careful to remember throughout 1983 was that Peter Jay's approach to breakfast television just didn't work. Even experienced television professionals of the calibre of the Famous Five had been unable to translate his theories about news presentation into an approachable, entertaining programme.

"Jay's model was wrong from the top," argues Peter McHugh. "The IBA sat down and thought, 'what kind of breakfast television should there be?' and concluded that it should be the *Today* programme on the telly." As for Frost and his colleagues, McHugh offers a blunt assessment: "I think those who came in at the start couldn't understand why they got it wrong, because they were the great and the good. They were five people who'd appeared on television and who believed that because they appeared on it, they knew about it. What popular breakfast television eventually became is a bit like a popular newspaper, and the opposite of a popular newspaper is an unpopular newspaper. I don't think they understood that. I think they tried to bring broadsheet television to the breakfast market, which hasn't got the time, whatever the inclination, at that time of day for that sort of approach."

"They had a rather pompous view of it," contests Dyke today. "The people most likely to watch breakfast television were parents and kids; therefore to try and do an upmarket programme was pretty unrealistic – especially on commercial television. You could've done it on the BBC, but not on a commercial station. In the weeks when I was watching it before I took it over, one time they had Yehudi Menuhin on. Who wants to watch Yehudi Menuhin at breakfast time?"

"TV-am had equipped itself with all these high-flying, intelligent young people from Cambridge or wherever, people who'd not got the experience of doing a continuous daily programme," adds *Breakfast Time* producer Mike Hollingsworth. "And I think day one had been planned months in advance, but nobody had remembered there was a day two and a day three as well." John Stapleton concludes, "There was a terrible arrogance connected with the previous management and, I have to say, some of the presenters, who thought that all they had to do was turn up. But then they soon realised that wasn't to be, because the BBC wiped the floor with them."

Whilst Greg Dyke's reforms had been drastic, it was never the case that his machinations and those of his peers had forced TV-am to abandon its so-called "mission to explain". Such dogma had simply proved impossible to implement in the first place. Jay and his cohorts were unable to realise as much, and the price was the unnecessary sacrifice of a score of personal and professional reputations.

FOUR

"Nothing should run for more than four minutes"

If Greg Dyke had succeeded in establishing a coherency to TV-am's on-screen identity by the end of 1983, the financial condition of the company was nowhere near as secure. In fact, throughout the entire first two years of its life, TV-am was in permanent danger of simply running out of money and falling off air.

"We were penniless. It was a bankrupt organisation," recalls Dyke. "We were going to go bust every week," adds the station's news chief, Peter McHugh. "The pay computer would break down frequently. [Weekday editor] Clive Jones came in one day and told us we couldn't go to air because we hadn't paid our bills. So, we had a whip round in the office. I remember being rung up on more than one occasion and told not to park my office car in the company garage because we were going to close down that day, so I might as well hang on to the car and try to use that as a lever to get paid. And that went on for months."

Unlike *Breakfast Time*, TV-am wasn't sheltered from economic crises by the protective arm of a benevolent, publicly funded corporation. It was a self-sufficient TV station, dependent on private investment and advertising sales to survive. As such, when it came to squaring idealistic vision with fiscal reality, the latter would always take precedence. "They'd undercapitalised it," contests Dyke, referring to TV-am's shareholders. "The people involved wanted big shares themselves and therefore didn't want too much outside capital. So, if [the station] didn't work on day one, it was in financial difficulties."

Thanks to its foundation and structure, TV-am was too fragile an organisation to broadcast output that nobody watched. Besides, the Electricity Board kept turning up to cut off the power. So, throughout 1983 and '84, a struggle raged behind the cameras for its financial survival, one that couldn't help but influence what viewers saw on their television sets. Its commercial obligations meant that TV-am's public profile would forever remain utterly bound up in the condition of its bank balance.

By November 1983, Roger Frye, the TV-am Director of Finance appointed by Timothy Aitken, had managed successfully to cut the station's first year expenditure from a budgeted £21m to £14.5m. However, to provide an additional £5.5m believed necessary for the company to survive the next 12 months, a search had to be launched for new investors. This resulted in Fleet Holdings agreeing to take a 20% stake of TV-am for £2m. Existing shareholders stumped up further amounts, while a final crucial million came from Kerry Packer, the Chairman of Australian Consolidated Press, who bought 10% of the equity and a seat on the board.

Yet it remained uncertain as to whether this was enough for TV-am to function in the long term. Some further savings were made by reducing staffing levels, but the station was still suffering from the prolonged clash with the acting union, Equity, that seriously limited the number of commercials it was able to run. "At one stage we only had two ads on the whole station: Pond's Cold Cream and Wall's Pork Sausages," Dyke remembers, "and we just played them time and time again."

Presenter John Stapleton recalls how no one was exempt from the drive to attract more revenue. "As presenters, we were recruited to go in and meet the advertisers to try and get more commercials. We worked on that front too." Advertising agency Young and Rubicam had estimated that were it not for the dispute, TV-am would have secured a gross ad revenue of £19.2m for 1984. Now, with every likelihood of the stalemate rumbling on into the New Year, it predicted the station would find it difficult to reach a gross revenue of even £15m.

Sales Director Tony Vickers accordingly drew up a strategy intended to woo prospective advertisers through a series of startlingly generous deals. He decided to offer a huge 40% discount to any company prepared to advertise their products during 1984 solely on TV-am and nowhere else. A 20% discount was made available to businesses opting to use TV-am to promote a product or service that hadn't been advertised on TV for at least two years. An additional 20% discount was also negotiable for advertisers wishing to buy airtime to make special announcements to dealers, distributors and employees. Vickers structured his plan to tie in with a concerted push to add new viewers over the Christmas period.

To begin with, it was a strategy that seemed to pay off. TV-am used Christmas 1983 to mount an all-out attempt to pull in family and young audiences. Central to the campaign was the impressively ambitious *Roland's Winter Wonderland*, which ran daily for three weeks across the holidays. Here the Rat and his gang were on location again, but this time in Switzerland, busy insulting locals, contriving misunderstandings and entering skiing competitions. Back in Camden Lock, celebrities were conscripted for a bumper parade of items, including Barbara Cartland and Matthew Kelly 'Panic Buying With The Stars' and Wincey Willis delivering luxury hampers to five people nominated by the TV-am viewers as 'unsung heroes'. On Christmas Day itself, Chris Tarrant broadcast live from the Queen Mary Hospital; Cardinal Hume provided a suitable 'Thought For The Day'; and Judith Chalmers, George Best and Jimmy Savile travelled back to places where they grew up in 'There's No Place Like Home'.

This heady mix of piety and entertainment reeled in the audiences. On 23 December, more than two million watched *Roland's Winter Wonderland*, and during the whole Christmas week *Good Morning Britain* attracted a maximum audience 'reach' (the total number of people tuning in at various points throughout each programme) of 6.2m against *Breakfast Time*'s 5.3m. This was great news for both Dyke and Vickers, especially given how they'd pushed the station's budget to the limit in order to send Roland and his team to the Swiss Alps. The pair now faced the challenge of retaining all these viewers into the New Year. One way to do this, they reasoned, was to raise further the profile of TV-am's news output. Someone with a bit of stature and experience would help bring some authority to the station's somewhat lacklustre bulletins, besides going some way towards appeasing the ever-circling suits of the IBA.

The upshot of this was the arrival of former ITN newsreader Gordon Honeycombe on Monday 30 January. The man waxed lyrical about receiving the call. "It came just at the right moment," he began. "I'd been writing non-stop for six years. I felt I could do with having people around me for a while. Coming back to newscasting [was] no great shock to the system. Some people didn't even know I'd gone."

In time, Honeycombe became a hugely iconic TV-am 'face' and an enduring presence at the station, providing not just the sought-after gravity but also a little eccentricity. Moreover, his arrival helped distract from a rather messy period of comings and goings within TV-am's front-line of presenters. Michael and Mary Parkinson left at the end of January 1984 to go on another of their holidays – but they never returned. Henry Kelly and Toni Arthur replaced them as permanent hosts of the Saturday edition of *Good Morning Britain*, bolstered by regular appearances from the decidedly brash new TV-am chef, Rustie Lee.

Then, at the same time as Jayne Irving and Richard Keys joined to co-present features and read the sports news respectively, Diana Dors was hastily axed for breaching IBA advertising codes. Her crime was absurdly petty, but illegal all the same: encouraging viewers to invest in a special dieting calculator she mentioned on air. Feeling shoddily treated, she briefly threatened to take TV-am to court, claiming that letters sent to the station after the item went out (which IBA rules required TV-am to keep from her) were personal fan mail. In reality, the station had employed someone exclusively to open the huge amount of correspondence addressed to Dors, just to make sure the only letters that were withheld were those enquiring about the notorious calculator.

*Pat Phoenix sorts the bailiff demands
from the disconnection notices in the TV-am mailbag*

Greg Dyke quickly filled her place on the sofa with Pat Phoenix. The renowned actress had just quit *Coronation Street* after decades in the soap opera, but the exact nature of her new role seemed a little unclear, even to her. "I won't be an agony aunt," she insisted, "more a den mother, to use an American expression. I'll be talking as honestly and as intimately as I can about a whole range of subjects, using my experience of life to good effect. Maybe viewers can help me as well at times. At least, I hope so," she concluded, uncertainly. As with her predecessor, a raft of unimaginatively entitled features were constructed around her, including 'Pat's Week', 'Pat's Chat' and the memorable 'Pat's Tip'.

In financial terms, it looked like Roland Rat was becoming TV-am's most lucrative asset. Roland Rat toys had gone on sale in the giant London-based toy store, Hamleys, before Christmas 1983 and had sold at the rate of 800 a day. Now, after being test-marketed by Woolworth's, they were distributed through shops across the country and proved an instant success. As the cash-tills rang, TV-am stood on the verge of a highly remunerative windfall: under an agreement with toy manufacturer Hasbro Industries UK, the station stood to get 15% of all sales. Hasbro anticipated netting £1m, which translated into a massive £150,000 for TV-am. Perhaps, after much carping from critics, Roland would indeed turn out to hold the key to the company's future security.

There was certainly no harm in trying, and Dyke for one made a point of ensuring that Roland continued to make plenty of appearances on screen. Money was found to send him, his gang and some cameras out to Hong Kong to film *Roland Goes East* for transmission during the Easter holidays. A second series of *Rat On The Road* was planned for the summer, and a special adventure was scheduled for the autumn half-term, entitled *Operation FOGI,* featuring Roland, Kevin and Errol plotting to 'Free Our Glenis Immediately' from the evil clutches of Harrods' pet department. Thanks to some extra-curricular activity, Roland's profile was also boosted. He made a guest appearance hosting Children's ITV in March 1984 (and again in January 1985), and even released three seven-inch singles: 'Rat Rapping', 'Love Me Tender' and 'No. 1 Rat Fan'.

Although 1984 had got off to a strong start, TV-am's ratings had continued to oscillate dramatically from week to week. Money wasn't coming in anywhere near as fast as the management, especially Tony Vickers, had hoped. In public, Dyke put on a belligerent, assured face. "We haven't got the BBC's news resources," he conceded gruffly, "but, like everything else, news is about ideas – and I think that apart from foreign coverage, our news is much better than theirs, and now Gordon Honeycombe enhances the product. The real art of breakfast television is to mix the news and the frothy stuff with speed and variety. Nothing should run for more than four minutes." He also made a point of highlighting the advanced relationship TV-am now enjoyed with its viewers. When he temporarily dropped the daily bingo numbers run-down, Dyke claimed that the station got 5,000 complaints.

Yet, while his own attempts at reorganisation had led to a £400,000 reduction in the current programme gross monthly budget, Dyke had to admit that it would be well into 1985 before the company might see any trace of a profit. "We were in appalling financial straits," confirms John Stapleton. "Everyone was very concerned. There was crisis after crisis, and so much neurosis that cameramen were taking the cameras home with them so that in case it all went belly up they'd at least have something. There was one month when neither Lynn [Faulds Wood] nor I were paid, and Greg, bless him, offered to pay our wages himself. Several of us, mainly the freelancers, on a number of occasions weren't paid. They didn't have any money. I remember going on holiday at one stage to Kenya with Lynn and making a couple of phone calls back to ask,

'Are we still in business?' Because there'd been yet another crisis and we were seriously wondering whether we still had a job when we returned."

As much as he tried, Dyke couldn't keep evidence of the station's reduced circumstances off screen. *Rub-A-Dub-Tub*, the Sunday morning series for young children, now existed solely in the form of repeats as the money had run out to make any new episodes. Behind the scenes, Wiltshire, a firm of building contractors, were demanding around £500,000 for contractual work carried out on the station's HQ dating back to the days of Peter Jay. Worse was to come.

Handling business matters was not something he enjoyed, but it fell to Dyke to inform his staff on Thursday 26 January 1984 that voluntary redundancies were essential for the company to survive. For all the hype of the Christmas holiday period, TV-am simply couldn't meet its running costs – now standing at £1.5m a month – and, while the recent financial injection from investors was supposed to keep the company afloat until at least May, the continuing Equity dispute and subsequent low ad revenue had taken a terrible toll. Dyke concluded by presenting his colleagues with two possible outcomes: either 90 staff would have to be sacked; or half that number could leave voluntarily, dependent upon the securing of another outside cash sum.

Not unexpectedly, this news was greeted with strong resentment. The two trade unions based at TV-am, the National Union of Journalists (NUJ) and the Association of Cinematograph Television and Allied Technicians (ACTT), rejected voluntary redundancies outright. In response, Dyke argued that if TV-am went bankrupt and another company took over, the first thing it would do would be to axe jobs anyway. He even let the NUJ look over TV-am's confidential company reports to see the situation for itself. It was to no avail.

"There were weekly meetings of the ACTT," recalls Peter McHugh, "which were always about whether it should pull the plug or not. TV-am could easily have gone to the wall. And if we had gone to the wall, I don't know whether anybody outside would've thought us worth saving."

Refusing to give up, Dyke tried a second approach. On Monday 6 February, he told the NUJ and ACTT that redundancies would not be necessary if 15 posts currently unfulfilled remained vacant, conditional on investors putting up a joint loan of at least £2m to help cover the advertising shortfall of £800,000 so far that year. But this money could not be guaranteed. Neither, more importantly, could anybody's salary for February. Hearing this simply hardened the unions' resolve to fight any redundancies. The situation seemed hopeless.

Then, at the very last minute, and with the Electricity Board once again preparing to disconnect the station from its power supply, a cash injection was found. Over the weekend of 11/12 February, TV-am's investors swallowed their pride and agreed to pump in an extra £3m. McHugh explains, "I think then it was, well, as we've invested so much already, we might as well hang on in there to see if we can get something back, rather than just cut our losses." In response, the ACTT agreed to endorse staff reductions through natural wastage, and implement new working practices to ensure monthly running costs remained at £1.25m throughout 1984.

In the nick of time, TV-am's life had been spared. But its shareholders were clear: if the station ran into any more problems, it could not expect a single penny more. TV-am had to learn to survive on its own two feet. For Greg Dyke and his colleagues, what mattered most was that the money was there to pay an overdue rates bill for £200,000 from Camden Council. Besides, the ratings looked evermore promising. TV-am had already scored a number of victories over *Breakfast Time*. It now looked like the moment was fast approaching when they would not only draw level with their rivals but maybe permanently overtake them.

"I think we had a relationship with an audience by just addressing people's concerns," emphasises Peter McHugh today, attempting to explain the station's increasing following, "and by doing things that were important, but sometimes surrounding them with things that were unimportant, in order to try and persuade people to watch." "It was a very long haul to turn things round," adds John Stapleton, "but the template for success was created by Greg, Clive [Jones] and Peter, all of whom worked unbelievably long hours and extremely hard. I remember going in there at 4am and seeing Clive asleep on the couch in the green room, having been up all night. Equally, Peter would be there from sun up to dusk every day. And Greg was in every day of the week, working not just on the editorial side but to get money."

After much feverish anticipation, a watershed was reached during the week ending 18 March when both TV-am and *Breakfast Time* polled a consistent, average peak quarter-hour figure of 1.4m. This was the first time both had drawn level for a continued period of time. Exactly one year previously, the figures had stood at 1.7m for *Breakfast Time* and 0.4m for TV-am. At the same moment, news came in that projected airtime sales for April were set to hit the station's monthly break-even point.

But if Dyke sensed victory, even he was at the mercy of ongoing developments at the highest level beyond his control. Timothy Aitken had recently revealed that he was thinking of relinquishing most of his day-to-day responsibilities as TV-am Chief Executive in order to concentrate on his family firm, Aitken Hume. Word of possible changes at the top couldn't help but breed feelings of unease amongst the general staff, especially given the company's acutely delicate condition. Dyke shared these sentiments, conscious of how any restructuring might end up encroaching upon his carefully guarded turf.

The rumour mill continued to turn through April, until Timothy Aitken confirmed that he was handing over the running of the station to a new General Manager. This was to be Adrian Moore, an advertising director at News Group Newspapers. Aitken explained: "The time is now right for the management team at TV-am to be strengthened. Moore will become a member of a very effective team that has a proven track record. The situation is now widely recognised as having some real light at the end of the tunnel."

These would turn out to be highly fateful words. Conflicting agendas and a clash of personalities led Moore and Dyke to fall out from day one. There was confusion and disagreement over responsibilities, and on whose terms the station was to move forward. The turbulence was then compounded by the intervention of the previously unassuming figure of Kerry Packer.

When Packer had bought his 10% of TV-am in November 1983, it had seemingly been off the back of a chance meeting with Jonathan Aitken in the doorway of the Dorchester Hotel. But, within weeks, learning of the company's financial struggles, he had arranged for one of his top executives, Bruce Gyngell, to represent him at TV-am's board meetings. Arriving from Australia for the first of these in February 1984, Gyngell had been shocked by what he saw as the shoddy, terminal state of the organisation. He immediately indicated his intention to stay in London to better patrol developments and watch over his superior's investment.

The assumption that this was the first step by Packer in a bid to take over TV-am was partially offset by the IBA's clear rules stating that no TV station could be run by a non-EEC resident or company. But with the continuing uncertainty over Timothy Aitken's exact role at the station, and the burgeoning ill feeling between Greg Dyke and Adrian Moore, if ever there was time for another boardroom coup, then it was now.

Sure enough, when gossip began circulating in early May that Timothy Aitken was about to move sideways into the Chairman's position, talk turned to the likelihood of his managerial responsibilities being taken on by Bruce Gyngell. For starters, there was no other suitable successor on the horizon. Moreover, Kerry Packer had continued to be a persistent visitor to the station. On one occasion, he had arrived at Camden Lock, set up his own desk in the atrium, and quizzed every single person who came into the building as to his or her occupation and working hours. He had also pointedly increased his holding in the company while Aitken had concurrently reduced his stake.

In Peter McHugh's words, "I think [the board] thought Greg had done a great job but they thought he had no business experience. Therefore, they couldn't make him Managing Director; therefore, they brought in Bruce." Bruce Gyngell's appointment to the position of TV-am Managing Director in mid-May brought to a head the tension and animosity that had been building within the station for some months. It was a succession only possible following emergency discussions with the IBA. It was also, by definition, a sortie onto the territory of Greg Dyke. Indeed, some sort of showdown between Dyke and Gyngell, both tough personalities with utterly contrasting ideas about breakfast television, was almost inevitable. Dyke had been considering his position after the appointment of Adrian Moore, and had already been offered another job at the ITV company TVS. Matters now moved swiftly to a conclusion.

"Gyngell was a flamboyant bloke," recalls Dyke. "I liked him. He was quite charismatic, but I fell out with him in about three weeks because he wanted to run it all." During a stormy board meeting on Tuesday 22 May, Gyngell presented his plans for TV-am's development and expansion. The crucial matter proved to be the continuing monthly deficit. Gyngell wanted it down to nil and as such asked for all aspects of editorial planning and programming to be put under his direct scrutiny.

Realising this would leave him totally emasculated, and seeing the rest of the board members appearing to back Gyngell's wishes, Dyke resigned. His statement read: "It is with considerable regret that I have taken the decision to leave TV-am. It is my view that the policy that is now being pursued by the board is significantly different to that which has been pursued during the past year and this has made my departure inevitable."

When Greg Dyke joined TV-am, its ratings had been 200,000. The week before he quit, they reached 1.5m – 100,000 more than *Breakfast Time*. While it is foolish to ascribe the revival of an entire TV station to the actions of one man, it was Dyke above all who was able to infect his staff with enough courage and enthusiasm to pull off and sustain such a remarkable turnaround. He had his own incentive, of course: the extra £20,000 on his salary when ratings hit one million. He'd also had to surmount obstacles, not least the rounds of perilous negotiation with the unions. But, in Bruce Gyngell, he found himself up against someone who questioned his entire judgement, regardless of his track record since TV-am had hit rock bottom in the spring of 1983. So, as quickly and dramatically as he had arrived, Dyke departed.

"By the time Greg left, we were starting to see the formula of what we wanted," reflects Peter McHugh. "A template was in place, which was items in bite-size pieces, longer than radio often did, which went from the serious to the sublime and sometimes to the ridiculous. Trying to give people a laugh; trying to help people see the serious stuff; and trying to reflect their concerns."

Though Dyke's revolutionary ideas about the look and content of breakfast TV would survive his departure, his potent personality and inspiration would be sorely missed. "There was always great hope while Greg and Clive and Peter were around," explains John Stapleton. "They turned it round. They settled on accessible, easy on the eye, easy on the ear, news, current affairs and entertainment." "I'd learned an incredible amount," Dyke sums up today, "nothing to do with television, but an incredible amount about business and what it was like in a crisis, and I discovered I quite liked it. I quite liked going through crisis, and not many people did." Looking back now, he claims not to have any regrets about getting out when he did. "It's a limited form of television, breakfast television, so I didn't mind leaving it. I wouldn't have done ten years of it. But it was good fun. It was the funniest year of my life. I laughed all the way through it."

A few months after walking out of TV-am, Dyke became Director of Programmes at TVS. A career taking him to the very top of his profession – and the post of BBC Director-General – would follow. Yet, thanks to his basic grasp of what would work on television first thing in the morning, and just as crucially what would not, one of the greatest achievements of his professional life would always remain the fact that he 'saved' TV-am where some of the self-professed brightest and best had failed.

FIVE

"A complete and utter disgraceful debacle"

Bruce Gyngell arrived at TV-am the most mysterious television executive in Britain. To the majority of people, both inside and outside the company, he was a complete enigma. It was known that he had an impressive track record in front and behind the cameras, but in his native Australia rather than in the UK. He'd been the first ever face to appear on Australian TV, where he'd gone on to rise through the ranks and become a major industry player. However, except for a period in employment at Lew Grade's ATV in the 1960s, he had no other experience of working in British television.

All of this helped to foster an impression of Gyngell being something of an outsider and a potentially disrupting influence upon the becalmed conventions of UK broadcasting. Indeed, it was rumoured the man himself relished cultivating just this kind of reputation. Yet the manner of Gyngell's takeover at TV-am had also prompted widespread resentment amongst those who recoiled at the notion of a foreigner being in charge of a British television company. In time, Gyngell's status as an uncompromising maverick, trading in both the maniacal and the mystical, would become not just his chief calling card but also his greatest millstone.

Within hours of Gyngell's appointment as Managing Director, TV-am's Camden Lock HQ was awash with wild speculation. The staff was about to be halved. Everyone would have to wear yellow, or become a Buddhist. Trade unions (another pet obsession) would be barred. The place would either go bust in a month or make a million by Christmas.

In the event, all that happened was a short, sharp dose of rationalisation. Greg Dyke was not replaced, and instead the day-to-day running of the station was portioned out between Clive Jones, Peter McHugh and Michael Deakin – with Gyngell having overall responsibility. Meanwhile, the entire staff was subject to a course of vigorous pep talks designed to promote positive thinking and mental energy.

"Bruce had seen the place and fallen in love with it," explains Mike Hollingsworth, then still a producer on *Breakfast Time*. "He just thought, 'This is a chance for me to have a TV station that I can run, do what I want with, and have a real bit of fun with.'" Advertising agency Young

58

And Rubicam noted Gyngell's opening gambits and predicted TV-am would make £17m by the end of its current financial year. But, for a man by nature predisposed towards altercation rather than conciliation, his honeymoon period at the station was always going to be brief.

"Gyngell was seen by many as a hatchet man," recalls John Stapleton, "and in my opinion it proved to be the case. He came in with the brief, we were told, to chop TV-am down to size, under the notion that they did this kind of thing in Australia with three men and a dog. Some of us made it plain to Gyngell that people had been promised that their living was secure, but he wasn't very interested in that."

The first flashpoint occurred a matter of weeks after Gyngell's entrance. Anne Wood was Head of TV-am's children's section, and one of a staff of six. Given Gyngell's distrust of too much autonomy within his businesses, her department was a likely target for cuts.

Her most recent creation had been a new summer replacement for *Data Run* called *SPLAT* (*Soap, Puzzles, Laughter And Talent*). This lively affair made its debut on Saturday 9 June and was hosted by Roland Rat production assistant James Baker. It featured a strong line-up, including 'No Adults Allowed', an improvised soap opera performed by kids, plus an open-topped double-decker bus that doubled as a stage for live bands. Especially popular was 'Crack It', a quiz involving four contestants from different regions of the country battling it out for the title 'TV-am Egghead Of The Year'.

Gyngell took one look at *SPLAT* and saw only dispensable over-indulgence, totally unjustified in these times of financial hardship. He ordered that no new children's programmes were to be commissioned until a full review of the department's operations had been conducted. Anne Wood was initially pragmatic, but when it appeared that no such review was likely to take place in the near future, relations worsened.

By July, a stalemate had been reached and, with neither side appearing willing to negotiate, Gyngell simply resorted to penning forthcoming episodes of the Sunday morning kids offering, *Rub-A-Dub-Tub*, himself. It was typical of the man and his hard-nosed, rather flippant attitude towards his colleagues. Finally, when Gyngell got bored with scriptwriting duties, he promptly merged the children's department with the station's weekend section. Shortly afterwards, Anne Wood left. Predictably, she wasn't replaced.

The second big showdown was conducted on a far more epic scale. It had been intended that ITV, Channel 4 and TV-am would combine forces to present coverage of the 1984 Olympic Games in Los Angeles. This would be the first time the event had been broadcast in full on independent television, and was to feature within the schedules around the clock.

In the expectation of record audiences, TV-am set about drawing up some ambitious proposals. Sales Director Tony Vickers decided to raise the premium price of airtime to roughly twice the current top rate, a record £6,000 per minute. A combination of advertising packages was to be launched, dubbed Gold Medal, Silver Medal and Bronze Medal. On the production side, fantastical plans were made to use star guest commentators such as Telly Savalas and Michael Caine – and an exhaustive timetable was drawn up detailing how TV-am would show live events continually from 6 to 7am, then a five- to ten-minute highlights segment every half-hour from 7 to 9am.

But at precisely the point that these strategies were about to reach their fruition, a disagreement with the ACTT union about technicians' pay that had been simmering for several months suddenly blew up into an all-out dispute.

At the end of May, TV-am had been due to pay a 5% increase to its long-term staff. When the time came, however, the company announced it intended to pay only two fifths of the claim upfront, with the rest spread over the following nine months. For the ACTT, this smacked of duplicity and the thin end of the wedge. Moreover, it had already been indicated that engineers and technicians would not be paid a standard level of overtime to work on the Olympics coverage during the night. The union decided to make a stand and demand the whole claim upfront. A full-scale industrial dispute, the first in TV-am's history, was on the cards.

A meeting of the TV-am board ruled that the company could not meet the ACTT's demands in full. The station's debts were still in the region of £18m, and such a payout would add an extra £100,000 to its wages bill. Consequently, at the end of June, a shamefaced Gyngell had to announce that TV-am was pulling out of the Olympics. It simply couldn't afford to accommodate the costs likely to be incurred through mounting such an operation. As it turned out, finances were in such a parlous state that the station almost fell off the air during the first weekend in July anyway. But that wasn't all, for in turn the vacuum created by TV-am's withdrawal triggered the collapse of ITV's entire Olympics coverage. Rather than entertaining wall-to-wall footage, the network ended up with a shoestring service and a schedule full of empty slots.

For weekday editor Clive Jones it was the last straw. He walked out, stating, "The LA Games would have been the first real breakfast Olympics, and I have been involved in planning ITV's coverage for more than two years." A survivor from even before Greg Dyke's era, Jones' exit was a hammer blow to morale. While Peter McHugh took over as acting editor, the NUJ passed a vote of no confidence in Gyngell.

At the same time, the station's regional offices in Glasgow and Manchester were shut at the cost of dozens of jobs. Recent advertisements placed by LWT, for researchers to work on *The Six O'Clock Show* and *The London Programme,* reportedly prompted floods of applications from desperate TV-am employees. It looked like the entire infrastructure of the station was crumbling from within. An NUJ spokesperson commented ruefully, "It's horrific. The goodwill has gone completely. The days when management could buy us off with promises are over."

Gyngell assured everyone that he was not about to do anything provocative, but there seemed little chance of his imminent replacement. Behind the scenes, Kerry Packer was rumoured to have increased his shareholding in TV-am still further, while for his part, Gyngell acted as if he were there to stay, personally painting his office bright yellow and ordering a similar round of refurbishments for the station's foyer.

He did make one concession. In response to pressure from the IBA, unhappy that Gyngell was presuming to combine the roles of Editor-in-chief and Managing Director, he brought in a replacement for Clive Jones. To much surprise, this turned out to be a member of the opposition: *Breakfast Time* producer Mike Hollingsworth.

"I'd been rung up by Jonathan Aitken," Hollingsworth recalls, "who said, 'I wonder if you'd come and have lunch with me. I want to talk about the future of TV-am and whether you have a part to play in it.'" After meeting with Aitken at a private club in Park Lane and signalling his interest, Hollingsworth, a week later, received a call directly from Gyngell. "He said, 'Why don't you come round and talk to me?' But before I went to meet him, he insisted I gave the time and date of my birth so that he could cast my horoscope. And he rang me back an hour or so later and said, 'I've got good news for you: we are compatible; we will work well together!'"

Hollingsworth started at TV-am on 29 June 1984. He definitely had the experience, having already amassed many years' work in television production. He was also no stranger to breakfast TV, and such had been his success on *Breakfast Time* that representatives had actually approached him from the TV-am board to join the company before. But, now he'd made the jump, did he really have the right temperament to fit in with Gyngell's regime, or deal with the very different environment of a commercial broadcaster compared to the BBC?

He certainly hit the ground running. "What I found when I arrived at TV-am was, frankly, an administrative mess," he testifies. "Greg Dyke may have cleaned up the relationship between the management and everybody else, but there were virtually only two people working in the newsroom. It was an absolute bloody mess. From the point of view of a respectable television station, it should've been ashamed of itself."

Hollingsworth immediately axed the daily reading of the bingo numbers and stopped the practice of letting presenters have alternate days off. "I said to Anne Diamond and Nick Owen, 'At least do me a favour. For the first six months, work as a five-day a week team. We'll let you have the same week off once every six weeks, when we'll bring in the B-team, Jayne Irving and Richard Keys. But we can't possibly have the A-team not together; you are our strongest card.'"

Next he appointed Bill Ludford, a former colleague from Central TV, to run the newsroom and "put some life into the place." He also waded into reconciling what he believed was perhaps the station's biggest handicap: its poor relations with the ACTT. "The ACTT could've destroyed TV-am single-handedly," he argues. "Greg had said okay to some awful union agreements, but he said it was the only way you could get them to work. We never went live on Sunday mornings because of Greg. We had to record David Frost's Sunday programme on Saturday afternoon. It was the most appalling arrangement ever made for a live television company."

Yet, it wasn't clear whether Hollingsworth's fierce determination to undo much of what he saw as stifling workforce conditions would deliver the company from its troubles, or merely rekindle old antagonisms between management and employees. Besides, the station continued to face more immediate problems, not least the amount of revenue that continued to seep from the organisation.

In July, former Chairman, Dick Marsh, announced that he intended to sue TV-am for violation of his two-year contract. Marsh wanted a lump sum settlement, while TV-am hoped to carry on paying him quarterly. His contract with the company was due to run until 1986 at around £15,000 a year. Reflecting on his predicament, Marsh commented ruefully, "At the moment I regard a two-year contract with TV-am as being like one of the passengers on the Titanic trying to negotiate life insurance."

Then, while the IBA conceded it would have to write off a half million pound debt in rental charges TV-am had yet to pay, reports broke that whilst ITN newsreader Elinor Goodman allegedly got a 'frock allowance' of £300 per year, Anne Diamond had one of over £9,000. A final nail in the coffin, if one were needed, was the news that when the Olympic Games began, TV-am's ratings sank below those of *Breakfast Time* once more.

During this protracted turmoil back stage, events on-screen were far more orderly. Anne Diamond and Nick Owen did sterling work in papering over the station's troubles to bring viewers an increasingly jovial, endearingly amateurish breakfast service. Both were by now fully settled into their roles as TV-am's front-line double act and had developed their own respective television personalities. Owen had turned into a measured, capable and somewhat rakish foil to Anne's more forthright, slightly overbearing yet deeply concerned presence.

"Anne and Nick were a superb presenting team," stresses Mike Hollingsworth. "They did the job that was required of them and they did it superbly well. And they clearly got on on-screen in a way that the viewers liked." "I think people could relate to us because we dressed informally and chatted in a cosy style," recalls Owen, "rather than 'announcing', which often seemed to be the mode in those days. We were young and new to national TV, so I think people got to know us as we broadcast up to three hours per day. We had a phenomenal amount of post from people who regarded us as friends. It was wonderful."

Theirs was a different relationship to that of Frank Bough and Selina Scott. *Breakfast Time* was characterised by Bough's paternal charm contrasted with Scott's open-faced innocence. On TV-am, Owen often resembled a fresh-faced buccaneer, jousting with Diamond's matronly inquisitiveness and matching her dominance with a few dry one-liners. It was through their essential down-to-earth demeanour, however, that they had the greatest impact. "We talked amongst ourselves about everyday things that viewers could relate to," continues Owen; "boy and girl next door stuff. I believe we relaxed the whole manner of TV broadcasting in this country."

Charles Goldring, TV-am's new film critic, augmented the pair on the sofa. Goldring, 27, was the proud owner of over 169 bow ties and had been collecting them since he was 11. Although a trained barrister, he'd tired of the law and applied to TV-am for, as he saw it, a career move. Goldring possessed one of those on-screen personalities that you either warmed to instantly or found intensely irritating. The same went for Rowanne Pasco, who became a regular face in the somewhat tokenistic religious 'Thought' slot on Sundays.

These arrivals were counterbalanced, off camera, by the departure of Michael Deakin. One of the members of the original TV-am gang, he'd seen his responsibilities eroded by the appointment of both Bruce Gyngell and Mike Hollingsworth. Now only David Frost was left from the team who had first bid for the breakfast licence back in 1980. Hollingsworth assumed Deakin's responsibilities, with Peter McHugh taking on the formal role of editor.

When Maggie Nordon, the sole surviving member of the old children's department, quickly followed Deakin out of the building, Gyngell woke up to the fact that he was still at risk from a cumulative exodus of staff. He finally appointed a proper successor to Anne Wood as producer/director of all children's output. This turned out to be Nick Wilson, senior producer on the BBC's Saturday morning kids' programme *Saturday Superstore*. Wilson was to have a profound impact on TV-am's future, thanks chiefly to his careful exploitation of the one audience the company had really sewn up: the under-12s. When *SPLAT* ended on September 1, rather than bring back the somewhat tired *Data Run* for another series, Wilson decided a totally new format was needed.

What he came up with, *The Wide Awake Club (WAC)*, was easily the most impressive and robust programme TV-am had broadcast to date. For starters, it was fresh, exciting and funny – qualities you'd have been hard-pressed to apply to any of the station's previous output. It was blessed with three amiable and entertaining presenters in the shape of James Baker, Tommy Boyd and Arabella Warner, who talked *to* rather than *at* their audience. There were plenty of amusing features, such as the 'News In 90 Seconds', recipes from viewers in 'WAC Snax', and historical tales re-enacted with a knowing amateurishness in 'Ghosts, Monsters and Legends'. Above all, it was TV-am's first attempt at a live children's show, which meant that everything was infused with an infectious sparkle. *WAC* had bags of energy and personality, and quickly established itself as something that demanded to be watched.

Gyngell seemed particularly taken by the programme's attitude, and the fact that it cost so little to make. He was cheered further by the resolution of the Equity dispute that had for so long restricted the advertisements available to TV-am to those mostly fronted by company bosses rather than actors. It was predicted that TV-am's revenue might increase by as much as 25-30% as a result. If true, this suggested that things might be looking up for the beleaguered station. Gyngell, of course, maintained that he had never expected anything less.

Over at the BBC, the team behind *Breakfast Time* had continued to eye TV-am's fluctuating fortunes with a detached bemusement. The fact that their rival had performed a recovery, ratings-wise, was tacitly acknowledged, yet nothing much was done to really fight back. Happily settled into its tried and tested ways, *Breakfast Time* seemed content to trade on predictability to win viewers back from the unruly behaviour at Camden Lock.

"Our mix worked a treat," argues presenter Nick Ross. "Serious interviewees, and especially politicians, were enticed to participate in a relaxed and unceremonious way that, until then, only *The Jimmy Young Programme* [on Radio 2] had got near, and the red-sofa format stood the test remarkably well." Even more significant was the relationship the programme had formed with its audience. "Warm, friendly – and yet authoritative," is how Ross describes it today. "It was a difficult trick, and one that set the tone for a generation of different attempts at the same outcome. I was quite unprepared for how much we the presenters would become part of the viewers' extended families. I would get shoals of birthday cards, and when my first child was born even he became a mini-celebrity. Almost all the correspondence was cordial, as though I was a friend, not a remote TV presenter. I have never experienced quite that sense of intimacy with viewers."

In order to preserve this kind of rapport, editor Ron Neil's strategy was to keep *Breakfast Time* bright and attractive through a familiar, slow evolution of new features, rather than anything particularly radical or unexpected. So a daily 'Top 20 Workout' with Diana Moran was added to the schedules, along with a pregnancy segment entitled 'Mother To Be'. Alan Titchmarsh launched a gardening phone-in called 'Titch's Pick', familiar BBC face Bob Wilson joined to help read the sports news, and children's TV host Steve Blacknell took over the job of presenting pop and entertainment news.

Breakfast Time really came into its own whenever there was a big national event to cover. Back on Friday 25 November 1983, the programme had rather daringly transmitted a simulcast with Terry Wogan's Radio 2 breakfast show to commemorate *Children In Need*. The summer of 1984 saw an even more ambitious feat. To mark the 40th anniversary of D-Day on June 6, the entire programme came live from Normandy. Dame Vera Lynn joined Frank Bough and Selina Scott to croon some old war-time songs, Frank Gillard recalled his days as a BBC war correspondent, while Francis Wilson used his 'Weather Window' to show how the original Allied invasion of France was put in jeopardy by storms. Various recollections from veterans peppered the programme, and overall it made for a memorable and poignant broadcast.

An arguably less convincing stunt was the decision to spend the rest of the 1984 summer months unashamedly aping TV-am's seaside road shows. Various combinations of presenters were despatched to front '*Breakfast Time* Out', which began on Monday 13 August in Southend. A series of outside broadcasts moved slowly round various British resorts, encountering celebrities along the way. Comedians Little & Large turned up in Scarborough, while the edition from Ayr included a feature melodramatically entitled 'The Secrets Of The Andrea Doria' that involved the opening up of a safe that had sunk on board a luxury liner in New York in 1956. Though energetically executed and high profile, these events couldn't help but seem rather superfluous. While TV-am's seaside stunts had been born out of desperation, the BBC's effort just seemed a poor imitation and, frankly, rather pointless.

In contrast, one area where *Breakfast Time* still most definitely called the shots was merchandise. While TV-am had its tiny eggcups, *Breakfast Time* marketed itself ruthlessly. After just two months on the air, viewers had been able to send off for *Breakfast Time* mugs (a snip at £1.60); car stickers (just 50p); tea towels (£1.50); aprons (£3.50); T-shirts and, most striking of all, a *Breakfast Time* sweatshirt (£7.50). All came in a pleasant, bland, light blue. Later offerings included a 'Get Fit With The Green Goddess' book, priced at £2.50 or available on record or cassette for just £3.99; 'Russell Grant's Zodiac Jukebox' LP, an album of astrological tips and music personally selected by the man himself; and Glynn Christian's *Best Of Breakfast Time Cookbook*, retailing at £1.75.

It was a reflection of *Breakfast Time*'s inherent stability that over a year and a half passed before the first big shake-up of its production team took place. When the BBC decided to axe the hapless *Nationwide* successor, *Sixty Minutes*, Nick Ross resumed a place on the red sofas. To replace the failed current affairs package, the Corporation opted for a shorter, more serious presentation simply entitled *The Six O'Clock News*. Ron Neil was moved from *Breakfast Time* to oversee the new programme's development.

His departure was an occasion for much emotion on the part of both *Breakfast Time*'s presenters and crew, uncertain as to quite what would happen once their mentor was no longer around. "You naturally felt very affectionate towards something that you'd helped to start," Neil reflects today, "but the truth is, I wasn't given much choice. Initially, I refused to go, to which [Managing Director of BBC Television] Bill Cotton replied, 'Don't worry, Ron, we won't fall out for a very long time – we'll just fall out forever.' So it was actually, 'you're going'. So I went. But you've got to accept that if you move on, somebody else is going to come in and change things. That's just an inevitability. I'm sure I felt sad that I was leaving *Breakfast Time*, but better to leave it behind on a high."

Sixty Minutes editor David Lloyd was appointed as Ron Neil's replacement. Though, in part, this was simply a case of BBC musical chairs, the Corporation was careful to take the opportunity of Neil's departure to initiate a partial review of *Breakfast Time*'s format – not, it seems, out of fear of a resurgent TV-am, but more simply to satisfy the enduring concerns of some BBC senior staff.

"I was asked to toughen it up a bit," Lloyd recalls. "Its strengths lay in the way it reported overnight news, and it was felt they should be more to the fore. I think that the top management at the BBC were content with it, but they wanted it a bit stronger. There was very little pressure at the time, because TV-am was really nowhere. It was almost like a monopoly. TV-am was almost not competing, and to the degree that they did compete, they competed only for a children's audience. The pressures were more internal – judgements about what the programme should be."

The fact that, for all of Ron Neil's success, certain circles within BBC management remained uneasy about the core design of *Breakfast Time* did not bode well for the future. For the moment, however, David Lloyd busied himself with tightening up the show's newsgathering operation, whilst leaving the overall format relatively unchanged. The same high-quality star guests continued to drop by, including Gore Vidal, Kelly

Monteith, Peter Alliss, Sophia Loren, Tommy Trinder, and Rod Hull And Emu. Frank Bough and Selina Scott flew out to America to cover the 1984 Presidential Elections. The programme also inherited an old celebrated *Nationwide* staple: the Dr Barnado's Champion Children competition.

At TV-am, Mike Hollingsworth was beginning to find that, while there was a sense the tide might now be turning away from the BBC, his attempts to progress root and branch reform of the ailing company increasingly ran up against the bulwark that was the fiscal fortitude of Bruce Gyngell. "One of the things made very clear to me within about a month of my arrival was that the company was bankrupt," Hollingsworth remembers. "I was told we would have to sell all the advertising breaks for December ahead of time in order to try and get enough money together to keep going; and that the money would be collected in a van from the advertisers, Hasbro, since, if it was ever paid into a bank, they would immediately seize it because we were so in debt."

Ratings were now going up more consistently than ever before, but Hollingsworth was convinced that the recovery could not be sustained, let alone advanced, without his boss demonstrating a bit more flexibility when it came to investment. "We'd got some very good stories," he continues, "but the only trouble was that Bruce was still squeezing me in terms of the finance. We had no external correspondents and no foreign correspondents at all."

Hollingsworth also discovered that Gyngell had a predilection for intervening in any aspect of the service he chose, be it content, appearance or personnel. Having become convinced that her style was inappropriate to the kind of programme he wanted to promote, Gyngell decided to sack Lynn Faulds Wood as TV-am's resident consumer champion. "Lynn was told quite categorically there was no future for consumer journalism," explains her husband and co-presenter John Stapleton, "and that there was no place for consumer journalism on breakfast TV." She promptly transferred her regular slot more or less wholesale onto *Breakfast Time*.

An even more dramatic illustration of the consequences of Gyngell's interference came a couple of weeks after Lynn's departure. The IRA's attempt to blow up Prime Minister Margaret Thatcher on the night of Thursday 11 October during the Conservative Party Conference at the Grand Hotel in Brighton was one of the biggest events of the year. And the fact that it took place in the early hours of the morning meant it was breakfast television that broke the story to the wider world.

Breakfast Time responded admirably, with a news team on the scene from daybreak and a full report with film ready to air by 7.30am. TV-am's response, conversely, was a shambles.

"Bruce had decided that in order to save money, he'd pull our crew out on the Thursday night, on the basis that, in his words, 'nothing ever happened on a Friday'," recalls John Stapleton, TV-am's main conference reporter. "This was despite the fact that the previous year, on the Friday of the Tory Party conference, Cecil Parkinson had resigned, and that had been a major story. Anyway, the main crew were pulled out, and I stayed on. Then at 3am, I suddenly got a phone call from my researcher, Adam Boulton, who was sitting in London and who said, 'There's a bomb gone off.' I said, 'Where?' and he said, 'About 300 yards from your head.'"

"I'd been rung up just after 3am and gone into work," continues Mike Hollingsworth, "and I realised very quickly that we had to try and get as many people down to Brighton as we could. But our problem was that we had no outside broadcast vehicles. Bruce Gyngell had let the tyres down on the one outside broadcast unit we had – to make sure we didn't use it."

Hollingsworth quickly realised that to get any pictures back from Brighton at all, he'd have to negotiate use of whatever other OB vehicles were in the area. "The possibility then arose that we could use some other ITV outside broadcast units that were there to cover the conference." But, there was a catch. "They were owned by TVS. So I thought, right, if I ring the Director of Programmes at TVS, I might be able to persuade him to let me have use of the vehicles. So I looked up who the Director of Programmes was. And, who do I have to phone? Greg Dyke." Dyke's response to being woken up in the dead of night by someone from the company he'd walked out of just a few months earlier was predictable. "He said, 'If you can get into the vehicles you can use them, but don't bother me again,' and turned over and went back to sleep. And that was the end of that conversation."

It transpired that the TVS vehicles were inaccessible as they were parked inside the cordon the police had set up around the Grand Hotel. Meanwhile, John Stapleton had now realised the extent to which he was very much on his own. "I'd been out to investigate," he recalls, "but I had no crew, and they couldn't get a crew to me in time for the start of the show." When TV-am went on the air at 6.30am, viewers were greeted, not with any startling shots of the half-destroyed hotel or live footage of survivors being pulled from the wreckage, but a file photo of John Stapleton with a telephone receiver pressed helplessly to his ear, accompanied by a slide of a fully furnished, undamaged Grand Hotel gleaming in the sunshine.

"I reported the Brighton bomb, sitting in my hotel room, watching my old mates at the BBC, and, more importantly, listening to my old mates at the BBC because they were my prime source of information," he winces. "I regurgitated down the telephone what they were saying on the BBC. I had no other way of doing it. In the end the first moving pictures TV-am

A discomfited John Stapleton
struggles to phone in TV-am's coverage of the Brighton bomb

had was a package put together at 8.20am. We'd been on the air for two hours or so before we saw a single picture."

That TV-am had even been able to do that was thanks to ITN. Hollingsworth had gone cap in hand to the news organisation, desperate to use whatever resources they had based in Brighton. But, even this had proved a minefield of opposition, as ITN had not forgotten the way TV-am had beaten them to the breakfast licence.

"I'd rung ITN and spoken to the night editor, Steve Clark, who used to work with me at Central TV," explains Hollingsworth. "I pleaded with him, and, God bless him, he tried to help me, but the truth of the matter is that David Nicholas [ITN editor] wanted TV-am blown out of the water. Meantime I had Keith Harris and Orville on the [studio] sofa. And I just said to Anne and Nick, 'Keep them there, keep talking, and we'll try to cross over by telephone to John Stapleton whenever we can.'" Eventually, Hollingsworth was able to negotiate access to some footage, but greatly against the better judgement of the ITN management.

Speaking shortly after the event, David Nicholas was scathing: "If it had not been for ITN, TV-am wouldn't have had a single frame from Brighton. Is that the way a channel's news should be operating? What's going to happen next week, or the week after if something like this happens again and we are all off duty as we are supposed to be?"

"It was just a complete and utter disgraceful debacle from beginning to end," Stapleton concludes. "Bruce Gyngell would've told you that it didn't matter a jot because the ratings remained just the same, but it was the principle of the thing. It was dire, absolutely dire. And it was doubly embarrassing for me because it was all my old mates at the BBC who were cleaning up. The incident certainly didn't imbue me with the notion that TV-am was very interested in news and current affairs."

Within a matter of weeks, Stapleton had quit. The manner of his departure seemed in line with a more general clearout of a range of figures who had become associated with Greg Dyke's era at the station. "Circumstances came about whereby it became uncomfortable for people like me to stay there," says Stapleton.

Looking back, he recalls how, shortly after Gyngell had first arrived, a summit meeting had been held with spokespeople from each of the station's different divisions. "He called in representatives from each particular sector. Lynn [Faulds Wood] went in to represent the consumer desk. I went in to represent the presenters; Peter [McHugh] was there, and Clive [Jones], and several other people. About 12 in total. And about nine spoke out and said to Bruce in polite terms, 'You can't do this, mate, we've got certain standards to maintain. You could run cartoons and repeat star interviews over and over again and do it on the cheap – but we have a moral and ethical duty to maintain certain standards and we've also made people a certain amount of promises, which we shouldn't rat on.' And he listened to all that, and, interestingly, about three months later, around 80% of the people who'd spoken out were no longer with the company. That included me. It also included Clive, Peter, and my wife. A whole raft of people went."

The general feeling of scandal surrounding the entire Brighton bomb fiasco, compounded by the stream of high-profile departures and defections, prompted the IBA to act. Shortly after Stapleton's very public exit, the Authority announced that unless it saw evidence of widespread improvement across all areas of output, TV-am's franchise could very well be completely revoked. Ironically, the threat came at a time when a review of the finances for 1984 revealed that the company was once again teetering on the edge of bankruptcy. TV-am had lost a staggering £17.9m since it came on air. In a mood of reconciliation, the ACTT agreed to a pay rise of just 5%, compared to the 8% awarded to its colleagues throughout the rest of ITV. The NUJ also pitched in, accepting a marginally improved pay offer rather than pursue industrial action.

This seasonal spirit of goodwill proved all too short-lived, as Mike Hollingsworth recalls, "Because of this extraordinary union agreement that we couldn't put out live programmes on Sundays or bank holidays, I decided that we would record the Christmas Day programme on 15 December." Unfortunately, lingering hostilities between Hollingsworth and the ACTT now exploded into a fire of resentment. "The ACTT did everything it could to try and stop me doing this Christmas programme," argues Hollingsworth today. "Its members said you couldn't possibly do a programme of three hours length in three hours. Well, of course, we did that every day, only live."

Feeling in a bullish mood, he proceeded to ignore the union's protests and went ahead with the programme regardless. "We eventually got it done, and the ACTT was very angry about it," he continues. "But, on this programme, as guests, we'd had Bob Geldof and Paul Young. It was the Christmas of Band Aid. During the programme, Bob said something to the effect that, 'Now we've raised all this money for Ethiopia, the one thing I'd really love to do is to go to Ethiopia, but I can't spend any of the money that's been donated.'"

The admission planted an idea inside Hollingsworth's head. "When we came out, after the recording, I said to Bob, 'If I can send you to Ethiopia, would you go with our cameras?'" Geldof readily agreed, and plans were immediately set in motion to fly him and Anne Diamond to Ethiopia. Hollingsworth knew that the key to the whole enterprise passing off without too much expense was to keep the film crew to a minimum. When this got out, however, it was only a matter of time before he was summoned to attend another meeting of the ACTT.

"The union said it wanted three of everything," insists Hollingsworth. "Three cameramen, three directors and three PAs, because it was a war zone and people needed relief and cover and so on. I said, 'Look, Bob Geldof's not going in threes, Anne Diamond's not going in threes, there'll only be one lot of you.' And the response was, 'In that case, you can't go.' The union blacked it." Neither side was prepared to give way, so in the end, Hollingsworth resorted to persuading a researcher to accompany Geldof alone, armed only with a Polaroid camera.

Christmas arrived at Camden Lock with relations between TV-am management and union staff at an all-time low. What with rumours of bankruptcy, liquidation and termination of contract from the IBA, there seemed to be gloom at every turn. When Chairman Timothy Aitken came to deliver his Christmas message, he could barely conceal his despair. "The company's future depends heavily on the co-operation of its staff," he stressed, "and their understanding of the fundamental need for the company to continue to maintain its costs at realistic levels. I hope that good sense will prevail."

The omens could hardly have looked worse.

SIX

"I shouldn't think I'll be asked to interview Gorbachev straight away"

The winter of 1984 was a distinctly non-festive time for the residents of TV-am's headquarters at Camden Lock. The station dutifully went through the rituals of the season, inviting viewers to have a rummage in 'Rustie's Shopping Basket', pull some of 'Tina's Christmas Crackers' and visit 'Alison Rice's Christmas Breaks'. But, behind the glitz and the élan, paranoia ran amok. Staff were obsessed by a fear of the future, the predatory behaviour of the company's board, and the machinations of the IBA. Few looked ahead to 1985 with any confidence. Not even a special yuletide on-screen appearance by Roland Rat could rally the spirits.

For Managing Director Bruce Gyngell this was simply unacceptable. Sure, TV-am had problems, some pretty severe, but it was all just a question of the right positive attitude and a generous helping of mental energy. He decreed that the New Year was to be a time of hope and prosperity. TV-am would emerge from its torpor with renewed assurance and substance. To hell with the critics. What did they know about running a breakfast television service? They probably never watched TV-am, anyway. Drawing strength from the fire of the enemies he visualised baying at the gates, Gyngell set out to recast the company entirely on his own terms and purely in his own image. TV-am would survive. It had to.

Shifting the station's opening time back to 6.15am was one way Gyngell signalled that he meant business. Another was bagging a new heavyweight journalist to join his family of presenters. When Jonathan Dimbleby arrived in February to alternate Sunday morning hosting duties with David Frost, Gyngell deliberately promoted the catch as a boost to the company's ailing news and current affairs record.

Dimbleby showed up full of self-assurance. "I want to be a little different," he announced. "I will discard parts of what David successfully does and replace them with a few ideas of my own. There will be no more discussion of the week's papers. Instead, I will focus on three or four major stories which have run through the week."

Some of his ideas sounded eerily close to a Peter Jay-style approach to news presentation, especially plans for a feature contrasting the electronic and newspaper industry, and another to compare broadsheet cartoonists at home and abroad. But Dimbleby, a high-profile breakfast television devotee, was well known throughout the media as being one of those who originally endeavoured to plant the idea of early morning TV inside the heads of the IBA. Now he would have the opportunity to put his grand aspirations into practice. Why TV-am, though, and not the more estimable *Breakfast Time*?

"TV-am has offered me the space, the air time and the resources to do something which I enjoy," he reasoned, "so I said yes. I have a clear sense of what I am prepared to do and what I will not do. I am prepared to lie in bed with my kids and watch Roland Rat, but I am not prepared to make a fool of myself and be an incompetent rat." Dimbleby even appeared resigned to what he would do were his stint at TV-am to fail: "Tractor driving is one of the most satisfying jobs in the world. You can see things happening immediately and yet you can concentrate on anything you want."

The flurry of publicity accompanying Dimbleby's arrival was impressive, but was soon overtaken by familiar signs of unsavoury management bust-ups. Peter McHugh, TV-am's editor, walked first, a mere matter of days before Dimbleby made his debut on screen. "Bruce Gyngell wanted to run the whole thing," recalls McHugh today. "He didn't just want to do the business side; he really got a buzz out of the television side. Therefore, whoever the programme people were – Director of Programmes, editors – Bruce didn't mind as long as they did what Bruce said, editorially. It didn't work for me, so I took my redundancy."

Then, a few weeks later, rumours started circulating that Director of Programmes Mike Hollingsworth was also on the way out. Bad feelings that had whipped up during showdowns with the ACTT (most recently over the number of staff slated to cover Bob Geldof's trip to Ethiopia), culminated in a terrible breakdown in trust and communication between Hollingsworth and virtually the entire technical and engineering workforce. Now he'd fallen out with the very man who had gone out of his way to bring him to TV-am in the first place.

Bruce Gyngell had witnessed the worsening atmosphere around the station, observed the low morale amongst fellow personnel, and concluded that his former golden boy had become more of a liability than an asset. The crunch came when the pair disagreed over a proposed move to hire dozens of new staff to boost TV-am's weak news operation. "We advertised about 50 new jobs," recalls Hollingsworth. "I'd said to Gyngell, that apart from anything else, I wanted to use this as a big PR statement. So we took half a page in the *Guardian* and advertised these jobs. And also made a little statement across the top saying TV-am is improving its news coverage; it intends to appoint a Washington correspondent and a Paris correspondent, and so on."

The advertisement appeared on a Monday morning, a day before both Gyngell and Hollingsworth were due to attend a meeting with the IBA to discuss TV-am's future. On the Monday afternoon, Gyngell paid his trusted lieutenant a visit. Hollingsworth takes up the story: "I said, 'We're going to have to get special people in to handle all the enquiries and applications ...' And he said, 'What applications?' I said, 'In response to the advert.' He said, 'You're not *really* going to appoint anybody, are you?'"

For Gyngell, the whole operation had simply been an exercise to curry favour with the IBA. "'You're coming with me to lunch at the IBA tomorrow,' Gyngell said. 'We'll talk to them about what we intend to do.' I said, 'I'm not going to go to the IBA and lie. We've advertised 50 posts – you're not going to appoint any of them?' And he simply said, 'No'. So I said, 'Well, I'm not coming to the IBA in that case. I'm not going to be taken to the IBA to lie to them.' And he stormed out of the office."

The next day, Gyngell studiously ignored Hollingsworth until it was time for the meeting at the IBA. "He came into my office and said, 'Are you coming to the IBA?' And I said, 'I am not going to the IBA to lie.' And he walked out of the office, and I knew from that point that I was in dire trouble. From then on, it was only a matter of time before I was fired."

With hindsight, it's possible to argue that Hollingsworth had marked his card by deciding to tackle the ACTT head on from day one, rather than adopting a more conciliatory line until TV-am was in a financially strong enough position to afford to alienate and possibly lose a large portion of its staff. For his part, Hollingsworth insists that the ACTT had to be tackled from the outset; such was the appalling state of industrial relations inherited from Greg Dyke.

When the final axe came, it was swift and brutal. "It was interesting that Gyngell could never sack anybody himself," Hollingsworth concludes. "He would send you on a holiday somewhere. The day I came back, I went straight into the office, and [Chairman] Tim Aitken came to see me and said, 'The board have decided that you must leave.' And I said, 'I'm not going anywhere, you'll have to sack me. I will not resign.' He went away, and eventually somebody else turned up with a couple of security guards."

Mike Hollingsworth was escorted off TV-am's premises. His rancorous departure made for a pointed contrast with that of Greg Dyke the previous year. The latter had received acres of publicity on the occasion of his exit – whereas Hollingsworth merited a far more muted response, much of it unfairly playing up his off-screen relationship with Anne Diamond and ignoring the influence he'd had on improving the day-to-day fortunes of the station. He certainly didn't have as much impact upon the very fabric of TV-am as his lauded predecessor – there were no radical revamps during his tenure. He also readily admits that his temperament often got the better of him: "I made some wrong moves as an individual while I was there, while I was under this terrible pressure of tiredness. I used to come in every morning at 4am and still be there at midnight." Yet, Hollingsworth did secure a more consistent ratings revival than Greg Dyke, and did much to stabilise the appearance of the company on-screen, if not behind the camera.

"I don't want to detract from what Greg did," he argues today, "because if it hadn't been for Greg I wouldn't have ever gone there after him. But the period following my departure was a very bitter time for me, because I felt that I was responsible for a lot more of the success at TV-am than I was given credit for." Of all the grudges harboured against TV-am by ex-employees, Hollingsworth's was by far the largest. "Because Anne Diamond by this point was my wife, I couldn't get away from it! Bruce Gyngell interfered with my life whether directly or indirectly. I spent a lot of time that I should've spent just getting on with my life somewhere else, looking at what TV-am was doing," he concedes. "In fact, I should've just got on my horse and ridden off in another direction."

It was typical of Bruce Gyngell's dogged spirit that he refused to let either himself or his staff dwell on the significance of Mike Hollingsworth's departure. Instead, he pushed on ever more rapidly in his quest for sustained, successful growth in terms of both TV-am's ratings and profits. Ruthless cost cutting and hard-nosed management were to secure the latter. The former was to be maintained through careful development of the TV-am 'brand': its 'family' of well known, friendly 'faces' and equally amiable, recognisable features.

This meant hiring journalist Derek Jameson to air viewers' semi-humorous complaints in the slot 'Sounding Off'. It entailed heavy promotion for the ever-popular *Wide Awake Club*. It involved rustling up distinctive mixes of guests and unlikely features, such as the edition of *Good Morning Britain,* on 16 March 1985, which included Pam Ayres, Frank Carson and an 'Oyster Opening Race'.

But it also meant an attempt to leaven the station with less frivolous and throwaway content. A new Sunday morning programme for young children was launched: *Are You Awake Yet?*, hosted by Sally Dewhurst and Peter Gosling. An award-winning Australian kids' programme, *The Curiosity Show*, was also aired. Its sober take on science and crafts may have sat rather uncomfortably alongside Roland Rat, but it certainly won points with the IBA.

The extent of Gyngell's ambition at this time was amply illustrated by the revelation, in March '85, that TV-am was drawing up plans to float itself on the Stock Exchange. On the face of it, this seemed utterly absurd, especially given the company's repeated skirmishes with bankruptcy. Nonetheless, off the back of expected current year profits of no less than £1.5m, the TV-am board forecast profits for 1986 to be up around £6m.

This was a sound base, it was insisted, upon which to consider public flotation.

But what Gyngell saw as the essence of TV-am, and what often took place on camera, were two very different things. Editorially, the station was prone to drifting into near-rhapsodic obsessions with whatever happened to be currently winning tabloid headlines, particularly if it was to do with the royal family. Anne Diamond appeared no happier than when flicking through the papers and incessantly drawing viewers' attention to whatever Princess Diana was wearing.

Residual confusions over responsibility and decision-making continued to manifest themselves in on-screen gaffes and controversy. Some of the stories of incompetence turned out to be false, such as the rumour put about that TV-am was considering offering three hours of airtime to Lebanese terrorists if they agreed to release a British hostage. Most of the embarrassments, however, were all too real. A noteworthy example occurred the day after the riots in Handsworth in September 1985. Central TV had worked around the clock to file coverage of the night's disturbances, only to find TV-am choosing to screen an interview with comic actress Beryl Reid rather than a specially lined-up live link with a local Chief Constable in Birmingham.

Such incidents, when set against the talk of stock market flotation, suggested a TV station a long way from settling on a realistic path to success.

TV-am's travails were far removed from the order and discipline of the BBC's *Breakfast Time*. A few cosmetic changes and additions had been made to the programme at the start of the New Year, but, as ever, these were implemented with the emphasis on evolution rather than revolution. So, while 'Jobs 85' was launched to help get the country back to work, Glyn Worsnip presented wry extracts from his 'Events Diary'. Heather Couper attempted to popularise astronomy in 'Skywatch', and there was also a rather clumsy attempt to capture the younger viewer with 'Zoe's View', profiling the opinions of *Breakfast Time*'s 'teenage correspondent' Zoe Brown. Least successful, perhaps, was 'Save Our Soccer', a weekly series of bulletins fronted, a little incongruously, by ex-footballer Emlyn Hughes. Quite what this feature was meant to achieve remained forever unclear; those people who could help Hughes "improve the image of British football" were unlikely to be awake at such an hour.

Looking back, Mike Hollingsworth believes that the BBC fatally underestimated the dangers of not responding more vigorously to TV-am's resurgence throughout 1984 and '85. "There was complacency," he argues, "and I think a lot of the people in the BBC at the senior level felt that it was a little beneath their dignity to be running a breakfast television show, anyway. There was an arrogance, typical of the BBC at the time, that went, 'We showed TV-am a clean pair of heels; we've sorted them out.' It was an unfortunate thing because to my mind, once that had happened, the BBC, which felt it had to occupy this territory because somebody else was going to get there, almost gave up. But there was a real feeling that the job had been done, and people started looking around for the next great challenge. I still think that if the BBC had wanted to, they could've held onto their audience."

In contrast, David Lloyd, then *Breakfast Time* editor, maintains that at this point in history the threat from TV-am, despite its ratings success, remained minimal. "It was true that TV-am were starting to make some inroads, at least in terms of overall audience share," he contests, "but they weren't really making inroads in terms of the audience which *Breakfast Time* was trying to get. They were just simply accumulating numbers of people, but not sustaining them in the long term. So, it was possible to write a quickie piece, even in a broadsheet, that TV-am was closing the gap – but really they weren't. And the answer was certainly not to mimic them."

Breakfast Time was not entirely immune to a few doses of turbulence. Following the wishes of new BBC1 Controller Michael Grade, its hours were given an overhaul. From Monday 18 February 1985, *Breakfast Time* ran from 6.50 to 9.20am to better compete with TV-am in the lucrative post-9am slot. There was no doubt that this was rather unsettling for the programme's presenters and viewers alike. It was known that Grade didn't rate *Breakfast Time* that highly, and was a man famed for his tendency to recast TV schedules with unashamed verve and aplomb.

Even more disquieting, the show then picked up some negative publicity, thanks to its undignified pilfering of a TV-am interview between Nick Owen and Princess Michael of Kent. The BBC pirated portions of the conversation dealing with alleged Nazi connections of the Princess's father, and then syndicated the footage around the world. Stern words were issued from the highest level.

One area where *Breakfast Time* continued to beat its rival hands down was in covering major national occasions, and a fine example was the grand affair laid on for the 40th anniversary of VE Day, in May 1985. 'Reunion Desk' brought together old friends from the forces, Dame Vera Lynn looked in to deliver more wartime favourites, a giant street party was blessed with the presence of both Selina Scott and Russell Grant, and Frank Bough was live from Westminster Abbey for a service of commemoration.

That summer also witnessed a few new faces joining the team. Sue Carpenter replaced Debbie Rix as the programme's main newsreader, while Sally Magnusson, a former presenter of the BBC regional news magazine, *London Plus*, helped fill the sofa while the main hosts were on holiday.

The highest profile recruit, however, was the somewhat unlikely choice of a university graduate turned beauty queen. Recently crowned Miss Great Britain, Debbie Greenwood made her debut on Monday 13 May, and was immediately at pains to admit, "There's no getting away from the fact that beauty queens are expected to be stupid. In fact, I'd go so far as to say that I was chosen to do *Breakfast Time* in *spite* of having been Miss Great Britain, not *because* of it." The programme's production team had first spotted her as potential presenter material when she appeared as a guest the morning after she became Miss GB. "I remember that Russell Grant borrowed my crown to do the stars that day," she quipped.

Debbie seemed unfazed by the prospect of comparison with Selina Scott, instead recalling some advice her illustrious colleague had passed on. "She said, 'Whatever anyone else tells you, just be yourself.' That's what I'm aiming to do. I shouldn't think I'll be asked to interview Gorbachev straightaway, but I don't think there's any intention to shield me. Being a policeman's daughter, I'm very nosey, so interviews are right up my street." She would prove so popular with viewers that her temporary status became permanent within a matter of months.

Christmas 1985 was marked with various treats including the 'Giving Tree' charity drive, which purported to "spread its branches so that viewers can help others"; a competition to find Britain's most popular father (with a chance for the winner to go to Disneyland); and a glittering pantomime co-starring prominent politicians Jeffrey Archer and Ken Livingstone.

These unusually imaginative items capped an eventful if not wholly sure-footed 12 months for *Breakfast Time*. It was a year that had proved that the programme wasn't completely infallible, and also that it was prone to the whims of rival BBC departments. A few months earlier, when the Corporation cheerfully announced that it had wooed none other than Roland Rat from his Camden Lock home, it was the light entertainment division that landed the prize, not breakfast. Consequently, Roland never appeared on *Breakfast Time* outside of occasional guest slots and fleeting cameos.

This nifty piece of cross-channel poaching may have left some in Lime Grove slightly smarting at the behaviour of their colleagues in BBC TV Centre, but it had tipped Bruce Gyngell and his management team into a riot of confusion. There was suddenly nothing to run for kids on TV-am during the school holidays. Roland's erstwhile stamping ground, the popular post-9am slot, had recently been turned into a semi-separate show entitled *After Nine*, a place for wall-to-wall lifestyle and consumer-orientated material, hosted by Jayne Irving. But this had been intended

Roland Rat shamelessly scurries over to the BBC
and the promise of no more early mornings

to run during term-time only, and had clearly little scope as a children's programme.

It was Nick Wilson, creator and producer of *The Wide Awake Club*, who came to the rescue. He devised a quick and easy solution: a *WAC* spin-off show that could run daily for half an hour, share an identity with its successful weekend parent, but pioneer features and personalities of its own.

And so, on Monday 21 October 1985, *Wacaday* was born. It was to remain a recurring staple on TV-am for years. Ludicrously cheap and unashamedly disorganised, the programme revolved entirely around the energetic personality of its host, the persistently wired Timmy Mallett. Already a TV-am 'face', it was *Wacaday* that made Mallett a household name, thanks not least to a shameless deployment of trademark gimmicks: preposterous oversized pairs of spectacles, huge tasteless coloured shorts, a disturbingly mute parrot called Magic, and, above all, a stylised over-sized foam hammer dubbed, unsurprisingly, 'Mallett's Mallet'. This device was wielded during an eponymous quiz, a simple word association game played by two hapless children in perpetual fear of a clout whenever they paused too long for breath.

An incarnation of seemingly everlasting youthful exuberance, Mallett revelled in his notorious reputation. Perhaps children despised as much as liked him, but they still tuned in out of curiosity, compunction and because there was nothing decent on the other side. The man quickly became as much a breakfast TV icon as his rodent predecessor, and continued to trade off this reputation long after TV-am had passed from the airwaves.

As 1985 turned into 1986, both Gyngell and his company seemed to be growing more bullish by the day. Announcements tumbled from the station's press office, detailing far-reaching expansions of resources, buildings and output. An extra £3m was to be earmarked for the development of TV-am's news operation, while there was talk of more regional unmanned studios being established across the country.

Gyngell continued to exercise little patience with those he perceived as timewasters and whingers. When the latest Head of Programmes, John McColgan, quit in January, Gyngell simply took on all editorial duties himself, tired of this endless procession of, as he saw them, office juniors. For McColgan, the last straw had been a memo circulated by Gyngell on the subject of programme policy that had listed McColgan's name below that of several low-ranking engineers.

TV-am was now moving towards the point where it was completely orientated towards making money and nothing else. Gyngell's core belief had become that the best way to safeguard the station's future was through a huge profit margin. Tight control on expenditure had resulted in figures showing a dramatic turnaround in TV-am's economic fortunes. In the 12 months to 31 January 1986, the company recorded a turnover of £6.92m with profits totalling £4.83m compared to the previous year's losses of £2.09m. Even more astonishing, an 88% increase in advertising revenue had been achieved over the same period.

Satisfied with these results, and utterly convinced by Gyngell's financial strategy, the TV-am board bit the bullet and allowed the company, on Tuesday 15 July, to be floated on the Stock Exchange. 12.17m shares were up for grabs at 130p each. An amazing 41,000 applications were received, meaning the bid was almost 11 times oversubscribed. 339 of the company's 400 employees also put in for shares. The whole project seemed to be a ringing testimony to Gyngell's notion that TV-am was now a sound investment.

Back on-screen, efforts were made to render the station's output similarly lavish. The *WAC* brand was further expanded to incorporate a new Sunday show, *WAC Extra*, hosted by Michaela Strachan and Timmy

Mallett. Its Saturday counterpart now boasted the talents of stand-up comedian Neil Mullarkey and future Hollywood star Mike Myers in a double act entitled *The Sound Asleep Club*. The *WAC* show celebrated its 100th edition on Saturday 22 November in typical fashion with an attempt to bake the world's largest biscuit.

Earlier in the year TV-am's weekday presenting team had pulled out all the stops for the royal wedding of Prince Andrew and Sarah Ferguson in July. Gordon Honeycombe penned a special book, *TV-am's Official Celebration Of The Royal Wedding*, and Nigel Dempster introduced a 'Royal Lookalike Competition'.

The station also acquired its first 'show biz editor'. Jason Pollock was the son of a clergyman and liked "plants and gardening, animals and Shiatzu massage", (the latter being a predilection he shared with Gyngell). Pollock had begun his career with the BBC working on 1960s variety shows such as *Dee Time* and *The Black And White Minstrels*. Now he was responsible for co-ordinating all of TV-am's celebrity interviews. He certainly had a clear take on the company's strengths. "The most important thing is the manner in which they are treated at the station," he argued. "Very rarely will an artiste not enjoy a TV-am interview. That's because there is never any hassle." Indeed, the facts spoke for themselves: TV-am were now doing around 2,500 celebrity interviews a year, more than any other TV station in Europe.

Still, not everything was rosy in this cash-stoked pantheon of the stars. Feeling increasingly out of place amidst the bluster and the tinsel, Jonathan Dimbleby left for Thames Television and a new job hosting the revived *This Week* documentary series. His credentials as a smooth-tongued tenacious presenter had become increasingly out of place in an environment where the art of cross-examination and conflict belonged very definitely behind the camera. But Gyngell didn't seem at all bothered by his exit. He was far more concerned by the departure of another important piece within his jigsaw of TV-am 'faces'.

Nick Owen made his last appearance on the sofa on August 1, also bound for Thames TV and a place hosting *Midweek Sports Special*. This most sage-like of anchors had always been a rock of calmness while mayhem reigned around, and more recently had proved invaluable in curbing some of Anne Diamond's more controllable excesses.

"I believe we set the trend that others followed," he recalls today, "and stretched further once the walls came down. In the end, I think our style, because we were so close – Anne, Wincey [Willis] and me – appealed to people: to be extremely informal, and genuine." During his time at TV-am, Nick Owen had consistently displayed a remarkable grasp of what would and would not work within the constraints of breakfast television. His presence had ensured that the mid-80s became the first 'golden age' for early morning telly. His disappearance would hasten that era to an ignoble conclusion.

Owen's contribution to the fundamental style, tone and day-to-day functioning of TV-am was no better demonstrated than by the messy, prolonged difficulties the station experienced in finding his replacement. The somewhat non-charismatic in-house junior newsreader, Adrian Brown, was initially touted as the next big thing. "It's wonderful, and a great challenge for me," he smiled, on learning that he had inherited Owen's role. "I'm looking forward to it enormously. Nick is an excellent bloke and both he and Anne have been very helpful and kind while I have been finding my feet."

But the chemistry wasn't there; nor was there much trace of a screen presence. Brown lasted only eight weeks before being humiliatingly demoted back to the news desk. A series of undignified revolving line-ups followed, with Jayne Irving, Mike Morris, reporter Geoff Meade, Richard Keys and even *Treasure Hunt* star Anneka Rice all taking their turns to nestle alongside Anne Diamond.

Christmas 1986 afforded both the depleted team and Bruce Gyngell a chance to take stock and reflect on a dizzying, uncompromising 12 months. Ratings were at an all-time high and the stock market flotation had by all accounts been a success. But Nick Owen's exit and the ensuing confusion was a pointed reminder that, no matter how much was in the bank, the station remained in thrall to the impact and influence of its most prominent 'faces', and above all their relationship with viewers at home.

If Gyngell was excessively worried, however, he tried to mask it with his usual chipper temperament. He still had his biggest star, Anne Diamond, who had just been voted favourite female personality at the *TV Times* Top Ten Awards. And besides, there was the added and somewhat unexpected seasonal bonus of what was currently going down over on the other side. Was that a white flag of surrender flying on top of the BBC Lime Grove studios?

SEVEN

"Like falling off a log – if you can do it"

Just a few short years had passed since its noisy and precarious birth, but already British breakfast television felt like it had been around forever. The same faces showing up day after day with the same diet of features and guests had given a ring of permanence to what was once dismissed as impractical and unthinkable.

It now seemed ridiculous that there was once a time when TV screens had been kept blank first thing in the morning. Both *Breakfast Time* and TV-am had learned to trade on the value of expectation and familiarity to hook in regular audiences. They knew it was important to offer people a breakfast television service with which they were happy to share their early mornings.

But there was a down side to this. Giving audiences what they wanted could just as likely encourage broadcasting that was as slick and ultra-confident as it was lazy and listless. Success breeds complacency, which in turn prompts hasty, sometimes drastic remedies. All long-running programmes have to evolve, but 1986 would see an increasingly panicked BBC trying to force *Breakfast Time* into a direction that didn't suit it – or its viewers – at all.

The year had begun pretty much as usual. The show had linked up with BBC1's *Hospital Watch* venture in February to present a week of outside broadcasts from the Queen Alexandra and St. Mary's Hospitals in Portsmouth. *EastEnders*' first birthday was marked with a trip to the soap's Elstree set on Tuesday 25 February. There was also a jaunt to Paris to cover the French elections in March, with Frank Bough, Selina Scott and Debbie Greenwood joined by a plethora of celebrity guests including Leslie Caron, Charlotte Rampling and Elton John.

Then came the truly massive jamboree mounted for the Royal Wedding of Prince Andrew and Sarah Ferguson. The revelry began on Monday 21 July when Frank Bough and Selina Scott were joined by the poet Pam Ayres who recited special verse for the bride-to-be, and by the esteemed commentator, Godfrey Talbot, for some suitably rarefied conversation. On Tuesday, the day before the wedding, Debbie was installed in a special studio outside Buckingham Palace, and, in a textbook *Breakfast Time* feature, Beverly Alt introduced suggestions for what viewers could wear on their own honeymoons.

On the big day itself, coverage ran from 6.15am to 1.30pm without a break. Selina Scott was now at the Palace; Frank Bough and Sally Magnusson helmed proceedings in the studio; David Dimbleby was posted at Westminster Abbey; and Guy Mitchelmore was stationed out in the Falklands. It was an epic production and represented *Breakfast Time* at its very best: rising to major occasions, matching the sombre with the frivolous, and all the while maintaining a friendly, respectful relationship with its audience.

Yet, aside from all these set piece stunts and national events, there was a nagging sense that *Breakfast Time* had started to grow increasingly pedestrian, even a little dull. Gone was the seamless blend of the everyday and the extraordinary. An early *Breakfast Time* trademark was its remarkable elasticity: it could stretch to incorporate high politics and low farce, and neither would feel out of place. Come 1986, there was less poise and rather more clumsiness on display. Leaks in the press about an impending radical revamp didn't help, but neither did the occasionally clunking sequencing of items. For instance, on the day the Greater London Council was abolished, an interview with its leader, Ken Livingstone, was awkwardly juxtaposed with a pithy TV review from the journalist, Anne Robinson.

Then there was the matter of morale and management pressure behind the scenes. After quitting TV-am in 1985, Peter McHugh spent several months at the BBC working on *Breakfast Time*. His recollections of the programme under the tenure of David Lloyd are far from positive. "I think they thought I'd arrived because the BBC had some grand plan, which they didn't. I was totally the wrong sort of person, but I wanted to know what the BBC was like. And it was awful. It was like the civil service. It was full of middle-rank people who were deeply unhappy and didn't want to be there. There was no motivation. I took away from *Breakfast Time* the sense that a lot of people at the BBC had inflated views about themselves. Not only did they have no view about popular journalism, or journalism that appealed to more than their group, but also they had no interest in appealing to people beyond their group. In fact a majority of them probably thought that *Breakfast Time* should be closed down."

Maybe it was simply the fact that the programme had changed so little from day one, compared to its ITV rival; or that several of its originators such as Ron Neil and Mike Hollingsworth had by now moved elsewhere. Nonetheless, there was an undeniable impression that *Breakfast Time* had drifted into the habit of appearing to be simply going through the motions. And, while Frank Bough seemed as comfortable on the leather sofa as ever, his co-hosts looked as if they were treading water while waiting for another job to come along.

All too soon, that threat of an exodus turned into reality. First to go was Mike Smith, who left on Friday 18 April to take up a new role as breakfast DJ on Radio 1. While Smith had become a regular *Breakfast Time* face, he'd never attained that primary, indispensable status of either Bough or Scott. So, it came as something of a blow when, three months later, Selina Scott herself decided to take her leave. Her unhappiness at the anti-social working hours and the somewhat demanding nature of the medium had become well known, both within the BBC and, thanks to constant tabloid speculation, throughout the media. Still, it was a great shock when she actually bade farewell to the programme that had made her a national icon, especially as she had no new job to go to.

Acutely aware of the publicity that would follow from confirmation that the BBC were prepared to carry on paying Scott an enormous retainer even though she was doing nothing at all, BBC1 Controller Michael Grade more or less assigned her, overnight, to a new fashion series called *The Clothes Show*. It would keep Scott in the public eye for many more years, but she would never again attain the heights of ubiquity and influence she had enjoyed as the first honorary queen of breakfast television.

News that Nick Ross was also about to bow out of the programme suggested that a culling of the old guard was underway. Sure enough, confirmation came in late summer that a total overhaul of *Breakfast Time* was on the cards, scheduled to coincide with the start of daytime programmes on BBC1 towards the end of the year. It had become self-evident that something needed to be done to refresh the Corporation's breakfast brand. However, was a complete relaunch really the right way to handle an institution like *Breakfast Time*?

Dave Stanford seemed to think so. A former *Nationwide* and *London Plus* producer, Stanford was the man the BBC installed as editor of *Breakfast Time* to replace David Lloyd and take the programme into a bright new future. He was quick to articulate his ideas. "The [new] programme will have a strong political thread," he revealed, "but it won't all be head-bangingly serious; it will be a good popular mix. There is a wider audience for breakfast television than currently switches on. The bedrock of breakfast television has been established and inevitably, people will tend to switch on their television sets more and more over the next few years. We intend to capture those people." There was talk of a more brisk format, a "good mix of light and shade", and a programme in the style of *Nationwide*. So far, so good – after all, in its mid-1970s heyday, *Nationwide* had ruled the roost as far as accessible, inclusive magazine programmes were concerned.

But then word began to filter out about the scale of the operation being proposed. First, and most dramatic of all, was the disclosure that the studio sofas were to be ditched. These pieces of furniture had been central to Ron Neil's founding idea of an approachable, palatable breakfast service. Now they were to be replaced with a suite of rather more conventional, but also somewhat formidable, semi-circular desks.

Next came news that the running time was to change. To give the programme a more business-like and functional feel, *Breakfast Time* would now air from 7 to 9am only. Some of Stanford's other ideas seemed less precise. One particularly hazy and fanciful promise was that there would be "less loose chat in the future". This was matched in vagueness by the observation, "Everybody will be there for a specific purpose," implying that the current version of *Breakfast Time* featured a lot of people standing about for no particular reason.

When it came to presenters, matters were clearer. Frank Bough was to stay, as would Sally Magnusson. However, they would be joined by a new regular co-host: another graduate of *London Plus*, Jeremy Paxman. Sally Jones, formerly of Central TV's evening news, was to become the new sports reporter.

This fascinating stream of information was abruptly halted when the entire project was put on hold, thanks both to a delay in the launch of daytime television and a clutch of unresolved union issues. Trouble sparked off over arrangements regarding the allocation of staffing and resources on overnight shifts. An impasse culminated in the NUJ repeatedly boycotting the new programme's pilot broadcasts. There were more union complaints when Stanford confirmed he was axing Sue Carpenter from her role of *Breakfast Time* newsreader in order to have bulletins read by the show's three main presenters. In the end, a messy compromise had to be reached. The BBC's main daytime service began on Monday 27 October, but *Breakfast Time* Mark II had to wait until Monday 10 November before reaching the air.

After all this palaver, the first morning of the reworked show proved to be something of an anticlimax. Little felt right with the new format. A painted gauze dawn scene on the studio walls looked tacky and lifeless. The sight of Frank Bough in a suit – after almost four years of pullovers – looked contrived and not a little unbecoming. The fact that the presenters had to double up as newsreaders meant there was scant trace of a relaxed atmosphere, despite the continued presence of familiar figures such as weatherman Francis Wilson. Overall, while it was clearly an ostensible 'alternative' to TV-am, it seemed a very definite step backwards. It also felt like it was a change on someone else's terms – a reaction rather than an innovation.

From inside a regulation itchy suit, Frank Bough mourns the loss of the Breakfast Time sofas

Radio Times readers were quick to speak out. "Since its inception, I have faithfully watched and mostly enjoyed [*Breakfast Time*]," complained one correspondent. "Now, however, it has become dull, dreary and diabolical. Not a smile, not even a titter, and the weather map seems to have become browned off. Perhaps it will be dinner jackets and black ties next, as it was 50 years ago." Another correspondent muttered, "Please bring back the sofa. I miss the friendly atmosphere and Frank's pullovers; even the steam rising from the coffee pot."

Speaking with hindsight, Nick Ross ascribes the reasons for the less than satisfactory overhaul to familiar behind-the-scenes tensions. "There has always been a trace of self-importance and pomposity in newsrooms – I know, I was there for long enough – and earnestness is often confused with authority. Maybe the old guard – and new, young farts – were uncomfortable with the informality. Maybe, as happens in evolution everywhere, there was simply a change in fortunes. Naturally, TV-am improved, and eventually turned into a workmanlike facsimile of *Breakfast Time*. With Ron Neil gone, perhaps *Breakfast Time* was no longer seen as a key battleground and no longer able to attract the talented management."

Ron Neil has a more measured take on the episode. "Replacing the sofas happened on *Nationwide* as well, towards the end," he explains ruefully. "It's always the same: 'Things are all fine and jolly, but let's make it a bit more serious.' There is a tendency for programmes seen to be 'light', in the views of their ultimate masters, to prompt people [to] say, 'Let's get a little more bite into them.' I felt the very difference that we'd created in the mornings – pullovers and red sofas – was more appropriate for the mornings. However, I don't think there are rights and wrongs with these things; I think programmes go through different stages and progressions, and different editors see it in different ways. What's right for one period is not right for another. I don't kind of see it as right or wrong, I just see it as the way programmes evolve."

For his part, Dave Stanford held his ground. Fighting back, he claimed at the time: "Criticism of *Breakfast Time*'s new style did not come as a surprise to me. After all, it is a bit of a shock when an old friend disappears and then reappears in a new guise. But the demise of the red sofa – which incidentally will raise thousands of pounds for the BBC's *Children In Need* fund – and the farewell to Frank's woolly pullovers don't signal the end of *Breakfast Time* as a popular current affairs programme. Far from it. The BBC has to offer a distinctive product from the other channels – not more of the same. If we did not, we would be failing to fulfil our obligations as a public-service organisation."

Yet, fulfilling remits and obligations did not and does not have to be a joyless and stuffy procedure, involving stripping programmes of their character and personality in order to satisfy a cluster of bureaucratic demands. While the new model *Breakfast Time* was probably the best news service on TV at that time of the day, a bit of magic died when the sofas and coffee tables were cleared away, never to return.

Over at TV-am, Bruce Gyngell was understandably jubilant. "It's a gift from the Gods," he boomed. "I just don't know how we could be that lucky." According to recent figures, his station already enjoyed several hundred thousand more viewers than *Breakfast Time*. Now, thanks to the BBC's behaviour, he predicted TV-am's ratings would increase to around a 75% share of the total breakfast audience.

Moreover, that audience would find a company supposedly at the peak of its game, with "Ten-minute news bulletins and a lot more current affairs input in the whole show". Gyngell continued, "[We've brought] in more experienced news editors and high profile reporters with a depth of experience. We now have 27 on-camera reporters. We now have two reporters in every region."

This was all very well, and no doubt appeased the ever-watchful critics within the IBA, but did seem somewhat at odds with Gyngell's well-documented reluctance to invest in genuine news staff. Besides, TV-am's beating heart remained its obsession with celebrity. In this, Gyngell was honest: "Frankly, if you've got Joan Collins in town and she's prepared to come in, then that's good enough reason in itself. If people are stars, that's a big enough peg. TV-am is a current affairs soap opera. We run a family and familiar organisation. People like continuity and security, and within that they like a few surprises." TV-am's 'cosy relaxed atmosphere', Gyngell concluded, was something the BBC had forfeited at heavy cost. Indeed, only a few months after the relaunch, TV-am was sometimes pulling in a peak audience of 2.7m viewers a day compared to *Breakfast Time*'s 1.1m.

When viewed on a wider scale, the enforced sobering up of *Breakfast Time* reflected the way the wind was blowing throughout the BBC. Within just a couple of months, an entire regime change had been enacted at the very top of the Corporation and an avalanche of upheaval begun. Chief architect of the insurgency was none other than the co-author of Peter Jay's "bias against understanding" treatise of the 1970s: John Birt.

In April 1987, the new BBC Director-General, Michael Checkland, announced that he intended to close the Lime Grove complex within four years, with all existing operations, including *Breakfast Time,* moving to new premises next to Television Centre. The impetus for this decision lay with Birt who, as the new Deputy Director-General, was also in charge of the Corporation's entire news output. His chief ambitions, of which he made no secret, were a speedy and business-like merging of the previously separate news and current affairs divisions, plus a complete restructuring of the way news was reported on the BBC. Regardless of Peter Jay's failures at TV-am, Birt was still on a "mission to explain", and now he had an entire corporation to play with.

Ironically, the man he appointed as his own deputy was the pioneer of the lighter touch in current affairs: Ron Neil. Representing the more human and approachable side to the Birt revolution, Neil had some influence in ameliorating the tide of anxiety sweeping across the BBC during 1987. Privately, however, the new management conceded that many existing current affairs programmes had ended up as an awkward hybrid of styles and agendas, and needed urgent reform.

This was thought especially true of *Breakfast Time.* Its trio of presenters seemed continually unsure of whether they were fronting a hard news bulletin or a chatty magazine show. Matters weren't helped by the programme's closing time shuttling variously between 9am, 8.40am and sometimes even 8.35am, depending on whether there was anything scheduled to fill the gap up to the hour. When Pamela Armstrong was seconded from the lunchtime chat show *Daytime Live* to fulfil the role of co-host from mid-June through to October, it was presumably to add an element of 'summer' to the programme. In truth, it looked like a rather desperate salvage operation.

Nonetheless, there were still moments when *Breakfast Time* came into its own, albeit not in the most expected or upbeat of circumstances. 1987 was a year marked by a series of natural and man-made disasters in Britain, and two in particular had direct impact on the fortunes of the BBC's breakfast service.

On the night of Friday 6 March the ferry, the *Herald Of Free Enterprise*, sank in the English Channel just off the port of Zeebrugge. In response, both the BBC and TV-am rushed out special editions of their breakfast shows the following morning. It meant that *Breakfast Time* made its first proper appearance on a weekend, and forced regular children's programme *Saturday Superstore* to start an hour later than planned. Frank Bough fronted the vivid and unsettling edition, at one point muttering, "We apologise if you're waiting for *Superstore* – in fact, we don't apologise."

More drama followed in the autumn. Famously denied by weatherman Michael Fish beforehand, the night of Thursday 15 October saw fierce storms rage across England, uprooting trees, felling power lines, crushing buildings and leaving most of the south east without electricity. The following morning found Lime Grove completely blacked out. Instead of *Breakfast Time*, a now-legendary shoestring breakfast programme had to be broadcast, hosted by the BBC newsreader living closest to Television Centre.

This turned out to be *Six O'Clock News* presenter Nicholas Witchell, who recalls, "I was rung at some unearthly hour by Robin Walsh, the then deputy editor of TV News. I recall trying to switch the bedside light on and telling him that for some reason it wasn't working! He explained why (in no uncertain terms!) and told me to get myself into TV Centre asap."

Witchell was forced to take refuge in the only BBC studio working at the time. By a wonderful stroke of fate, this happened to be the so-called 'Broom Cupboard', the tiny continuity presentation room at Television Centre utilized as a 'studio' for the Children's BBC output, where current presenter Andy Crane linked kids' shows surrounded by children's drawings, small toys, cards and posters. "There was no script," continues Witchell, "and very little information. There was a real sense of being Corporal Jones on *Dad's Army,* and of going on and telling those who were watching 'don't panic'. I was joined by John Kettley from the weather studio and various BBC correspondents, and we wittered away for an hour or more until *Breakfast Time* relocated to a TV Centre studio.

"It produced one of the most gratifying responses from people that I can remember in 27 years of broadcasting: dozens of letters from people, many of them elderly and on their own, who'd spent a very frightening night, and who had switched on in the morning and found a face which I hope was friendly (if a little bemused) and reassuring. It was certainly one of the oddest situations I've found myself in, but also – looking back – one of the most satisfying because it was a moment when people wanted and needed information, and we were able to give at least some of it, even if it was from the 'Broom Cupboard'!"

A more light-hearted and wholly anticipated stunt was staged on Friday 27 November 1987, when *Breakfast Time* incorporated part of Anneka Rice's special *Children In Need* 'challenge' to arrange a performance of Tchaikovsky's *1812 Overture* on the River Thames in the space of 12 hours. Yet, by this point, a year after its revamp, *Breakfast Time* was being piloted by an increasingly weary-looking and restless Frank Bough. Little seemed to hide the fact that his patter and demeanour were a pale imitation of what they had once been. Almost five years' worth of early mornings appeared to have taken their toll on the man. In the wrong light and an unflattering camera angle, he looked his advancing age and a world away from the smooth, welcoming gentleman of 1983.

Speculation had been rife throughout the year that he was considering quitting *Breakfast Time* for good – so it was not a great surprise that Friday 18 December turned out to be Frank Bough's last show. He'd never really fitted into the remodelled programme, the memories of red sofas and pots of coffee being too hard to dispel. But he was a broadcasting institution, and one of that tiny handful of people genuinely responsible for making breakfast television viable and successful in Britain.

Paddy Haycocks – at the time a producer at LWT, though soon to become a leading face of Channel 4's own breakfast service – rightly sums up his legacy: "You'd see Frank working, and watch people throw 90 things in his ear at the same time, another 23 through his eyes, another 16 through his body, and you wouldn't know. He was a very accomplished live presenter. He once said, when asked whether it was difficult being a presenter, 'It's absolutely simple; it's a piece of cake. It's like falling off a log – if you can do it.' And that said it all." After *Breakfast Time,* Frank Bough spent just one more year at the BBC, presenting the *Holiday* programme, before moving to Sky Television. His calming presence on the nation's screens was sorely missed.

Former TV-am reporter John Stapleton was the man chosen to take Bough's place behind the *Breakfast Time* desk. "After leaving TV-am, I'd worked for a variety of ITV companies, including LWT, before coming back to the BBC," Stapleton recalls. "I'd done *London Plus* for a while, and then *Watchdog* with Lynn [Faulds Wood, his wife]. Then, Ron Neil said to me, 'Would you do *Breakfast Time*?'" Stapleton soon struck up a convincing on-screen partnership with another new presenter, Kirsty Wark, although it was telling that, within a few years, two of the three new breakfast 'team' – Jeremy Paxman and Kirsty Wark – were fronting *Newsnight*, a programme as far removed from the traditions of breakfast TV as it is possible to imagine.

It had been a bumpy 12 months for the one-time giant of current affairs broadcasting. Yet, for all of its pretensions and increasingly poker-faced approach towards news presentation, *Breakfast Time* was still by no means beleaguered, or on the rocks, or a national joke. Indeed, those particular distinctions had just been reclaimed – and on a profoundly breathtaking scale – by the opposition.

EIGHT

"I know a lot of people can't stand me"

1987 should have been a triumphant year for TV-am. The company's finances had never been healthier with profits up by 42% in the 12 months to January and expected to carry on rising. Ratings showed the station often pulling in as many as 2.4m viewers at any one time – double the figure for *Breakfast Time*. The disorderly procession of substitute presenters that had followed the departure of Nick Owen had also been curtailed, thanks to long-serving co-hosts Mike Morris and Richard Keys taking up alternate weekly residencies on the sofa.

Yet despite all these indicators, before 1987 was out, TV-am would see itself collapse from a position of extreme buoyancy and excess into one of total calamity. Everything that been so carefully and audaciously put together was to fall apart, and crisis revisit the station on an epic scale. Headlines and coverage would be of a kind not witnessed since those nightmare days of early 1983. This time around, however, because the company had climbed all the higher, the fall was all the more dramatic and its consequences played out, not over months, but years.

No trace of storm clouds blew across the station for the first six months of the year. Even the disappearance of Anne Diamond on maternity leave failed to derail operations, with Jayne Irving and new recruit Caroline Righton proving more than adequate as stand-ins. TV-am's 'family' continued to grow: charismatic chef Patrick Anthony joined the team, as did reporter Kay Burley, while Trish Williamson, Anna Walker and Carol Dooley all took turns in front of the revolving weatherboard. Comic actress Su Pollard, well suited to the increasingly ribald ethos of the station, also turned up to preview TV highlights. A somewhat more sober testimony to TV-am's achievements came in the form of a BAFTA award for best children's factual programme, given to the enduringly entertaining *Wide Awake Club*.

TV-am staged the first ever international conference on breakfast television in June. In a similar move, the 'news hour', one of the first things Greg Dyke had scrapped in 1983, was symbolically restored between 6 and 7am in July. As before, so again, it became the least-watched and most unconvincing strand of the station's output – but that was not the point. It was supposed to show that TV-am was serious about news, as was the introduction of an expanded bulletin on Saturdays.

Nonetheless, this didn't stop the IBA continuing to castigate the station for what it perceived to be persistent and serious failings. At the end of July, the Authority handed out more stinging criticism, citing TV-am's regional coverage and investigative current affairs as being particularly poor. TV-am countered by claiming that it had already pre-empted such complaints by boosting its sports coverage and upping the number of regional spots to 90 a month.

For further examples of responsibility, the company argued, consider Saturday mornings, where *Countdown* presenter Carol Vorderman now hosted a regular science slot, or the fact that the station had already agreed to hand over part of its weekend to the Open College, a Channel 4-based learning initiative similar to the Open University. And if that wasn't enough, there was the appointment of Rowanne Pasco as full-time Religious editor, and the impending launch of TV-am's first ever religious show *Fables, Parables And Miracles* presented by Alvin Stardust.

Such gestures were significant concessions towards TV-am's statutory remit to mix celebrity with information and education. Yet, at the same time, they inevitably seemed terribly worthy and, by the standards set in British breakfast television to date, more than a little out of place. Partly out of lingering shame at handing TV-am a licence to broadcast in the first place, and partly in response to petitions from other ITV companies, the IBA continued to try to influence as much of the station's output as possible.

One thing the Authority had no control over, however, was the behaviour of TV-am's Managing Director. Bruce Gyngell's profile soared during 1987, and it was all down to events of his own making. As the year progressed, he set about advancing an even more pronounced role for himself as gun slinging outsider and maverick entrepreneur. His public outbursts grew more frequent, and his self-styled troublemaker persona more extreme and relentless. With money rolling into TV-am's HQ at Camden Lock, he could afford to mix occasional genuine investment – such as hiring an extra 12 reporters and creating four journalist traineeships – with outrageous speculation.

He very purposefully voiced an interest in competing against ITN to provide a full night-time news service for ITV. Then, not satisfied with sniping at one company, Gyngell laid into the entire ITV network, accusing them of making programmes for themselves and not their viewers. Also, at the Conservative Party Conference, he aired his long-held views about the lack of competition and archaic practices within British television, and was given a rapturous reception.

All of this rabble-rousing won reams of publicity, but simultaneously sharpened long-harboured sentiments of suspicion towards Gyngell throughout the rest of the media. The man was rapidly turning into a hate figure, and the walking embodiment of all that was loathed about TV-am. There was undoubtedly a degree of jealousy to this sniping, not least regarding TV-am's financial and ratings success. Yet Gyngell seemed just as much to blame in the way he continually cultivated hype and attention; revelled in the fact he was Prime Minister Margaret Thatcher's favourite TV executive; and actively sowed seeds of confrontation.

The reasons why it did eventually go so wrong for TV-am in 1987 lie with Bruce Gyngell and his deliberate show of calculated, aggressive brinkmanship. The spark was unfinished business left over from TV-am's launch: the poor relationship between the station's technical staff and its management. But instead of these bad feelings being resolved quietly and methodically, they had, over time, been dangerously agitated and intensified through Gyngell's bravado and grandstanding. In retrospect, a showdown was almost inevitable.

What followed was one of the most notorious industrial disputes in TV history. It all began with a single incident involving TV-am's annual 'Caring For Christmas' charity campaign. A film shoot had been planned as part of the appeal, which the ACTT (the main production and technical union at TV-am) intended to cover with its usual five-man crew. The station's management, however, wished to employ a three-man crew for the shoot, containing neither a separate director nor producer, in contravention of standard working practices then in place at TV-am.

In response, the ACTT balloted its members over the possibility of registering its disapproval in the form of a one-off strike. Over 80% of the workforce voted by four to one for industrial action and accordingly, a 24-hour stoppage took place on Monday 23 November. But Gyngell, feeling combative, took one look at this protest and decided to teach his employees a particularly vicious lesson. Come the following day, he locked the station's doors, barred all entrances and refused to allow the strikers to return to work. The ACTT, stung by this unexpected rebuke, immediately set up a picket line outside TV-am.

So, a one-off dispute turned into a stalemate and a short-term showdown became a long-term battle. Both sides made it quite clear they were in for the duration, and neither was interested in backing down. All good feeling at the company completely evaporated and in a stroke, TV-am became the focus for a maelstrom of media hyperbole, negativity and ridicule.

Gyngell was instantly seized with a zealous sense of righteousness. He didn't care that he'd lost most of his staff: he believed TV-am could operate a normal television service indefinitely. Faced with the sight of no proper technical personnel whatsoever – no producers, floor managers, electricians, camera operators or editors – his response was typical. He personally took charge of the entire broadcasting operation himself, 'directing' each edition of TV-am single-handedly while enlisting anyone still left in the building, including secretaries, tea ladies and teenagers on work experience, to help him in the gallery.

The idea was preposterous and the results were little better. To begin with, seeing as few presenters were willing to cross the picket lines, Gyngell could only run a skeleton service consisting almost entirely of repeats of veteran shows like *Batman*, *Flipper* and *Happy Days*. Such was the haphazard manner in which this was organised that no attention was paid to transmitting any of these imported programmes in the correct order. Nor were they properly timed or sequenced. Consequently, if one episode was over-running, the tapes were simply fast-forwarded during a commercial break to catch up, and then switched back to the right speed as if nothing untoward had happened. Two-part stories were left unfinished with the second instalment never aired, or sometimes the concluding part was aired before the first. Indeed, the same episode was often shown two or three days running. Tapes were also played at the wrong speed, appearing on-screen slightly too fast or too slow. Most famously of all, part of an episode of *Flipper* was shown backwards, apparently due to the clumsiness of TV-am Sales Director Tony Vickers who claimed to have mistakenly loaded the film into a machine the wrong way round.

Despite this catalogue of mayhem, Gyngell and his troops were quick to enjoy the support of the tabloids ("RATS! Striking TV Men Hold The Needy To Ransom" screamed the *Star*) and his close friend, the Prime Minister. Plus, he wasn't the slightest bit worried about losing money. All of TV-am's advertising space up to Christmas had been sold and there were enough forward bookings to be able to continue with a management-run service at least until the end of February 1988.

He soon had the added bonus of Anne Diamond. From Monday 7 December, Gyngell was able to switch from a 100% prerecorded schedule to one that featured a 30-minute live segment in the middle. Anne was the host and typically, one of her first interviewees was Margaret Thatcher herself. Other guests weren't so co-operative, however, following the example of Adam West who refused to cross the picket line to talk about his memories of filming *Batman*. When this half-hour live segment was increased to an hour from Monday 14 December, Tommy Boyd and Timmy Mallett started turning up to explain, from the TV-am sofas, why repeats of *WAC* and *Wacaday* were being aired, and also why viewers should not enter any of the featured competitions.

With each passing day, the off-screen acrimony grew. Both management and union fired smears and allegations at each other and heaped blame on their opponents for prolonging the dispute. Watching from afar, former TV-am Director of Programmes Mike Hollingsworth viewed events with a

A resolute Anne Diamond
defies the massed ranks of the locked-out TV-am workforce

keen sense of irony. "I had a mixture of feelings, because I clearly saw that at last, Gyngell, who had always said I was being too hostile towards the ACTT, had turned against the union himself, and had thrown the ACTT out on the street. He was being urged on this route by the other ITV companies who felt powerless to do anything about the ACTT themselves. But it set a precedent, because TV-am would now go straight to the transmitters; it didn't have to go through any regional companies, so the signal couldn't be blacked in any way. The ACTT could no longer affect TV-am and its transmissions."

The stand-off was made even worse when the *Sunday Times* printed details of an alleged 'dossier' compiled by TV-am Controller of News Jeff Berliner, which listed supposed recurring instances of malpractice by the ACTT dating back several years. The document included: mention of Mike Hollingsworth's abortive attempts to film Bob Geldof in Ethiopia; suggestions that technicians had deliberately sabotaged pictures of the Queen's 1986 trip to China; and how a report by Kay Burley on a microlight flight around the world by one Brian Milton was halted, with only a 20-second shot left to record, because there was no official 'director' present.

Tim Wight, ACTT shop steward, issued a long rebuttal of the charges, point by point, arguing, amongst other things, that, "The ACTT did not at any time request that a director or a production assistant be assigned to the Ethiopia trip. The ACTT did request that a freelance producer be employed for the trip because at that time no member of TV-am staff had experience in supervising a crew in a Third World country and a war zone."

Such disagreement over rival interpretations and agenda would dog the formal negotiations between TV-am and the ACTT when they finally began on Thursday 14 January 1988. At the talks, management formally unveiled a 'Ten-Point Plan' listing the precise terms and conditions under which the union would be allowed back to work. The ACTT promptly rejected it, arguing that it paved the way for a further weakening of employees' rights. Both sides were left to withdraw and consider their next move.

Somehow, in the middle of all this, the means were found to ship Anne Diamond and Mike Morris off to Australia for a week to mark the country's 200th anniversary. There was even a celebration of sorts to coincide with TV-am's fifth birthday on Monday 1 February, with Anne joined by Richard Keys, Gyles Brandreth, Su Pollard and Jimmy Greaves for a Blitz-spirited toast to the good old days. Su marked the occasion with various outbursts, including the declaration that the early months of TV-am were, "Pathetic! Let's face it!" and the weather so cold as to "freeze your tits off". Viewers were also treated to Gyles' special birthday cake jumper, plus protracted reminiscences about the presentation of the TV-am boat, *The Diamond Lady,* on Bondi Beach.

This fifth anniversary programme was the first time management had been able to get the total amount of daily prerecorded output down to just one hour. It was also the final deadline set for the ACTT to accept the 'Ten-Point Plan'. The 234 locked-out employees held another ballot to determine their response. The result was unequivocal. The union rejected the Plan outright, and refused to consider returning to negotiations unless substantial concessions were offered.

Yet, for all the ACTT's belligerence and tenacity, the fact was that TV-am's transmissions had steadily increased, not declined, during the course of the dispute. Gyngell seemed in total control of events, able to outflank the union time and again through a combination of judicious announcements and good luck. By way of a spoiler tactic, he contrived to proclaim the opening of new TV-am bureaux in Moscow, Cyprus and Hong Kong on the same day as the ACTT's vote, and deliberately encouraged rumours that those technicians still inside TV-am HQ were being paid up to £70,000 a year.

As far as Gyngell was concerned, the only damage really being done by the dispute was to TV-am's image. Thanks to the continuing press interest, the station had once more acquired a reputation for incompetence and disorder. This was not good enough. So, utterly tired of all the gossip and tongue wagging, Gyngell suddenly – late on the night of Tuesday 16 February – sacked all the locked-out personnel in one fell swoop. The following morning he called a meeting of all remaining TV-am staff and, rather melodramatically flanked by half a dozen specially hired bodyguards, announced that the ACTT would never again be allowed to organise inside his building. No advance warning had been given to the ACTT of their impending dismissal; members learned of their fate on the television news.

This was the epitome of Gyngell's clinical and ruthless approach to management: a decision he felt was harsh but necessary. It turned a constituency of the media against Gyngell for good, and established a solid bank of ill feeling towards TV-am that would remain at large for years. Yet sacking the ACTT staff did not in any way resolve matters in the short term. The picketing continued, as did the rickety television service run by the management, hampered by gaffes, mistakes and embarrassments.

The chaos rapidly intensified. Later in February, news broke that a percentage of TV-am was actually owned by the Saudi royal family. This was a complete contravention of IBA rules, and the Authority ordered the shareholding to be sold immediately. It transpired that the stake, worth around £14m and totalling 14.9% of the company, had been acquired by its owners under a complicated array of anonymous credentials. As a result, both Jonathan and Timothy Aitken resigned from the TV-am board and Ian Irvine, another executive, was hastily promoted to the position of Chairman. Finally, and as 54 Labour MPs signed an Early Day Motion in Parliament asking the IBA to suspend TV-am's franchise, Bruce Gyngell suffered a heart attack and had to absolve himself of all duties for a couple of months to recuperate.

It was quite remarkable, given this string of crises, that there was only one occasion when there was no TV-am service whatsoever. This was on the morning of Monday 30 May 1988, when ITV were holding their first *Telethon* charity appeal. The ACTT had asked all its members across the ITV network to boycott the programme. For fear of triggering a nationwide dispute, TV-am's acting Managing Director Adrian Moore had simply washed his hands of his station's airtime, giving the hours between 6 and 9.25am to the rest of network to use as they pleased. Relations between TV-am and the rest of ITV had always been strained. Now they hit rock bottom.

Reviewing all the events of the previous few months, the company could draw some comfort from a consultation of the books. Somehow or other, TV-am had managed to make £13.1m in profit for the year ending January 1988, while advertising revenue across the same period had risen 30% to a record £54.1m. But although Gyngell and his cohorts talked of a TV-am made stronger through adversity, their schedules were still packed with repeats of dusty shelf material such as the ancient jungle series *Daktari*. The recent turmoil had wrought terrible damage to the company's already chequered legacy and, within both media and industry circles, TV-am was regarded as a ludicrous anachronism. Morale within the surviving workforce was very low. Management had only been able to recruit 40 people to replace those 234 sacked.

The Piper Alpha oil platform fire off the east coast of Scotland in July exposed the extent of TV-am's present condition in pitiless detail. The crew, which assembled to mount a live outside broadcast from Aberdeen, set their camera 60 feet up in the air, on top of a building surrounded by a moat, thinking this would give a good background view of the sea. They failed to account for the presence of an elderly priest among the guests booked to appear. Consequently, the entire broadcast was delayed while the ageing man of the cloth clambered across a hastily erected moat bridge, before gingerly scaling two vertical ladders. Then it was decided that the location was unsafe anyway, and the whole shoot had to be re-mounted in the street.

After more delays, the transmission was ready to begin. The first guest, a doctor, was wired up with an earpiece to allow him to speak with Anne Diamond back in London. The interview began, but Anne was puzzled by the fact that the medic didn't seem to be hearing anything she said. She pressed on regardless, but to no avail – the GP remained resolutely mute. Utterly bemused, the entire link-up was brought to a premature close, and technicians called over to check the wires. It turned out the electrical connections were fine. Only when they noticed the doctor still waiting patiently to speak to Anne Diamond did the crew realise that their guest was completely deaf.

The IBA, when similarly reflecting on recent events, was appalled. It had witnessed TV-am drop virtually all its news content in favour of imported repeats, top up its accounts with a secret Saudi Arabian treasure chest, and replace experienced, accomplished technicians and producers with unqualified or half-trained handymen and secretaries. Accordingly, the Authority used its annual report on all ITV companies to launch a withering attack on TV-am, reserving particular scorn for its weekend news service and children's programmes. Standards may have slightly improved since the day Gyngell locked out his staff, the report observed, but overall output was "below that required".

A special crisis meeting followed on August 19, the outcome of which was an even more explicit warning threatening to review, early in 1989, the nature of TV-am's entire franchise unless immediate improvements were made. In private, however, the Authority had been at pains to assure the station that the IBA and TV-am would, "sink or swim together". This telling admission confirmed that matters were not as clear-cut as they seemed.

The IBA was in a tricky situation. On the one hand, it was under pressure to deal quickly and properly with the perceived failures of TV-am. On the other, it was anxious to preserve the ITV network intact through to the next round of franchise renewals slated for the early 1990s. It was also desperate to show a government, keen on deregulation, that the Authority could discharge its responsibilities at arm's-length and without too much intervention. While the IBA was urged to act tough by voices across the industry, it couldn't afford to ignore the intrigues of the one person who had final say over its own survival: the Prime Minister, who, as fate would have it, was one of Bruce Gyngell's closest allies.

For its part, TV-am did not wait for the IBA to sort out its priorities. Back in July, the station's Foreign editor, Stephen Barden, had been appointed the new Managing Editor. Now he acted swiftly to re-establish at least an appearance of confidence and credibility to TV-am's output. Some familiar fixtures were hastily restored, including *Frost On Sunday*, while a scattering of new programmes and features were launched. Chief of these was *Saturday Sport*, a sprawling 60-90 minutes of sports news fronted by Geoff Clark. Barden supervised a joint initiative between TV-am and the Training Commission, called *Success '88,* intended, ironically, to provide young people with advice on job opportunities. The number of weekend news bulletins also increased and transmissions of the Open College, suspended since the industrial dispute began, returned to the schedules.

However, despite a sense of the company having come through the worst, more foundational problems demanded attention. For one thing, the quality of children's programmes was embarrassingly dire. Just 12 months earlier, *WAC* had won the station its first BAFTA. Since then, virtually no new shows had been made, and the IBA had instructed that the deluge of repeats and imports must now come to an end. Accordingly, a revamped *WAC* made a rather subdued return in October, now called *Wideawake* and resembling a pale imitation of former glories.

Secondly, and of potentially far greater significance, was the news that Anne Diamond was considering quitting TV-am for good. At the time, she went on record as believing, "The image I have is not the image I particularly like. The impression is sometimes given that I'm hard-faced, and deserve every comeuppance I get. I know a lot of people can't stand me. I know I get up a lot of people's noses."

Her decision to leave was, reportedly, much to do with her continued treatment by the tabloids, the stress of working through the dispute with the ACTT, plus the feeling that now, after five years, it was definitely time to move on. Still, for many, Anne Diamond was the absolute embodiment of breakfast television, loved and loathed in equal measure, and it had been assumed that she would be a part of TV-am forever.

In a typically emotional and unsubtle display, she made her farewell on the morning of Tuesday 1 November 1988. This was no random date: it was the occasion of the British Film Institute's *One Day In The Life Of Television* project, which was recording and documenting for posterity everything broadcast on British TV over the course of 24 hours. The terms under which she left Camden Lock dictated that she would never again work for the station as a full-time presenter, but on Gyngell's insistence, allowed for an occasional return at some future date or even some kind of executive position.

This would turn out to be a rare instance of sound judgement from a man increasingly obsessed with thoughts of destiny and retribution. Gyngell had emerged from the ACTT dispute a more steely, outspoken and headstrong individual. He believed he had fought for and won the right to take TV-am into the 1990s and beyond. The more isolated and ridiculed he became, the more he convinced himself he was right. The fact that the money kept rolling in (helped no end by the multiple sackings and the minute number of replacements taken on) was – to him – a total vindication. Besides, with an ally such as the one Gyngell had sitting in Number 10 Downing Street, surely nothing could threaten the one ITV company that had dared to stand up to the unions.

But Gyngell had also become blinkered as to just how deep the scars ran amongst his contemporaries and rivals. After triumphing, as he saw it, in this most brutal and final of conflicts, he refused to countenance the possibility that TV-am would ever be on the losing side again. It would prove to be a fatal miscalculation.

NINE

"Did you get the package from Ronnie Kray?"

At the same time that TV-am was struggling to keep itself from tumbling off the air, another network was busy preparing to make its debut on early morning screens. Back in September 1986, Channel 4 (C4) had first signalled an interest in introducing its own breakfast television service to compete alongside the BBC and ITV. The station may have been only four years old, but had quickly established itself as a key player in British TV, proudly and imaginatively exploring its remit to transmit alternative, challenging and minority programmes at peak times. Now it was eyeing up those hours of the day it had yet to colonise. A breakfast TV programme, C4 reasoned, would do wonders to increase its profile, besides demonstrating the channel's relevance and ambition to a government intent on implementing major media reform.

C4's breakfast television was always going to be a curious creation. In order to fulfil its statutory remit, the station had to provide a contrast to existing networks, to innovate and to experiment. This virtually guaranteed that its breakfast service would be unlike anything seen on TV so far. Understandably, the speculation that greeted confirmation that C4 had begun planning for such a programme was intense, yet it also prefigured a less than easy ride for C4's team of executives and commissioning editors.

An early stumbling block was the relationship that the new service was to have with TV-am. C4 was funded by advertising revenues paid for and collected by ITV companies. Surely the channel's proposed breakfast output would therefore invoke some kind of financial combat with TV-am, independent television's sole breakfast license-holder? The IBA were quick to broker a solution. It proposed that TV-am enjoy all the rights to sell advertising airtime during C4's breakfast service, and in turn would help fund the new operation from the resulting revenues collected. C4, meanwhile, would commission and retain editorial control of all its own programming.

Bruce Gyngell thought this a nonsense. Why have different production companies battling it out against each other when only one had the rights to sell airtime? Far more sensible, he argued, would be for TV-am to control C4's breakfast service completely. It would be a useful showcase for its supposedly burgeoning news resources, while allowing limited investment of the company's amassed fortunes. Mindful of Gyngell's handling of the ACTT dispute, however, the IBA was quick to reject this rather far-fetched notion. The Authority gave C4 the green light in the summer of 1988.

The man ultimately in charge of creating the new breakfast service was Michael Grade, who had left the BBC to become Chief Executive of C4 in January 1988. Grade had been no great fan of breakfast TV while in his previous job and carried some of his suspicions into his new position. But the environment of a commercial broadcaster was very different to that of a publicly funded Corporation – and Grade's decision to introduce a breakfast programme was an honest acknowledgement that, in his own words, "Our blank screen in the morning was an invitation to the regulators to take those hours from us."

Michael Atwell, then Channel 4 Commissioning editor for business programmes, expands on this view: "The Conservative government of the day was threatening to sell off spare airtime to the highest bidders in order to earn money for the Treasury. Channel 4 took the view that if they didn't increase the number of hours they used, some of their airtime would be taken away and sold on to other people."

After lengthy consultation with his colleagues, Grade decided to go for, "a television version of the Radio 4 *Today* programme. Channel 4 Daily was the title I chose to signal our aim, which was to give the viewers authoritative global news, city reports and arts reviews." The parallel with radio was emphasised by Grade's second-in-command, C4 Director of Programmes Liz Forgan: "One of the reasons that early morning television is still a minority area in Britain is that early morning radio is so good, offering many different choices to a disparate audience." C4's seven-day breakfast service was to be similarly eclectic, yet purposefully aimed at special interest groups: "I'm only asking people to make a brief date with us," she continued; "perhaps ten minutes each day, to watch what they are really interested in."

Channel 4 was unique in British television in that, save for the viewers' feedback show *Right To Reply*, it did not make any of its own programmes. It was the TV equivalent of a publishing house, commissioning output from other independent companies and then scheduling and broadcasting it as and when it saw fit. The breakfast service was no different. C4's proposal for the Channel 4 Daily became the largest and most complex tender the station had ever handled – and the man charged with directly overseeing its development was former *Breakfast Time* editor David Lloyd, now C4's Commissioning editor for News and Current Affairs.

Michael Atwell recalls, "David Lloyd was the person who was given the responsibility for running the early mornings, because I think it was automatically assumed that, as it was an early morning programme, it would have to have news in it. And, as he was the person responsible for news, he was given charge of it."

It was Lloyd himself, not Grade or Liz Forgan, who came up with the idea of running the Channel 4 Daily as, to use Atwell's phrase, a "compendium of programmes". In other words, rather than comprising one continuous broadcast, the service would resemble a patchwork of different strands and commissions. "I tried to design it, not as a sort of general mix of everything," concurs Lloyd today, "but instead to give everything specialist slots." The thinking was that, by doing this, Channel 4 would open the field for contributions from as many independent production companies as possible, besides guaranteeing a finished product that was assuredly different from any other breakfast TV programme.

When a deadline of 19 September 1988 was set for the receipt of interested proposals, the C4 offices were deluged with mountains of paperwork. David Lloyd grappled with pitches that suggested everything from newspaper reviews, a weekend leisure strand and live music to a religious or secular 'pause for thought', a consumer programme and even a youth-TV style show. In total, almost 700 programme ideas were submitted. Lloyd estimated that all the documents stacked on top of each other would reach a height of between 15 and 20 feet.

Perhaps understandably, the final service was slow to take shape. Mentorn Films, who produced the regional review series *01 For London*, was commissioned to supply an arts news strand; and a consumer slot entitled *Streetwise* was ordered from the small production company, Roach & Partners. This was to be fronted by former *Breakfast Time* face Debbie Greenwood along with erstwhile *Six O'Clock Show* editor Paddy Haycocks, and was intended to be one of the key elements of the new service. The only sports-related content that made the cut, however, was the amusingly frugal *Kickback* involving a member of the public delivering an opinion piece to camera (the calibre of which turned out to be performance poet Attila The Stockbroker reciting a rap about Liverpool's 9-0 defeat of Crystal Palace).

ITN was awarded the contract for supplying news content, and appointed Carol Barnes as chief newsreader. "I'd been presenting *News At Ten* for several years with Alastair Burnet and Sandy Gall," Carol recalls, "and had let it be known at ITN that I wanted to front a programme on my own. So when ITN got involved in the Channel 4 Daily, it asked me to be the main news presenter. I agonised over this for quite some time, since I would have to get up at 3am to travel in each day from my home in Brighton." In the end, however, she couldn't resist the spirit of the occasion. "ITN was very excited about this new venture and I got caught up in the enthusiasm. I think we really believed this was going to be the definitive breakfast TV programme."

As the launch date approached, Channel 4 decided to mount an unusually glitzy press conference to publicise the service. It was a rather heady occasion. "I remember going along to this launch," recalls Paddy Haycocks, "feeling like a very minor star. It was in a wine bar in Charlotte Street, just north of the C4 building, and lots of people were there from the channel along with members of the press. Liz Forgan got up, stood on a little plinth and made a speech about how the service was going to reflect exactly what C4 was franchised to do. It was going to be distinctive and very different from the breakfast fodder that people had watched up until then. And then, suddenly, she said, 'Well, we've got these little toothbrushes here...'"

It was C4's idea of an appropriate promotional gimmick: customised toothbrushes, embossed with the Channel 4 Daily logo, packaged in their own clear plastic presentational boxes. "I thought it was incredible!" Haycocks continues. "It was almost rattling a sabre at the TV-am eggcup. It was quite amusing that C4's version was something worthwhile and useful – something to clean your teeth with. The box was even branded with some of the segments – news, weather, arts, and so on. They produced a few hundred, but I never saw them given out anywhere else again."

At 6am on Monday 3 April 1989, after a few last hectic weeks of preparation, the Channel 4 Daily finally began. The first thing to greet viewers was an extremely eye-catching and glossy opening sequence based around a motif of people opening roller blinds, blessed with a distinctive and very hummable title theme. The omens were good. Next up was Carol Barnes with the first of the regular hourly news bulletins. This did not look quite so promising. She was seated in what resembled a cheap, sparsely furnished TV editing suite, and looked rather abandoned as she cued in reports from Michael Nicholson in Washington and James Mates in Tokyo, both of whom were also stationed in poky-looking cupboards, ostentatiously referred to as 'bureaux'.

The next surprise was that the whole service did not have any proper presenters, relying instead on an off-screen anonymous continuity announcer to introduce each of the individual items. These included: the arts strand, *Box Office,* hosted by former Central TV presenter Garry Rice; *Streetwise*; *Business Daily,* fronted by Dermot Murnaghan; a cartoon; and, most familiar to regular C4 viewers, *Countdown Masters.* This was a spin-off from the stalwart quiz show featuring long-serving presenters Richard Whiteley and Carol Vorderman overseeing rematches of former champions.

Weekends were an entirely different proposition. Michael Atwell remembers, "David Lloyd said to me, 'I'm not going to run news at the

Carol Barnes salutes the arrival of the Channel 4 Daily

weekend, there isn't a team geared up for it, it's going to be too expensive. So, do you think you could look after the weekends?' My starting point was to go to TV-am, who would be selling the airtime. I spoke to Tony Vickers, Head of Sales for TV-am, and said, 'You've got to sell the advertising – you tell me, what would sell?'"

Vickers suggested that the most effective way of maximising revenues would be to offer up complementary programming. When TV-am was airing serious, news-based output, Channel 4 should go for kids' shows, and when they were broadcasting their own children's programmes, Channel 4 should try for the adult audience. "So, it was actually very simple," continues Atwell. "We bought children's cartoons [branded Just 4 Fun] and played them while TV-am was showing its early morning sports programmes. Then, when TV-am had kids' shows, we bought in other stuff."

So it was that C4 weekend breakfast audiences were treated to a mixture of natural history in *Ark On The Move*, more from *Streetwise* and *Box*

Office, plus repeats of the chat show *Oprah Winfrey* and old clips of jazz performers from the 1930s. "For Sunday mornings, we bought weird things," claims Atwell, "because we had no money. I bought a thing that ran for about a year called *The Bobby Jones Gospel Show*, a black gospel show from America, which cost very little. Later, the British Black Gospel Churches actually invited us to go to an awards show for having run this – the only place on British television that it had ever been seen. And probably still is!"

The Channel 4 Daily was definitely unlike anything previously seen on breakfast television. It was unique, that was for sure, and felt very 'Channel 4'. The entire enterprise was even blessed with a typically stylised on-screen clock, far more complex than the BBC or TV-am, in that it not only displayed the time but, thanks to four little illuminated bars, each quarter-minute. But for all its peculiar charm, eccentric mix of features and charismatic presenters, the Channel 4 Daily's appeal quickly turned out to be sorely limited.

One problem was the service's piecemeal structure, which relied a lot on prefilmed content. "We were making all sorts of compromises by having to prerecord various links," remembers David Lloyd. "That's a poor start to the design of any programme that's claiming to be live and that wakes you up in the morning." "It should have been more live," adds Paddy Haycocks. "It should've had more of a human face. It was a bit disjointed. When they constructed it, and decided how they could make the thing roll for three hours, they depersonalised the links. An anonymous continuity man sat in a cupboard at ITN, and when it went from one segment to the next you'd hear this disembodied voice saying 'Coming up next...' Apart from the news, he was the only live element – and he was out of vision! There was nobody sitting on a sofa driving the whole programme, so there wasn't a sense of family or unity about it."

For those who did have to turn up to broadcast every morning, the experience soon proved to be something of an ordeal. "I have to say that once the programme was up and running, I found it disappointing," confides Carol Barnes. "I think our news content was dull, with all the foreign sections prerecorded. And nothing else sparkled either – perhaps because most of that was prerecorded as well."

"Carol was sitting on her own in a studio," explains Haycocks. "I remember going over one day to meet her. *Streetwise* was recorded the day before, so everything was very separate. There wasn't a huge amount of mixing. The one day I went over to ITN, I remember hovering outside the studio while Carol was doing a bulletin. I just thought, 'You must be very lonely in here.' Carol was quite high profile at the time, and now she was suddenly in the world of breakfast without big audiences and feedback. The potential for being slightly demoralised for just doing the job was pretty great."

Its tapestry-like structure also lent the Channel 4 Daily an ever-shifting, somewhat ambiguous profile. "The Channel 4 Daily was effectively aimed at a *Daily Mail* sort of readership," explains Michael Atwell; "an intelligent adult audience who wanted intelligent news but also wanted some sort of consumer features. But the real problem was that BBC1 provided a very good news service for middle class so-called ABC1 viewers, and had a huge newsgathering operation worldwide, so you couldn't really compete with that. And TV-am was providing more populist news, which included a great number of consumer features. So, fundamentally, there just wasn't enough of an audience between those two for us to get."

From the outset, the Channel 4 Daily never really possessed enough of a coherent identity to ensure a stable and sound basis for its long-term existence. Individual programmes tried to develop their own personalities, but were somewhat undermined by the fractured character of the parent service. Some sections did better than others. "*Streetwise* consistently outperformed the other segments in terms of numbers," laughs Haycocks. "But let's get that in perspective – in other words it might have had 300,000 viewers while other segments got 200,000. But it was more popular, because it was easier to digest and more user-friendly. It was consumerist. I'm not saying it was down to the packaging and presentation; it just happened to strike a chord."

Streetwise was party to some of the Channel 4 Daily's more unconventional aspects. "Hilariously, our show came from a converted ball-gown showroom in central London," Haycocks continues. "The set was knocked up for a few bob by an art student-cum-aspirant designer, utilising scrap metal, hub caps and not a little steel sheeting. But because it was a conversion, the studio ceiling was very low, and the lighting rig was only about 18 inches from your head. So you can appreciate the recordings got pretty hot. One of the problems for me was that I'd sit under these lights and start to perspire, which bled through on my shirt. So I developed a thing I called the chest nappy. I used to go into the little loo off the studio, fold a number of paper towels and stuff them inside my shirt. And I would offer them to other interviewees, members of Parliament, captains of industry, leading heads of charities. You might have looked a little bit puffy in the chest but, of course, you got no bleed-through. One or two guests took me up on this. Most who came in would look aghast."

Aside from regrettable incidences of technical foul-ups – the very first *Business Daily* stalled in transmission, leaving a flustered Carol Barnes to fill for 90 seconds – the Channel 4 Daily attracted little publicity. Advertising agencies were fearful from the outset about the prospect of falling viewer numbers. The levy on TV-am's advertising revenue was slated to give C4 a budget of about £11m during the service's first 12 months. This would obviously decrease, however, if audiences tailed off, and lead to cutbacks and a less enticing product, which would in turn drive away more viewers, and so on.

As it turned out, the Channel 4 Daily attracted about 10% of all potential viewers in its first week on air, its audience peaking at 400,000 compared with TV-am's current average of 2.2m and *Breakfast Time*'s 1.2m. Yet by June, viewing figures had already fallen to 200,000, and initial audience research was revealing that few people even knew of the service's existence. Liz Forgan grimaced, "The biggest problem we have found is that nobody knows it's on. I think the concept's good, right and different from the other two. It's quite distinct, but some tweaking is needed." Michael Grade is more explicit: "We researched it carefully and promoted it widely. The only problem was that virtually nobody watched it."

The service did have one rather unexpected fan, as Paddy Haycocks reveals: "On *Streetwise* I had to wear a shirt, and it had to be done up, but I wasn't allowed to wear a tie. This was the Channel 4 style of the time. Then after two or three months of being on air I received a jiffy bag, and inside was a silk tie with a Harrods label. There was a note attached, which simply said, 'Dear Paddy, please wear this for me, I enjoy your programme.' There was a signature I couldn't make out. I thought this was clearly a very old person who's very kindly sent me a tie and who's not a great speller. But I had to put it to one side, because there was no way that C4 at that stage would let me wear a tie.

"Anyway, two weeks later we had our regular guest lawyer on the show, and he said, 'By the way, did you get the package from Ronnie Kray?' I said, 'I beg your pardon?' He said, 'Did you get the package from Ronnie Kray? The tie?' It transpired that the lawyer had been doing some work, representing Ronnie Kray. One day, Ronnie had asked what other business the lawyer was doing, and he replied he was doing a bit of telly, including this thing called *Streetwise*. So Ronnie started watching it. Hence the tie! Ronnie Kray was a viewer of the Channel 4 Daily. And he liked it! As a postscript, six months later I decided that a report I was doing about British Rail needed me to wear a tie. I made sure it was Ronnie's. You could argue that the biggest number of the Channel 4 Daily's audience were either in prisons or hospitals for the criminally insane."

As news about poor ratings continued to arrive, David Lloyd tried to strike a calm note. "There is no crisis," he declared publicly. "This is a long, long haul. My view was that we had to place ourselves somewhere between *Breakfast Time* and TV-am. We haven't broken into the duopoly as dramatically as I would have wished. But overwhelmingly, when people find the service, they like it." He described the biggest problem facing those currently working in breakfast television as the medium's "eccentric history", especially how *Breakfast Time*'s "comfortable, relaxed, tabloid format" had established a precedent that would take a long time to overcome.

"We always expected that it would be two or three years before we achieved any kind of parity with the others," Lloyd continued. Nonetheless, he ordered the service to undergo a limited revamp, together with a renewed publicity campaign. *Box Office*, perceived to be the least well received of the segments, was instructed to become more topical and shift from looking solely at the arts, to entertainment. The line-up of Saturday output was bolstered with: *Tree House*, a programme for young kids hosted by Floella Benjamin; the long-running factual cartoon series *Once Upon A Time...Life;* and LWT's racing programme *The Morning Line.*

But even once this process was complete, there were still only 200,000 viewers tuning in at peak time. This was nothing short of humiliation, so after another round of head scratching and brainstorming, Grade and his team proposed a course of more radical surgery. "It was controlled in a very Mafia-like way," notes Paddy Haycocks. "Those of us who had slightly broader experience of telly knew what was going on behind closed doors, yet nobody would admit to the fact that *Streetwise* might not be recommissioned. There was quite a long period, four to six weeks, where it was like you were waiting for the diagnosis to some dreadful test to tell you whether you had a terminal illness or not."

When word finally came, the news was not good. "They went for the ground zero approach," Haycocks continues, "and decided to clear the cupboard out." *Streetwise* was to be completely dropped, while Carol Barnes' news slot was to be shown on the hour rather than half-hour, pitching it against the main bulletins on TV-am and the BBC. *Box Office* was to be reduced in length and switched from being prerecorded to live, and a proper children's strand entitled *Early Bird* was to be introduced. Made by Mentorn Films, this would resemble a sort of junior version of *Box Office*, but using only child presenters and aimed at kids between eight and 12 years old. Last but not least, the service's overall start time was to move from 6 to 6.30am with the spare half-hour filled with excerpts from *The Art Of Landscape*, a slightly absurd avant-garde music and pastoral pictures medley.

"This was a moment of sourness," concedes Haycocks. "We were led to believe that *Streetwise* was reasonably successful in ratings terms. I think we felt very cheated that – given what was being proposed, with more business, news and live-ness – we couldn't be part of it. Instead, the rest of the service hadn't been axed completely, and now there was this 'son of the Channel 4 Daily' going on."

The Mark II Channel 4 Daily began on Tuesday 17 April 1990. There was now a proper studio, based at the Trocadero in London's Piccadilly Circus, featuring four separate desks for news, sport, *Box Office* and business. *Kickback* was incorporated into *International Sports News* segments read by David Bobin. David Roper took over presenting *Box Office*, sometimes sharing duties with Larry Sullivan and Joanna Kay. It was a radical overhaul, and it did feel more like a lively and accessible programme – yet audiences remained at a stubborn 200,000.

Whether too diverse, too anonymous or too enigmatic, it appeared the Channel 4 Daily was stuck with an exclusivity it would never quite be able to shake off, which was a shame, because there was an eternal quirkiness and humour to its presentation that flourished in spite of the occasionally earnest content. This became more pronounced when Carol Barnes left at the end of 1990 and the main news-reading duties were taken over by the waspish Dermot Murnaghan. The arrival of the slightly wry and reassuring Caroline Righton from TV-am to take up the post of co-host made her at the time the only person to have worked on every single British television breakfast programme, even the shows on the satellite stations Sky and BSB.

A very different tone and line-up was adopted from January 1991 when the Gulf War began. *The Art Of Landscape* was dropped for half an hour of CNN, while the rest of the service featured increased news content and no *Countdown Masters* or *Early Bird*. Extra news bulletins were also added at weekends, complementing additional output run by C4 every weeknight. Viewing figures rose accordingly, though once the schedules returned to normal at the start of March, ratings dipped back to their usual depressing 200,000.

Whatever changes came, whether by accident or design, it looked like the Channel 4 Daily was cursed to remain a minnow in the breakfast television pond. "I think it was very brave and ambitious to have a relatively large and heavyweight news content," recalls Carol Barnes. "However, that may have been one of its weaknesses when push came to shove. It should be said, I never watched the whole programme through. When I was working, I was 100 percent involved with the news sections. When I was not, I was having a lie-in."

Paddy Haycocks remembers the whole project with great affection. "There were plenty of laughs, and ludicrous situations. Sure, we'd all hoped it would do better than it did. Wearing my producer hat, I was very unsure of the direction they were taking the service in. And they were very unhappy about popularising it. But it was a fund of fun, and I remember it all with great fondness." Michael Atwell argues, "It was a sensible, intelligent and rational strategy; we just never quite knew whether the audience was there or not. It turned out that a lot of them just did not watch television in the mornings. And as we didn't have a lot of money, we couldn't market the service very heavily, and we couldn't draw them in."

For David Lloyd the story had been one of seeing his initial, rather grand predictions and promises fall at a criminally early hurdle. Looking back today, he acknowledges, "Perhaps the mix was a little bit too grafting. The Channel 4 Daily tried to find different audiences, and probably missed finding different audiences. And you can now say that it did fail, because it didn't do as well as I'd hoped it would. I'd thought I'd found a way of delivering something different for Channel 4, which would rate – but in the end, unfortunately, I wasn't right."

Facing the prospect of becoming a self-financing organisation at the end of 1992 and losing the safety net of its regular ITV subsidy, Channel 4 began to wonder if its breakfast television strategy needed not just a makeover but complete and fundamental revolution.

For those at the BBC, the pressing concern throughout this time was not so much the threat of competition from Channel 4, but more simply trying to figure out just how they had let things go so far off the rails.

The Corporation was once the master of early mornings, pioneering and popularising the very notion of breakfast television with flair and runaway success. By the end of the 1980s, however, all was confusion. John Stapleton explains: "The BBC had been out-sofaed by TV-am. The BBC had created the sofa, but TV-am came along and in the end got the bigger ratings. Bruce Gyngell had turned it round from a business point of view, but he'd stuck with the template that Greg Dyke created and made a huge success of it. And the BBC just fell by the wayside, it lost that cutting edge."

At the time, the BBC Head of News and Current Affairs, Tony Hall, had tried to put it into context when he mused: "There are two poles of the breakfast market. First: there is what TV-am is doing and what the original *Breakfast Time* did – sofas, astrologers and show biz. Second: there is news, a briefing for the day. We are delivering the second." Yet, while the "second" may have been an obvious "pole", it did not follow that the BBC would naturally do it very well. In truth, *Breakfast Time* Mark II gave the impression of having accepted its limitations and settled into comfortable inertia.

John Stapleton is scathing when recalling the period he spent working on the programme: "I didn't think it worked. I thought the format of the programme was just far too serious, intense and rigid. It was formulaic and far too repetitive. We would sit there doing the same reports over and over again, with boring VT packages about the economy in Timbuktu or somewhere. It had nothing to do with a lot of people, and in my view, it was just far too upmarket. I know the BBC has a duty to be a public service broadcaster and do serious news and current affairs, but this was unrelenting."

Perhaps unsurprisingly, Stapleton himself chose to move on from the programme in the spring of 1989, to be replaced with BBC newsreader Laurie Mayer. Other than that, little changed to the *Breakfast Time* core presenting team, with Kirsty Wark and Jeremy Paxman in charge, supported by Sally Jones, Francis Wilson, Sally Magnusson, Bob Wilson and new recruit Jill Dando.

By this point, the Corporation was gripped in the thrall of Deputy Director-General John Birt's hugely controversial ideas regarding the reorientation of news output solely around the presentation of facts and analysis. As *Breakfast Time*'s first editor, Ron Neil, now recalls, "John thought that the BBC's news journalism needed an injection of expertise and specialism – that it needed to be much more effective, and needed to have much more invested in it than it had hitherto." Reviewing the current state of the BBC's breakfast service in mid-1989, Birt and Tony Hall decided to seize the moment. The pair installed *Six O'Clock News* boss Bob Wheaton as a new editor, and together agreed to push through a complete relaunch. Nothing was to be sacred. There would be a new name. There were to be no more resonances of the old sofa or Frank Bough and Selina Scott, and the entire operation would be moved from Lime Grove back to Television Centre in Shepherd's Bush.

This new effort ended up being called, rather unimaginatively, *BBC Breakfast News*, and first appeared on screen at 6.30am on Monday 18 September 1989. For a supposed relaunch, a surprising number of existing presenters remained: Laurie Mayer, Kirsty Wark and Sally Magnusson all stayed, as did Francis Wilson, Bob Wilson, Sally Jones and Jill Dando. Only Jeremy Paxman was given the push, leaving to host *Newsnight*.

To take his place, a new front man was booked: Nicholas Witchell. Arguably the epitome of the unflappable, stoical newsreader, Witchell was at that time most famous for two things: his emergency breakfast broadcast the morning after the 1987 storms, and for sitting on some lesbian protestors who'd hijacked an edition of the *Six O'Clock News*. Now he was to spearhead a new chapter in the BBC's six-year history of breakfast television. "I was asked by Tony Hall if I would be the main presenter of a relaunched BBC breakfast programme," he recalls. "He told me that it was to be the first 'rolling news' programme on BBC Television, which would be edited by Bob Wheaton, with whom I'd worked on the *Six*. After some thought I agreed to do it."

Wheaton certainly went to great pains to sell his new creation. "It's important to freshen the look of the programme," he contested at the time, "but the main change is in its texture. It will have more pace and punch. Just half an hour with *BBC Breakfast News* will keep you abreast of all you need to know. The BBC has at its disposal the finest and certainly the most comprehensive news service available, with more foreign and domestic correspondents than any other network. We're going to harness these resources to produce a first-rate news programme that will tell people what's happened since the previous evening and everything that's likely to happen during the day."

As it turned out, for all its credentials and resources, there was often precious little warmth and reassurance to *BBC Breakfast News*, let alone humour. This was a straight, no-nonsense news service – no more, no less. There was the odd glimpse of a magazine format in the shape of regular newspaper reviews, but that was as far as it went for either wit or vibrancy. Its agenda seemed most typified by the way its first half-hour was entirely given over to uninterrupted business news, which eventually turned into a separate programme in its own right, entitled *Business Breakfast*.

The somewhat clinical and occasionally cold tone to the programme lay chiefly with its design and its architects, and not necessarily its presenters, who did their best to grapple with an unwieldy format that did not look too kindly on exuberance. As Nicholas Witchell explains, "It was a news-rolling programme with analysis and interviews. It is the only time BBC Television has attempted to mount a TV version of the Radio 4 *Today* programme. Its overwhelming strength was its ability to cope in depth – yet in a style that was accessible to the audience at that time of the morning – with the news agenda; and indeed, through its interviews, to add to that news agenda in the way that the *Today* programme so successfully accomplishes. *BBC Breakfast News* was not as 'dense' as the *Today* programme, or as preoccupied with domestic politics. It offered, we hoped, something more digestible."

Witchell also defends what was at the time a very niche programme style: "It seemed to me then that there [was] little point unless the BBC offer[ed] something distinctive to its rivals. They were news-light and full of froth. *BBC Breakfast News* made use of the BBC's huge news-gathering machine to offer a serious and proper TV news programme at that time of the morning."

Sporadic occasions of national importance or emergency brought the programme out of its shell, such as the 1991 Gulf War, which added extra substance and viewers. "My greatest memory [of *Breakfast News*] is of the Gulf War," adds Witchell. "We were extended to seven days a week and ran from 6 to 10am. Many of the major military developments – the start of the air war and the start of the land campaign – happened at night. People were waking up and switching on the television – for some reason, when there's a really big story, the radio is not sufficient – and they were hearing about these momentous events from [us]."

Nevertheless, at heart, *BBC Breakfast News* seemed like a programme created out of line graphs and pie charts, the kind it was possible to imagine being wholly designed for citing in strategy sessions or meetings of the BBC board of Governors. It was such an unassuming affair that, despite the fact that it would survive the entire 1990s, it was not unusual to hear people in the year 2000 refer to it as *Breakfast Time* or ask after the whereabouts of "the red sofas". Viewing figures remained stubbornly static around one million, but that didn't matter, not officially anyway, as *BBC Breakfast News* was about informing and explaining, rather than entertaining. It was a symbolically Birtian way of kick-starting a TV station's schedule, akin to a dose of cod liver oil to clear out your insides.

"It was a straight news programme, and that was the mood of the times," Ron Neil explains matter-of-factly. "John Birt believed that the journalism should be strong in the morning." "It could've worked if it had been news that people were interested in," argues John Stapleton; "but it was far too political, with far too much economics and foreign news. Unless you're a real news junkie, you've not got much appetite for that at that time of the morning." Nicholas Witchell retains a more pragmatic view. "Those members of the breakfast audience who did not want that sort of news-led fare would have found it too lacking in 'snap crackle pop!' But there was lots of that on ITV."

Ironically, ITV was also a place where you could find a plentiful supply of intrigue and controversy, for, by the end of the decade, TV-am had given up trumpeting the downfall of its BBC opponents and instead become engrossed in one last, grisly, desperate battle for its own survival.

TEN

"It had become like being in the Politburo"

By the end of the 1980s, the fortunes of the IBA and of TV-am had become deeply entwined. In its endless deliberations over how to 'deal' with TV-am, the Authority was acutely aware of being watched very closely by a government in the process of drawing up plans for a major round of broadcasting legislation and reform. A sense of being on probation and of time running out was felt at the highest level.

Battle-weary IBA Chairman Lord Thompson stepped down at the end of 1988. He'd been in the job almost eight years and used the occasion of his retirement to take stock of the turbulent relationship his organisation had endured with the beast it created back in 1980. Thompson made a point of observing how the IBA's original vision of breakfast television had been, to a degree, erroneous: "The kind of people our specification catered for were those who listened to *Today*. But it turned out the real breakfast time audience was composed of stay-at-home people of one kind or another." He was honest in conceding that mistakes had been made: "The IBA's view of what the British public wanted at breakfast time was an overly high-minded one." However, he continued, "If TV-am had come to us with the present programme mix and board, they would not have got past the first interview."

Thompson departed his position, firm in the belief that, for all its previous failings, the IBA – and only the IBA – could properly set breakfast TV on a safe and practical road for the future. He, like most in the British television industry, had no idea that it would turn out to be the Conservative government that would shape the course of independent breakfast television in the 1990s, and that Prime Minister Margaret Thatcher herself would fashion both the means and the ends that would lead to the downfall of her favourite TV executive, Bruce Gyngell.

The government published its much-trailed Broadcasting White Paper on Monday 7 November 1988. The compass of its proposals was vast, leaving almost no sector of the media untouched by the threat of radical reorganization. Its most contentious clauses included: renaming ITV as Channel 3; the replacement of the IBA with a less rigorous body called the Independent Television Commission (ITC); and a new Channel Five. Most controversial of all, however, was the suggestion that the next round of

ITV franchises should be awarded by competitive tender (in other words, by auction) and not at the discretion of a regulatory authority.

Throughout 1988, TV-am Managing Director Bruce Gyngell had laboured long to influence the contents of the White Paper, working his government contacts for all they were worth. He had lobbied most hard against any kind of competitive tendering, speaking at the Birmingham Press Club in August of how, from the evidence of similar cases in Australia, auction-based franchise rounds led to over-valuation and bankruptcy. He even met Mrs Thatcher in person in the autumn, enjoyed a warm welcome, and tried to sell her a variation on the tender option that involved the IBA choosing winners on quality grounds but then inviting the lucky company to match the highest overall cash bid. If they could not, then the offer would be passed on to the next ranking bidder. Although Mrs Thatcher was keen, the Treasury vetoed the idea outright.

Once it became certain that some kind of auction process would be involved in the renewal of all ITV franchises, Gyngell's tunnel vision, ruthlessly honed by the ACTT dispute, manifested itself into one sole burning desire: to fashion TV-am into the kind of organisation guaranteed success in any franchise war. Nothing else mattered. One early idea, quickly rejected because of the high costs involved, was to engineer a full management buy-out of the company. Gyngell then turned to smartening up the performance of his rickety station, which was still reeling from the departure of its most famous presenter and running its operations on a skeleton staff.

The two female presenters Gyngell had hired to replace Anne Diamond – Kathy Rochford and Kathryn Holloway – had failed to gel with male hosts Mike Morris and Richard Keys. This had led to an unusually tense, fractious on-screen atmosphere, all-too reminiscent of the days of David Frost and Anna Ford. When Frost himself disappeared at the beginning of 1989, off on another of his American trips, TV-am listed badly – and a substitute Sunday show, *TV-am Reports,* fronted by Political editor Adam Boulton, failed to shine.

Gyngell decided to swallow his pride and issue a grovelling appeal to Anne Diamond. He banked on the fact that, on leaving the previous November, she'd mentioned that she might one day be interested in reappearing on TV-am in a semi-regular capacity. Indeed, she'd already done four live reports for the station, entitled 'G'Day Britain', marking the end of Australia's bicentennial celebrations. His ploy worked, and Anne duly returned on Sunday 19 February to fill Frost's shoes and, as journalist William Phillips described, "salvage the segment".

Next, Gyngell had to deal with the exit of newsreader Gordon Honeycombe. He'd been a loyal and enduring member of the team, working right through the industrial dispute and ending up as one of

TV-am's most iconic and famous personalities. But now he was off. Knowing Honeycombe was a hard act to follow, Gyngell opted for the complete opposite as his replacement: an almost unknown 26-year old woman named Lisa Aziz.

Her appointment, however, could not help but reinforce the impression that TV-am's family of presenters was something of a shadow of former years. None of the current weekday hosts had the weight or charisma of an Anne Diamond or a Nick Owen. Mad Lizzie was still around, joining Tory MP David Mellor to promote her latest fitness campaign: "I was a state in '88, but I'm feeling fine in '89!" Yet children's programmes, once home to some of the station's strongest personalities, had been reduced to an over-eager George Spanswick introducing *Mr Men* and *Portland Bill*, while elsewhere, the unassuming Kathy Tayler had replaced Jayne Irving in charge of *After Nine*.

Perhaps conscious of a widening feeling of malaise, Gyngell hurried through a couple more appointments: new co-host Lorraine Kelly, who shared Anne Diamond's ability to evoke feelings of both tolerance and torpor in viewers; and weathergirl Ulrika Jonsson. Formerly Gyngell's secretary, Ulrika was quickly and energetically promoted as a major new TV-am 'face', no better demonstrated than when she married cameraman John Turnball and the ensuing on-screen celebrations lasted a whole week.

Yet, for all such efforts, Gyngell found his attention increasingly distracted by matters off camera. Fellow ITV companies began publicly demanding that the breakfast franchise be effectively abolished in the next round. Granada, HTV, Scottish and Grampian TV all included in their submissions on the Broadcasting White Paper the suggestion that the hours between 6 and 9.25am be given to individual companies rather than maintained as a separate licence. Gyngell was dismissive of their carping, but such an issue was reflective of how, even though it was still a few years away, the occasion of the franchise auction was coming to dominate the media agenda.

Mindful of the White Paper's emphasis on ITV companies demonstrating profitability and efficiencies, Gyngell declared in May 1989: "We are streamlining the company down to a publisher/broadcaster", following through such words with actions. All TV-am children's programmes were promptly contracted out to Clear Idea, a new independent production business set up by former head of children's output, Nick Wilson. The first fruits of this deal came in September, when Wilson launched a revived *Wide Awake Club* called *WAC '90*. It boasted a new presenter, Shelagh Ferrell, plus various new features including Sybil Ruscoe with environmental news from her 'ECO-Emergency Desk' and 'The History Of The World In 52 Parts'.

Rather embarrassingly, Shelagh was dropped by the end of the year, leaving the programme back in the hands of Tommy Boyd and Michaela Strachan. More promising was the start of *Dappledown Farm* in March 1990, which featured veteran children's presenter Brian Cant introducing cartoons from a studio farm set. But Wilson then decided to scrap *WAC* once and for all and start from scratch with a new cartoon and competition show called *Hey Hey It's Saturday* hosted by Mike Brosnan. Yet another new offering followed in autumn 1990, in the guise of *Top Banana*, again with Brosnan in charge, and once more comprising a distinctly *WAC*-esque mix of features. Sundays were given further Clear Idea treatment in the shape of *It's Stardust*, featuring songs, cartoons and religious fables introduced by the eponymous Alvin.

Offloading the responsibilities of producing children's output, even if it did lead to a jumble of programming, was cited by Gyngell as proof that, "all of the energies at TV-am [are going] towards news and current affairs." Chairman Ian Irvine chimed in with the epithet, "We are now creatively driven rather than technically driven," a statement that could also be interpreted as an admission that there was still a shortage of technical staff.

In some aspects it was true that the company was getting its house in order. It consented, in September 1989, to settle its long-running stand-off with the ACTT, getting the union to drop its boycott of TV-am with a £700,000 settlement that left the sacked employees with around £3,000 each. It also continued to rake in bumper profits, which had risen to £20.23m in the year ending January 1989.

Yet there seemed to be mixed opinions amongst Gyngell's management team over just how to handle the upcoming franchise round. Gyngell continued his manic outbursts, writing to both the new IBA Chairman George Russell, and to the Home Secretary Douglas Hurd, raging, "Ultimately it is the viewer who will suffer because, in the wake of all the financial wheeler-dealing, programme budgets must be slashed." In contrast, Bill Ludford, now TV-am Director of Programmes, advocated a less hysterical approach. "You won't see any dramatic changes at all," he promised, responding to speculation that TV-am was about to revamp its output in order to hang onto its licence. "It is a winning format. And it's crazy to change a winning format."

Which is precisely what TV-am then proceeded to do. Throughout 1990 and 1991, the station tried to remodel itself as nothing less than a professional news channel. There were sudden, uncompromising injections of topicality, such as 'Westminster Watch' featuring footage from the newly televised House of Commons, and Dr Hilary Jones' daily 'Doc Spot'. From September 1990, *Frost On Sunday* was broadcast on both TV-am and BSB and expanded to run for 30 weeks, conveniently tying in with the lead up to the franchise auction, while another new programme, *News Week*, was introduced from Sunday 7 October. Controller of News Jeff Berliner claimed: "It's our biggest news and current affairs development since we began opening our four overseas bureaux two years ago," and that, as a consequence, the amount of airtime devoted to show business stories in *Good Morning Britain* was being vastly reduced.

Yet this mad dash for news seemed to be proving something of a turn off, for the station's ratings started to go down. This was an ominous portent that someone should have picked up on. TV-am still scheduled items on subjects like the royal family's fashion sense, John Lennon, and the 30th anniversary of *Coronation Street*, but these sat awkwardly alongside more earnest fare such as a 12-part series on truancy, and week-long studies of the food industry and Romanian babies. For all Gyngell's blustering about how TV-am would retain its franchise by "demonstrating we are providing a popular, quality service and by coming up with a competent business plan," once more it felt like he was too bound up in affairs of the future to notice what was happening under his very nose.

He wasted months toying with various ambitious and not very realistic projects intended to render TV-am more than just a breakfast television service. For a period, he contemplated the idea of developing the station into a 24-hour news operation to challenge ITN for the right to provide news for ITV. Then he changed his mind and announced that he was intending to apply for one of three new independent national radio licences. When this lost its appeal, Gyngell mooted a plan to buy a stake in the then troubled Australian Channel 9 where he was previously Chief Executive. Each of these proposals disappeared as quickly as they came, and left the residual impression of a man all too prone to getting lost in the realms of conjecture and hyperbole.

By late 1990, the stage was set for the breakfast franchise battle to begin in earnest. Surveying the field ahead of the impending hostilities (and casualties), William Phillips astutely identified three areas where TV-am would be open to attack: it made more money than was "diplomatic", it did so by keeping its style of programming noticeably cheap, and was "populist without being very popular". He also stressed how viewing figures for breakfast TV in general had not risen at all for the last two years. As such, "Whatever lofty aims a successful rival [to TV-am] professed, it might have to eat its words, staying cheap and cheerful to defend its share of early-morning advertising."

Indeed, the draft breakfast licence issued in December by the ITC, the IBA's replacement, set high and detailed criteria. It insisted all bids address six strands of programming: news, sport, factual (including current affairs and features), education, religion, and children's. Applicants were required to set down the average amount of programming they would provide for each category. Proposals had to include a minimum of 30 minutes of high quality national and international news on each weekday. Finally, news had to be specially prepared for the service and must include regional material.

These were unexpectedly rigorous demands, yet TV-am was convinced it could win, and that countless initiatives and revamps would deliver up the franchise on a plate. The station received an unexpected fillip in the shape of the Gulf War at the start of 1991, which gave it a chance to further demonstrate its supposed reportage credentials. Extended news-based programming was added to both weekdays and weekends, and presenters Mike Morris and Lorraine Kelly were moved from the sofa and put behind a desk. Morris was even forced to wear a suit. As had been the case with the revamp on *Breakfast Time* in 1986, this sudden and artificial change in TV-am's on-screen appearance and tone was never that convincing. In addition, the station suffered the ignominy of being followed by a special *Gulf News Report* every day at 9.25am, almost as if ITN were setting out to correct any mistakes TV-am had made in the previous three and a half hours.

But Gyngell wasn't bothered. After all, he'd received a special letter from George Russell, now Chairman of the ITC, personally commending the station on its Gulf War coverage. As audiences continued to switch off, TV-am spiralled ever-upwards into aspirations of high culture that were positively Peter Jay-like in their loftiness. A sequence of Passion Plays from Salisbury Cathedral retold the Easter story in medieval costume. The daily news hour from 6am was rebranded *First Reports*. Even the cartoons seemed to take on an ultra-highbrow and worthy stance, with *Captain Planet And The Planeteers* featuring a team of 'eco-heroes' protecting the world from environmentally unfriendly villains.

By this point, TV-am was sitting on a chest of more than £40m. Pre-tax profits for 1990 were £24m, and forecasts were for more than £30m in 1991. "It had money coming out of its ears," argues erstwhile TV-am editor, Peter McHugh. "At that point the BBC had gone back to doing what the BBC does worst – or best – which is a boring programme, to attract an older and non-commercially important audience. You had the Channel 4 Daily, which was another example of the Peter Jay school. I watched it and couldn't believe it had got on the telly. BBC2 were doing Open University, a total audience of 1%, and satellite and cable hadn't developed. TV-am had all of the popular audience, kids as well as parents. The franchise was a licence to print money."

Such reasoning was an obvious incentive to those outside parties interested in bidding for the breakfast franchise. Yet Gyngell was convinced he could see off all opposition and that his company would easily pass the specially contrived "quality threshold" added to all the franchises to ensure high standards of programming. Besides, could the ITC risk awarding the licence to a more self-consciously heavyweight and abstract consortium that, like TV-am's original pre-Gyngell incarnation in 1983, would then face plummeting ratings and have to start changing schedules? He was sure the answer was no.

It had long been anticipated that TV-am would face some competition for its licence, not least because of its notorious history and the number of enemies it had made along the way. Sure enough, on Wednesday 15 May 1991, the closing date for all franchise applications, those suspicions were confirmed. TV-am was one of three bidders for the breakfast television licence. Its opponents were two new consortia, Daybreak Television and Sunrise TV – both initiated by former TV-am personnel.

Daybreak was the brainchild of ex-TV-am Director of Programmes Mike Hollingsworth. He'd long nursed an intention of exacting some kind of appropriate gesture of revenge upon his old boss, and this seemed to be the perfect opportunity. "Clearly I wanted to take the franchise off them," he confirms today. "Resentment had burned in me for a very long time."

He'd already irked his erstwhile employer by registering the name 'Good Morning Britain' at Companies House, something Gyngell could do nothing about as long as the 'company' remained dormant. Now Hollingsworth unveiled what he believed was "a very, very powerful franchise application" in a bid to unseat his nemesis. It had taken quite a few months of serious planning, kicking off with the assembly of a team of eight former TV-am and *Breakfast Time* managers who then met regularly to swap ideas. The end result was an association of a number of companies and broadcasters each with a different stakeholding. ITN, which would provide news bulletins for the station and would house it within its new offices on Gray's Inn Road, had a 20% share. Carlton Television had another 20%, as did the *Daily Telegraph*. NBC Europe pitched in 15%, MAI Broadcasting 20%, and the construction firm Taylor Woodrow 5%.

Although Daybreak presented a united front in public, behind the scenes the involvement of ITN had proved something of a problem for Hollingsworth. "Bob Phillis, who had been my last boss at Central, had just been appointed Chief Executive of ITN, and he'd rung me up to say 'we would like to be part of your consortium'. And I thought, 'Great, ITN – that's rock solid.' Then I remembered all the troubles we'd had in the past, and the resentment that was there towards me inside ITN over what had happened over the Brighton bomb." To avoid confrontation, Hollingsworth agreed to take a more low-key role and let others become the main faces of Daybreak.

But the consortium then proceeded to swap one controversial media figure for another, in the shape of respected TV executive Sir Paul Fox. His agreement to become Daybreak's Chairman was a major coup, but he'd chosen to signal his arrival in the job through an ill-advised stream of high-profile abuse targeted at TV-am: "Nothing more than cheap couch television," he railed of his opponents. "They are the outsiders of the commercial television family, going their own cheap way and thinking they are wonderful." Furthermore, TV-am was "incompetent" in its news delivery. "We will bring them back to the fold," he concluded dramatically.

Daybreak's plans specified a segmented magazine format, featuring two presenters and one newscaster with a total of five hours and 50 minutes a week devoted to topics such as health, fashion and the environment. Sports would account for one hour and nine minutes a week, arts for one hour and 15 minutes. Children's programming was to be provided in a magazine show called *Comix* and around five hours and 30 minutes per week would come from independent production outfits including Initial Film And Television and Mentorn. To complete the package, deals had supposedly been agreed with The Children's Channel to provide four more kids' shows for the new service. These proposals actually conspired to make Paul Fox's already rather tactless remarks look even more foolish, adding up to a breakfast format very similar to the TV-am model he'd been so quick to decry.

The second rival bid, Sunrise, was the personal pet project of none other than Greg Dyke. Now Managing Director of LWT, Dyke and his Chairman, Christopher Bland (chief IBA advocate of breakfast television back in 1980), were convinced that the incumbent broadcaster could be unseated. Dyke recalls, "It was pretty obvious to me that TV-am wasn't going to win. Once it was only going to be about the figure you could put in the envelope, I never believed that TV-am would get accepted. Therefore I always believed they were vulnerable, largely because it was so much cheaper to run [the franchise] on another operation [like London Weekend] compared to how they'd run theirs."

In the lead up to 1991, Dyke and Bland had toyed with the idea of bidding for a number of different licences as well as their own, yet increasingly found their discussions always leading back to the breakfast franchise. Economically and logistically, it made sense. The pair certainly had the know-how and experience to put together a convincing pitch. Plus there was the fact that here was a chance to get one over on an old industry adversary.

"We had a spare *World Of Sport* studio which sat downstairs doing nothing," explains Dyke. "We had a transmission system, and you could rent offices in our building. So, for London Weekend, it was a very attractive prospect. In other words it could lose quite a lot of money each year and still make profits for London Weekend." Ex-LWT producer Hugh Pile masterminded the bid, which was kept top secret and code-named 'Apollo'. Roped in as shareholders were the *Guardian* (20%), Scottish Television (15%) and the Walt Disney Company (15%), alongside LWT themselves (20%). Dyke had personally suggested involving Disney, aware of the quality children's programming they would be able to supply. News was to come from the wires service, Visnews; and Harry Roche, the *Guardian*'s Chairman, headed the consortium.

Sunrise's proposed schedules were based around a programme named *Daybreak*, cheekily named after the short-lived news hour that opened the first incarnation of TV-am in 1983, but unwittingly echoing the name of their rival bidder. *Daybreak* would be a rolling news service, running from 6 to 8.50am, when it would be followed by *Daybreak Plus*, a supplemental slot that would apparently "inform and entertain in a popular but authoritative way". A strong emphasis was placed on local news, weather and travel information for each of the ITV regions. *Sunday Break* would offer religious content and a major political interview, and the whole service would be linked by two presenters handling news and lighter material including celebrity interviews, arts features and human-interest stories. At the time of bidding, Sunrise still had to find a shareholder for the remaining 30% stake of its company, yet its £3.4m planned investment in regional opt-outs was interpreted by many as highly significant and a potential winning card.

It turned out that TV-am, meanwhile, had tried to play the franchise game with a hail of promises and an extremely brazen level of self-confidence. Its bid detailed a startling intention to establish a £10m fund "earmarked for programmes of especially high quality". From this would flow new series including: *Displaced People; Family Of Europe* (on the lives of families in different countries); *Educational Minutes* (a strand for young people using experimental broadcasting techniques); *Through The Eyes Of Children; Faith* (a weekly half-hour religious programme); and *Speakers' Corner* inviting viewers into regional studios to sound off about various contentious topics. Mersey TV, makers of C4 soap *Brookside*, would also be commissioned to develop and pilot a half-hour drama series for young people.

This kind of distinctly highbrow, ambitious and aspirational programming was as astonishing as it was laughable. It represented the climax of Gyngell's three-year campaign to mould his company into a byword for financial security, wholesome responsibility and unequivocal respectability. It was also a load of hot air. Such a line-up would never have sustained viewer interest, and maybe deep down Gyngell knew as much, but he refused to admit to himself or anyone that he'd put a foot wrong. "The camaraderie has been fantastic," he cooed after finalising TV-am's bid. "We had an all-day session where we sat around making affirmations of our success, saying things like 'wake up with winners' and 'licence to win'." He'd even insisted his staff think positive by rubbing a good luck plaque inscribed, "A winning team for '93."

The submission of the competing franchise bids had given rise to a near unprecedented period of intense bitterness, deception and resentment throughout the TV industry. Greg Dyke characterised proceedings as being, "Nothing to do with business [and] nothing to do with television. It has been pure poker." The mood of all the principal players in the auction swung between elation and despair with each passing rumour.

Gyngell, in particular, revelled in the melodrama of the moment. As soon as he learned of the bids from Sunrise and Daybreak, he assumed the mantle of a doom-laden soothsayer, forecasting great ills to befall British television should TV-am be beaten. The company would have to close completely if it failed to win back its licence. Its profitability, he wailed, depended upon its ability to sell airtime, and without this, its 400-odd staff would immediately have to start looking for jobs elsewhere. He reminded all and sundry that his station's coverage of the Gulf War had been "immaculate", while disclosing, not a little erroneously, that TV-am's submission to the ITC contained no proposals to change the service. "You tamper with a format with great trepidation," he boomed.

What none of the bidders – or the public – knew was the sum of money each of the consortia was willing to pay in its attempt to 'win' the auction. The figures were submitted to the ITC inside sealed envelopes, not to be made known until all the franchise winners were announced in the autumn. As is always the case, however, gossip quickly began circulating, and the nub of the speculation was that Gyngell had bid too low. Moreover, it was thought his two competitors had entered bids almost double that of TV-am. Surely Gyngell, the arch-tactician, could not have made such an elementary mistake – could he?

If Gyngell felt at all agitated by the possibility that he had blundered, he did not let on, nor did he allow others in the company to entertain any concerns or pessimism. On the contrary, he insisted that TV-am continue its blissful mission to upgrade its output. He even launched a whole new programme. *TV-MAYhem* was hosted by former radio DJ Chris Evans, who had recently made his TV debut fronting a breakfast show on the BSB satellite channel Power Station, and Gary Monaghan. It began in a blaze of glory on Saturday 21 September, less than a month before the franchise results were due. It was as if the station had already won and, worse, was celebrating as much.

On Thursday 10 October 1991, George Russell convened the meeting of the ITC that would decide the fate of TV-am. Though their debate was lengthy, their final decision was quick and to the point. All three bids

A whirring fax machine dispenses judgement
on Bruce Gyngell and the future of TV-am

passed the so-called "quality threshold". Was there any exceptional factor within the incumbent's bid that warranted it being handed the franchise regardless? No. So it came down to money. The ITC looked at the figures. By TV-am, they saw the figure £14.13m. But by Daybreak, the amount was £33.26m – and by Sunrise, £34.61m. Consequently, because Sunrise bid the most, it won the franchise. That was how it worked, because that was how it had been designed to work.

On Wednesday 16 October, the results were announced. When the news spooled out of the TV-am fax machine, Gyngell almost collapsed in shock. Recovering his composure, he lit a cigarette (despite having given up smoking years ago) and then strode outside Camden Lock to confront reporters.

"I do not believe Sunrise will be a profitable company," he began. "I predict they will be bankrupt by 1994." He slammed the auction system as "disastrous", before concluding with the boast, "It's business as usual. We will continue to serve faithfully and honestly our 17 million viewers." This was a woefully misleading remark, as only two million or so people ever watched TV-am at any one time. A more measured response came from David Frost, who met the media with a well-prepared soundbite: "When I was at school I was always told that the important thing is not the winning, but it's the taking part. I didn't believe it then, and I don't believe it now."

Why had Bruce Gyngell bid so low? In part, it was to safeguard TV-am's huge profits; but in part, it was, as ever, out of foolish bravado. Gyngell, nicknamed 'The Pink Panther' after the colour of his shirts, had become convinced that his courting of the government and the broadcasting establishment had landed him the licence. Yet ultimately, they weren't the ones who decided who won or lost. It was the ITC, headed by George Russell and peopled with figures immune to the lobbying of seasoned television company directors. Gyngell's fanatical, dangerous perception of TV-am as an unimpeachable success, which had fought and won its right to exist long into the future, had blinded him to the realities of the changing media environment. It was with acute irony that the one factor Gyngell had placed at the centre of his management strategy right from day one – money – had proved his ultimate undoing.

"I think Bruce honestly believed that the ITC would make an exception for TV-am," suggests Peter McHugh today. "And he sincerely believed that Mrs Thatcher would pick up the phone to the ITC and say, 'I don't care who has won it; you will give it to TV-am.' I never thought TV-am would win, on the basis that I always thought they'd bid low, because I thought Bruce would gamble on this relationship."

Mike Hollingsworth, who saw his own bid for the licence lose out to that of his fellow ex-colleague, was nonetheless pleased to see Gyngell emasculated. He remains similarly dismissive of Gyngell's bid. "Bruce had helped to break the unions, and he'd been in and out of Downing Street. But I didn't expect him to win it. The saga of Bruce at TV-am had not been viewed by everybody with a single accord. I think that he made quite a number of enemies inside the IBA/ITC. Bruce's way of doing things was not always approved by some people. They thought he was bringing brashness into ITV – and to a degree he was."

"TV-am could never have won," agrees Greg Dyke. "I never understood the TV-am bid. The only way TV-am could have won was to have said, 'Look, on this date, TV-am changes, and TV-am Mark II starts – we've got all this cash, we'll give it all back, we'll have new shareholders, we're going to do it in somebody else's building.' Bruce wasn't up for that. I don't think he was up to speed with the finances. But he must have known he wasn't going to get [through on] exceptional circumstances. I think he thought that Margaret Thatcher would pull him through, but of course she had no influence – none."

What of the woman behind it all, who had singled out Bruce Gyngell for personal endorsement, hailed his treatment of the trade unions, but then, in the form of the Broadcasting Bill, helped TV-am to sign its own death warrant? A few hours after the results were announced, Gyngell had received a commiserative phone call from the now ex-Prime Minister herself, followed later that evening by an equally regret-filled letter. The next day, Gyngell was due to appear at a TV-am broadcast journalism awards ceremony. Despite all the furore of the preceding 24 hours, the event had to go ahead. So Gyngell took the opportunity to talk candidly and emotionally about the significance of TV-am's defeat. He'd just finished speaking, however, when David Keighley, TV-am's Head of Corporate Affairs, reminded his boss about Mrs Thatcher's letter. Keighley suggested Gyngell read it out to the assembled reporters. Perhaps it would help focus attention away from TV-am and back onto the whole franchise process itself.

Gyngell initially dithered, and then eventually took his colleague's advice. He read the document aloud: "Dear Bruce. When I see how some of the other licences have been awarded I am mystified that you did not receive yours, and heartbroken. You of all people have done so much for the whole of television – there seems to have been no attention to that. I am only too painfully aware that I was responsible for the legislation. Yours sincerely, Margaret Thatcher."

The incident made all the main TV news bulletins, and the following morning's front pages. As for provoking any sympathy for Gyngell's plight amongst the rest of the media, however, the gesture was a complete misfire. Richard Dunn, Head of Thames Television which had also been deprived of its licence, chose to ignore TV-am altogether and focus on the aution itself. He noted how the former PM "is not as painfully aware as we are at Thames Television" that the legislation was her doing. There were precious few tears amongst other broadcasters, especially those who had served under Gyngell at various points during the previous seven years.

Reflecting on the outcome, Peter McHugh admits, "I was pleased, not for the people there, because a lot of individuals were friends of mine, but pleased that Greg had won it. Greg was a founder of breakfast television, and now I thought he could move it on journalistically to a better place than it had been before." Dyke is clear about his response towards TV-am's loss. "I felt rather pleased," he recalls. "I didn't have any regrets. I disliked the way Bruce had written us all out of history. It had become like being in the Politburo: you'd been airbrushed out because Gyngell didn't want anyone to know."

As for LWT's successful bid to unseat TV-am – well, that "wasn't revenge; it was a straight business decision. And if it meant we put the boot in, then that wasn't such a bad thing either."

ELEVEN

"Whatever it is, just make it stand out"

The fall of TV-am was as undignified as it was swift. Rather than strive to maintain a professional operation right to the end, the station slumped into a confused melee of repackaged reportage, celebrity tittle-tattle and hundreds of repeats. An unfettered air of spite, bitterness and petty jealousy seemed to pervade the company. It was not a pretty sight.

Within hours of learning he'd lost his franchise, Bruce Gyngell submerged himself totally in the business of reversing his planned programme of expansion, and of doing what he could to save money. Chris Evans' *TV-MAYhem* was axed after just six weeks on air. All news output was binned off and replaced with a service direct from satellite channel BSkyB, branded somewhat fussily "From Sky – the TV-am news". This £10m deal involved around just 20 TV-am journalists, including presenter Lisa Aziz, being kept on under the auspices of BSkyB, while the remaining newsroom workforce was junked. A wider round of redundancies was also initiated, which saw a quarter of the station laid-off by spring 1992.

As far as the schedules were concerned, all semblances of consistency seemed to vanish overnight. A spokesperson noted: "The elements of the show which used to react to breaking news will be greatly reduced. We are going to give the audiences what they want, and that's a magazine show with emphasis on the show business elements." And how. TV-am ditched all pretence of being interested in serious current affairs and went flat out for entertainment. Ironically, this halted the ratings decline that had set in thanks to the station's dalliance with hard news, and the subsequent rise in viewing figures removed an obligation to refund an expected £1m to advertisers for falling revenues.

David Frost swiftly cut all ties with the ailing wreck he'd once helped to create. He left TV-am in June 1992, his last interviewee being, rather symbolically, Mrs Thatcher. Ever the smart negotiator, Frost quickly landed a deal with the BBC to go on hosting more or less exactly the same show under the new name *Breakfast With Frost*.

Gyngell suffered. His anger and distress manifested themselves in a persistent flu that lasted for weeks. "Finally, I decided enough was enough," he recalled. "I remember lying in bed on Sunday evening, reading a book, and I thought to myself: 'It's about time I gave all this up and got on with my life.' I woke up the next morning and the cough and cold were gone."

For a brief period, it looked like he had found his second wind when it was announced that TV-am, in association with Virgin, had won a new national independent radio licence. But this was quickly overshadowed by another slew of cutbacks. The leases on TV-am's eight regional studios were sold. Staff were awarded pay-offs ranging from £10,000 to £80,000. A messy legal row over TV-am's involvement in rival consortia for the new terrestrial station, Channel Five, was eventually settled in the company's favour, but at a cost to morale and the sensibilities of its leader. A weary Gyngell resorted to rounding on ITV and C4 at a Royal Television Society dinner. Channel 4 was "bullshit" and "truly appalling. I would give £1,000 to anyone who can list ten good things about it."

Bit by bit, TV-am's schedules fell apart. Individual strands were abruptly scrapped or left to die slowly. Fancy names like 'Cartoon World' and 'Cartoon Carnival' were concocted to mask hasty recycling of whatever animation the company had left on its shelves. No new children's programmes were commissioned, their place being taken by old episodes of *Wacaday* dating back to the mid-1980s. David Frost's slot was filled by the American import *Saved By The Bell*. Special sports coverage on weekends was discontinued, while all the station could contribute to that year's ITV *Telethon* was a desultory package entitled *Michaela's Cartoons*.

As the wind-down continued through 1992, however, ratings kept rising, eventually hitting a peak of 30% more than the previous year. Though this was a somewhat hollow victory, given that TV-am only had a matter of months to live, it was still a salutary reminder, to anyone interested, of what appeared to 'work' on breakfast television and what did not.

At least there was always the land. TV-am owned all of its buildings, offices and equipment. At one point, this potentially lucrative piece of real estate was thought ripe for turning into a 'new media' village, or maybe rented out to another broadcaster. Yet, despite the fact that the site had been valued at £9m, a buyer was proving difficult to come by, thanks to the then-rampant economic recession. In the event, £26.7m of TV-am's fast depleting cash stockpile had to be handed back to shareholders after the company was unable to find any way of either investing or shedding some of its remaining capital.

On screen, presenters Mike Morris, Lorraine Kelly and Kathy Tayler soldiered on until the end of the year. Christmas 1992 was twilight time, with most of the station's seasonal programmes made up of clips from the archive. Then came the final curtain on New Year's Eve, when TV-am's 119 months on the air came to a close. Survivors from both in front of and behind the camera gathered around the sofa to cue in a bombastic and cheesy visual montage of presenters, crew and producers past and

Pathos runs amok as Mike Morris
loses the battle to bid a dignified farewell from Camden Lock

present accompanied by the tune 'Simply The Best'. "We'd like to thank everybody who's been watching TV-am," blubbed Morris; "we've enjoyed your company. But from TV-am, sadly, we now have to say it, finally, thank you, and goodbye." Brash, vulgar and uncompromising, it was an utterly appropriate tribute.

That wasn't quite the end of the story. A few TV-am administration staff were kept on until March 1993, to complete the closure of operations. Then there was the matter of that 50% stake in what was now officially called Virgin Radio. Initially, there was talk of the company investing up to £6m in the station over the next four years. Gyngell even mooted the idea of becoming Virgin Radio Chairman. However, when the stake was discussed during a full meeting of TV-am shareholders in March, the unanimous verdict was to sell up and draw a line under everything. Virgin bought the stake; the TV-am buildings were sold to the satellite music channel MTV; all involvement in bids for Channel Five was terminated, and Gyngell departed for Australia.

The only thing left was to liquidate what remained of the company. A final meeting of shareholders green-lighted a reverse take-over of TV-am's residual assets by the Mayfair casino, Crockfords. "There's just a bit of cash," explained a departing spokesperson, "about £9m of which will be used to pay off remaining Crockfords debts after the rights issue. Crockfords plc has no plans to continue any involvement in television." And that was it. The last few pennies of Gyngell's empire of "eternal summer, [where] lost, lonely people turn on and feel warm and bright" ended up rattling around gambling tables and slot machines.

When Bruce Gyngell died in September 2000, aged 71, fulsome tributes made much of the revolution he supposedly wrought on British breakfast television. And it was true that for a time he did succeed in maintaining a service that was dazzling in its self-confidence, unforgettable in its homeliness, and unapologetic in its pursuit of the cheap and cheerful.

But it wasn't his creation. Others who had come before had constructed the foundations upon which Gyngell sought to fashion his place in history. His apparent unwillingness to concede either credit or respect for the actions of his peers led to a sequence of unsavoury conflicts and crises. A host of influential figures from behind the scenes – Greg Dyke, Clive Jones, Peter McHugh, Mike Hollingsworth and many more – had their contributions to TV-am's success compromised, belittled or simply ignored. In consequence, scores of high-ranking media executives vowed they would rather run a mile than have anything to do with TV-am.

Eventually, this fondness for self-promotion and of revelling in the role of a maverick outsider proved Gyngell's undoing. He thought his anti-union, entrepreneurial credentials made TV-am a shoo-in for a place at the top table of the Conservative government's broadcasting establishment. In fact, he took his eye off the ball, preoccupied with modelling TV-am into something it couldn't be: a full-time news service. Obsessed with his own audacity, he then let his rivals bid more than twice as much as he had for the breakfast licence, convinced the ITC would realise such a cost would never prove sustainable. He blundered, and lost everything. The result was a chaotic, graceless demise for what was, once upon a time, a truly innovatory organisation.

Another breakfast television service came to a conclusion in 1992. The Channel 4 Daily had continued to be an awkward, though inventive, patchwork of features and programmes. It had experimented with puppetry in the shape of Earl E Bird, an avuncular spin-off character from the titular daily children's slot; then from the start of '92 it had aired 52 new *Magic Roundabout* cartoons specially written and narrated by Nigel Planer. Yet its ratings had remained stuck at 200,000, which C4 boss Michael Grade considered "risible, compared to TV-am's couple of million".

Mindful of how his channel would have to start paying its own way from the start of 1993 rather than rely on advertising sold by the ITV network, Grade realised the Channel 4 Daily could prove a serious drain on revenue and resources. "I was determined that breakfast television should stand on its own feet," he recalled. "I had no intention of diverting cash from peak-time output, so something had to be done. Now that the toothpaste was out of the tube, there was no way of squeezing it back and reverting to blank screens in the morning as in pre-breakfast television days. We had a statutory obligation to provide alternative viewing, and that was what I intended to do."

Grade ordered the formation of a small committee of C4 commissioning editors to discuss how and when to replace the Channel 4 Daily, chaired by Director of Programmes Liz Forgan. Among its members were News and Current Affairs editor David Lloyd, Arts and Entertainment Controller Andrea Wonfor, and Business and Features editor Michael Atwell. All agreed on the need to act quickly, yet opinions varied on just what kind of programme they should be looking for.

Atwell recalls, "My argument was, on the basis of what I'd already shown on the Channel 4 Daily on weekends with the kids' stuff, that we probably ought to be aiming for a children's programme." He talked through his ideas with the channel's newly appointed Director of Sales and Marketing, Stuart Butterfield. "I asked him what he thought of the idea of doing a children's programme," Atwell continues. "He said it probably would be difficult it if was just a children's programme because there were already kids' shows on ITV in the afternoons, which accounted for a lot of children's advertising. He didn't think there was enough children's advertising to really sustain two hours every day in the early morning as well. But then he said if you aimed at doing a programme for children and their parents, young families – if you can find a way of bridging those two worlds, we could then advertise cereals and washing powder and all sorts of domestic things." Atwell took Butterfield's analysis back to the committee and, after some healthy discussion, managed to get the group to agree to pitch the new breakfast programme at precisely that audience.

So it was that a briefing document was circulated early in 1992 amongst independent production companies, which specified that C4 was looking for a self-financing, entertainment-orientated replacement to the Channel 4 Daily, aimed at "families with children – that is, children and young adults, mothers particularly". It was to be "essentially an entertaining feature-led service", weighted towards neither news nor sofa-based lifestyle content, but which would make a point of maintaining "C4's innovative approach". It would also be a single programme, rather than a collage of commissions like its predecessor, and would be allotted an estimated budget of no more than £10m over 15 months.

This was major news. The significance of what was implied within the document – a major reorientation of C4's breakfast output – was not lost on many throughout the TV industry, in particular ITN who wondered what would happen to its 40 members of staff currently employed on the Channel 4 Daily. However, Michael Grade wanted to move things along speedily, and set February 14 as a deadline for the receipt of programme proposals.

The feverish interest that greeted the invitation to tender suggested that enthusiasm in breakfast TV was no less great than it had been ten years earlier. A total of 31 companies submitted bids, far more than both Grade and Channel 4 had ever expected. Among them were pitches from various ITV companies including Anglia, Yorkshire, ITN and HTV, alongside joint proposals from Thames and the production outfit Mentorn, and Central TV in alliance with programme makers Wall To Wall and Initial. Several independent companies threw their hats into the ring, such as Jonathan Ross's Channel X. There was even, as Grade recalled, "one from a company that proposed presenting the show from one of Harrods' shop windows, while another thought the main concourse of Waterloo station would be an ideal location for a wacky, noisy programme".

Time was very much of the essence. Grade and his committee needed to have the new show up and running as soon as possible, ready for the channel's switch to self-funding status on 1 January 1993. As such, they spent only a few weeks deliberating before drawing up a shortlist of four bids: ITN, who proposed a revamped version of the Channel 4 Daily; Bernard Clark Productions; Central Television; and the small independent producer, Planet 24.

Michael Grade remembered how "Andrea Wonfor passed along the proposal from Planet 24, a company part-owned by the founder and driving force behind Live Aid, Bob Geldof, for something called *The Big Breakfast*. Everyone round the table thought it sounded great fun, but of course it wouldn't work." Still, there was something about Planet 24's bid that the commissioning group found impossible to ignore. It was just so unusual, and such a departure from the norm. After further discussion they decided it came down to, in the words of Grade, "A straight choice between *The Big Breakfast* and a proposal from Central Television for a show that would be in the mould of TV-am – all sweaters and sofas. The consensus was that we should plump for [Central], though there was also a sneaking feeling that if Channel 4 didn't take a risk with *The Big Breakfast*, no one else would. And it was different, which put it squarely within our remit."

Some had serious doubts about even funding an official pilot of *The Big Breakfast*. "Quite a lot of people on the committee were very dubious about it," remembers Michael Atwell, "and I had my reservations, too. On paper, there wasn't much of a proposal. It had a concept, and I quite liked the concept, yet there wasn't much flesh on it. So we really had no idea how it'd look. But everyone could see that *The Big Breakfast* was very very different. I'd had a conversation with Michael Grade when we were trying to write the briefing document, where I'd gone, 'Michael, what the hell should we be doing?' He just said, 'I don't know what it is, but make it different from anything else on television. Make it stand out, whatever it is, just make it stand out.' And *The Big Breakfast* was the thing that stood out most from everything else."

Live pilots of both the Central and Planet 24 productions were mounted and relayed back to Channel 4. "I went to the house where Planet 24 was running the pilot of *The Big Breakfast*," recalls Atwell. "They'd rented some place in the middle of an ordinary terraced street. From the moment I walked in the door, there was electricity in the air. It was just buzzing. It was fantastic. We asked all the commissioning editors to come into C4 early and watch [the pilots]. When I got back everyone said they'd all been in one corner watching this one." "After five minutes of the Central production," noted Grade, "my eyes glazed over, but *The Big Breakfast*, and particularly its presenter, Chris Evans, transfixed me. In places it was crude, even amateurish, but it had immense energy and there was no danger that the casual viewer who switched on could mistake it for any of its competitors."

It didn't take long for the committee to reach a verdict. David Lloyd for one was completely convinced: "I'd looked at the original proposal, and then the tape, and there was absolutely no question from the material that this was the best idea. If ever you'd seen something leap off the page – that was it. It was a very able piece of work. And so it didn't cause me any pain to slaughter the Channel 4 Daily and go for *The Big Breakfast*, as did most of my colleagues."

In June, it was announced that Planet 24 had it in the bag. Liz Forgan expanded on the result, explaining how *The Big Breakfast* looked: "Fresh, energetic and full of promise. We are not attempting to compete heavily with TV-am or its successor, but we think Planet 24's concept will give everyone in the business something to think about."

The modest company that had landed the most lucrative commission in recent television history had been formed in February 1992, following the merger of two separate organisations – 24-Hour Productions and Planet Pictures. It was best known, so far, for the notorious late-night self-conscious youth show *The Word*, but had also been responsible for a live televised performance of *Handel's Messiah*, the design quiz *Eye To Eye*, and a series on Japanese prisoner-of-war camps called *Across The Jade Divide*.

Veteran pop performer Bob Geldof had founded Planet Pictures with Tony Boland, a producer who had worked on Ireland's Live Aid and *The*

Late Late Show. Charlie Parsons, erstwhile presenter of another youth programme, *Network 7*, was the brains behind 24-Hour Productions, and brought with him Waheed Alli, a former head of investment, financial publisher and consultant to actuaries. Together, Geldof and Parsons made a formidable partnership: staunch, headstrong, and fervently passionate about what they believed in.

Now they had barely a few months to prepare and launch Britain's newest breakfast television programme. Parsons set about talking up the project for all it was worth, promising *The Big Breakfast* would be "a morning radio show on TV, with short news bulletins [and] lots of chat – but not like TV-am and with items for kids... If there is a feel to it, I suppose it will be middle market tabloid, or maybe the mainstream end of Radio One." Everything in the programme was to be accessible to anyone who tuned in, Parsons claimed. "And we won't repeat items through the morning – this will be a single, seamless programme, running for two hours, five mornings a week."

Away from the confident PR, however, it hadn't taken long for a palpable sense of unease to grip both C4 and Planet 24. An awful lot was riding on the performance of a relatively obscure company and its band of unknown personnel. A huge amount of work needed to be done in a tiny period of time, including hiring 70-odd production staff and finalising the location of the suburban house that was to double as the programme's studio.

Michael Atwell, now officially in charge of the project at Channel 4, found the tight deadline a plentiful source of panic. "We only had a very short period between commissioning and going on air," he recalls. "Planet 24 had to find premises, get the planning permission sorted, clear the site, gut the house, bring the stuff in. Yet the company had no television facilities. It was all unbelievably hairy."

Above all, nobody had a clue how the costs would work out in the long run. Would *The Big Breakfast* become the launch pad for C4 successfully paying its own way in the future, or a cumbersome albatross that dragged it into financial penury? Waheed Alli, in charge of balancing Planet 24's books, could only conclude, rather hesitatingly, that, "I would not say that we will make a loss, but the costs involved in setting up and shooting this programme are quite high. Our main hope for the first series is that it gets us an extended commission for a second run, on which we might start to see some return."

Just one week before going on air, the results of some focus group polling came through. "We'd booked a research company to go and do focus group testing with *The Big Breakfast* pilot," Atwell continues, "and basically they said it's going to be a disaster. The people they'd shown the programme to, hated it. We'd asked them to include children in their research, because *The Big Breakfast* was aimed at a young audience, but they said the children hated it so much that they'd had to lock the doors to stop them leaving." A sense of gloom descended over Channel 4. "We all sat around in a terrible state of despair," confesses Atwell, "and we didn't really know what to do. The first technical rehearsals were a complete and utter disaster. We were terribly worried – thinking, 'Will we ever get this show on air in one piece?'"

The reality would take everybody, up to and including Michael Grade himself, completely by surprise.

TWELVE

"That was funnier
than you'll ever know"

At the end of the final edition of the Channel 4 Daily on Friday 25 September 1992, the show's presenters good-naturedly threw their scripts into the air and wished their successors the very best of luck. It was a valediction dripping in sarcasm. Scepticism about *The Big Breakfast* was rampant throughout the TV industry. Unknown faces, untried formats, untested technologies … what kind of madness was this? It could surely only be a matter of time before events demanded a return to some of the values enshrined in its hapless yet dignified predecessor.

Those same demob-happy Channel 4 Daily hosts had no idea how quickly they, never mind their endeavours, would be forgotten.

The Big Breakfast arrived on television brimming with such overwhelming self-confidence and charm that it felt as if years had gone into its preparation. In reality, the entire programme had been knocked up in a matter of months. That the show was such a success – and so quickly – was down to a number of triumphs on the part of Executive Producer Charlie Parsons and his team. And the first, and most important, concerned the choice of presenters.

Chris Evans had only brief experience of breakfast television: the ill-fated *TV-MAYhem* on TV-am, but he proved to be the perfect host for *The Big Breakfast* virtually from day one. His striking, freewheeling presentational style, refined on Greater London Radio and Radio One, transferred remarkably effectively onto screen. He soon cultivated a freakish, rascally nature that was unpredictable in front of the cameras and famously perfectionist off. In turn, a format was shaped around him that allowed his strengths to be devastatingly realized, and amusing scenes and set-ups contrived with him at the centre. The end result was a potent broadcasting force, and an icon in the making.

Joining him as co-host was Gaby Roslin, or 'The First Lady Of British Television' as Evans dubbed her. She also had a previous TV career: first as a presenter on *Hippo*, a daily children's programme on the satellite-based Super Channel, and then on ITV's Saturday morning series *Motormouth* for three years. Despite being a last minute replacement for fellow kids' TV personality Emma Forbes, Gaby's experience and accommodating character proved vital in nurturing *The Big Breakfast*'s rapport with viewers.

The third member of the team was Paula Yates. Easily the biggest 'name' attached to the programme, she made her presence felt by doing what she'd done best on *The Tube*, the 1980s music show that had made her a TV star: swanning around not really doing much in-between entertaining high-calibre celebrity guests. This she did lounging on a gigantic and ludicrously upholstered double bed, indulging in gossipy chats, reading questions off cards, and flirting incessantly. Everyone, from Miss Piggy, Oliver Reed and Barbara Cartland, to all of pop group Take That, took turns on the mattress – though politicians Cecil Parkinson and Tony Benn preferred to sit on an adjacent chair, while Richard Branson stripped off to join Paula under the covers.

To begin with, her husband (and programme executive), Bob Geldof, also had a direct role in proceedings in the guise of a jet-setting interviewer flying the world chatting to leaders, presidents and other luminaries. Though much publicized, these interviews didn't really work, with Geldof coming across as less than his usual animated self, while the choice of guests, such as the Prime Minister of Turkey, was often absurd. The feature was quietly dropped from the show after a few months.

Charlie Parsons had appointed two key individuals to head up his production team: former *Network 7* colleague Sebastian Scott, and Ruth Wrigley with whom Parsons had worked on LWT's *The Six O'Clock Show*. Both had direct input into what was Planet 24's second big triumph: establishing an almost universally effective programme format for *The Big Breakfast,* which, unusually for British breakfast TV, would remain pretty much unchanged for several years.

For all the ostensible on-screen disarray, a carefully ordered sequence of items and features was in place from the beginning. "The single biggest thought we had when we were sitting round thinking, 'God, breakfast TV – will it work?' was that British people didn't generally watch television in the morning," recalls Ruth Wrigley today. "You'd listen to the radio and read the newspapers. So we'd said, 'how would you get British people to turn the telly on?' And we worked out that kids would. So the first half of *The Big Breakfast,* between 7 and 8am, was very orientated towards children."

The show opened with Chris Evans and Gaby Roslin welcoming viewers at 7am, usually from outside of their specially customized 'house' that doubled as a studio. A news bulletin followed, read by the affable Peter Smith. These were neat, snappy reports from ITN, replete with eye-catching graphics in lurid colour schemes. When Smith was absent, legendary figures from TV's past were hired to take his place, such as Jan Leeming – and, making her return to breakfast television for the first time in virtually ten years, Angela Rippon.

Next on was stand-up comedian Mark Lamarr who fronted 'Down Your Doorstep', a daily outside broadcast from an unusual location. Besides showing up at people's houses demanding to be let in, Lamarr would often position himself at a busy road junction, providing distraction and amusement for commuters stuck in traffic jams, such as a David Bowie impersonator hired to entertain travellers at Spaghetti Junction.

This somewhat relentless and exhausting role would see a rapid turnover in presenters, beginning in March 1993, when Lamarr was replaced with sunglasses-wielding Paul Ross, former editor of *The Six O'Clock Show* and *The Word*, and who himself was succeeded by enduring children's host Keith Chegwin in August. These OBs weren't always that effective but made for some memorable moments, such as the time Lamarr tried to get inside Fiona Armstrong's house shortly after she'd quit TV-am's replacement GMTV, or when he brought a camel onto a housing estate in Glasgow.

The rest of *The Big Breakfast* then unfolded through a number of slots. 'Meet The Family' charted the exploits of a real life clan who 'lived' in the studio house for a week at a time, and who joined in features such as 'Dish The Dirt' where they were encouraged to spill the beans on their siblings' worst habits. 'Whose Washing Line Is It Anyway?' was the most functional of quizzes, involving telephone callers guessing the identity of a celebrity from items hung on the eponymous line, while 'Snap Cackle And Pop' ran music, film and TV reports. After the eight o'clock news, the programme's tone was less overtly juvenile and boasted items such as a newspaper review, a laborious 'serious interview' by Gaby with a bereaved mother or wronged consumer, and celebrities offering handy tips for day to day living in 'Superhints'. Paula's interrogations filled the final quarter-hour up to 9am.

"In terms of style, *The Big Breakfast*'s greatest legacy was to ask the crew to be an audience for the programme," argues David Lloyd, C4 Commissioning editor for News and Current Affairs. From the outset, *Big Breakfast* technical staff, from cameramen to floor managers, were consciously encouraged to become part of the fabric of the programme. Viewers were just as likely to see shots of the production team as they were the presenters, and to hear them joining in call and response-style chants with the hosts. It all helped create a sense of community and inclusion, sentiments that were just as tangible for audiences watching at home as they clearly were in the studio.

The 'house' from which the show was broadcast was a fantastic achievement, being both a constantly evolving set and a resource. Seven weeks before *The Big Breakfast* went on air, the site was in total disrepair: three cottages left in ruins. It took £750,000 and 140 builders to convert them into the finished article. Interior designer Cath Pater-Lancucki then gave each room a distinctive identity and a brash, overtly modernist look, but it still functioned as if it were a proper house, with all appliances from showers to cookers in working order. Outside, a 30-ton OB truck doubled as a production gallery, which had been winched into place over the nearby canal.

No attempt was made to shut out the real world: ordinary people on their way to work were constantly seen walking past the windows and behind the presenters' heads. Neither was the location kept a secret. Anyone could turn up to watch the goings-on by heading down to 2 Lock Keepers Cottages, Old Ford Lock, London – the address regularly read out for competition entries and letters.

"*The Big Breakfast* was a revolutionary programme," argues its Commissioning editor at C4 Michael Atwell, "not only because it was anarchic or apparently anarchic and it was sort of 'zoo television', but also through the relationship with the viewers. People could phone in and take part in the games, and we had the 'Family Of The Week', so we had actual viewers in the house. And that was completely unlike any other breakfast television programme there'd ever been. What *The Big Breakfast* did was bring values from a lot of entertainment shows, such as *The Generation Game*, into early morning television and really make the viewers feel that it was *their* show. So it was a much more inviting show, simply because people were directly invited. When people found out where it was [filmed] you got armies of people by the canal, outside the gate, watching all the comings and goings. And they became part of the action. We used to include shots of them in the show and they'd all wave. In that sense, it set out a new relationship with the viewer."

Perhaps *The Big Breakfast*'s greatest triumph of all, however, had to be 'The Crunch'. This was a segment hosted by Chris Evans together with two aliens, Zig and Zag, who had crashed on Earth from the planet Zog and now lived in the bathroom. Noted for their distinctive brightly coloured 'zogabonds' (their pom-pom ears), the pair spoke English and were fully assimilated into British customs and practices, but displayed remarkably varied degrees of intelligence.

Zag was ultra-smart, cynical and clued-up. Regularly caught on the phone to a film producer or supermodel, he was an alien on the make (swindling Zig out of his pocket money or pestering Planet 24 for a raise). He schmoozed with guests, was in tune with popular culture (especially computer games) and was a versatile 'ragga' performer. Zig on the other hand was hopelessly dim, naïve and gullible, yet did possess a winning line in party tricks such as swallowing the camera or the top of his own head. From this unlikely scenario, a relationship developed between the aliens and Evans that was entertaining, hysterically funny, and often the highpoint of the entire show.

Chris Evans opens his bathroom to aliens from the planet Zog – just for fun

In reality, Zig and Zag were two puppets who had originally debuted on the Irish station, RTE. Their appearances on *The Big Breakfast* introduced them to a whole new audience and won them national appeal. Each morning they showed up in two separate slots: a five-minute section alone with Chris Evans and a range of meaningless features, often improvised; then a second, longer slot with the trio being joined by special guests.

The former was witness to some classic, unforgettable television of the kind that everyone would be talking about later at school and work. One such incident involved Evans being accidentally covered in chocolate icing when the gang attempted to bake a cake. Another involved Zag demonstrating the 'self-peeling banana' by jerking his hand up and down, to which Evans responded, "That was funnier than you'll ever know".

A number of regular items soon emerged, such as Zig's appearances as an 'Agony Alien', dispensing informed wisdom ("Pop down your local library, you'll find some booklets and pamphlets there, read them over a nice cup of coffee"), to 'serious' problems from viewers ("My umbrella is pregnant").

Zag developed a talent for palm reading, canvassing custom from viewers, while cautioning, "If you don't want your future to be sloppy, don't send me a fuzzy photocopy." Zig hosted a special 'Make And Do' slot ("Do you like it? I thought you would, missus!"), besides challenging his cohorts to guess, 'What's At The End Of The Bin, Jim?' When Evans started to learn the guitar, the three often lapsed into made-up songs, such as 'Only Five Days Left' – a tribute to it being February 23 and almost the beginning of March. There was also the on-running saga of Zig's pregnancy, culminating in his giving birth, live on television, to a pillow he named Pete.

When special guests were added to this confection, the results were not always that successful. Some entered into the spirit of the occasion, but others appeared totally at sea. Alan Freeman called in to offer tips on DJ-ing ("It's great fun, and it's number one!"), while Patrick Moore serenaded the aliens with his xylophone. Numerous pop and dance bands received early exposure, and Zag struck up quite a bond with the 'ragga' star, Shaggy, when the pair dueted on the part-spontaneous song 'Dem Girls'. Professional experts dropped by to inform the country about their vocation, only to end up the butt of engagingly bad jokes. A beekeeper was asked: "When you go into a petrol station, do you ever get embarrassed, asking them to fill you up with BP?" while a deep-sea diver was met with the question, "Have you ever blown off in your wet suit?"

Zig and Zag, along with Chris Evans, would eventually become – for many – the embodiment of all that was great about *The Big Breakfast*, and why the show was must-see television that people would set their videos for (an undoubted first for breakfast TV). But to begin with, possibly in light of such a dazzling potpourri of items and strands, press reaction to the programme was mixed. "Snap, Crackle, Flop" crowed the *Daily Express*; "Wacky Wakey!" concluded the *Sunday Times*; "A slap-happy slice of toast-modernism", muttered the *Guardian*; and "Sunny side up but it's no yolk at all", cracked the *Independent On Sunday*.

"For the first week, the press, on the whole, were quite sniffy," remembers Michael Atwell. "They were hedging their bets; they couldn't quite work out whether they liked it or disliked it. Their instinct was to dislike it, because they were all middle-class snobs and thought it was all terribly downmarket, though they sort of recognised that there was something quite exhilarating about it. But then, by week two, when the ratings were going up and all their children were talking about it, the press very quickly dropped the criticism and started really supporting it."

The programme pulled in 600,000 viewers on its first morning. "I thought we would probably double the Channel 4 Daily's audience," Atwell continues, "then on the first day we ended up with three times as many viewers. And it started building very fast after that." Ruth Wrigley recalls the mood in those early days as being a marked change from the tense, anxious weeks preceding the launch. "Channel 4 and nobody else was particularly interested in their new breakfast show. And as long as it got a few hundred thousand viewers, the broadcaster was going to be happy. We were a very small team, but when the show worked, morale obviously was good. There was no expectation, and yet suddenly people started to take notice."

Sure enough, ratings rocketed during October and November, until soon the show was threatening to break the one million mark. Ed Forsdick, then researcher for 'Down Your Doorstep' but someone who would go on to have a long association with the show, remembers these first few months as, "Probably the most exciting time to have been involved with *The Big Breakfast*, as we saw it become a national obsession as the weeks went on." "Publicity was quite important," Atwell adds, "but word of mouth was definitely the most effective thing – I mean, every kid in Britain was talking about it."

Opinion amongst fellow broadcasters and the rest of the media was not so uniform. Paddy Haycocks, former standard-bearer for the Channel 4 Daily, remembers, "My first reaction to *The Big Breakfast* was one of amazement, shock and horror. I couldn't see it ever working. But I think that was because it was so far away from my perception of what breakfast television could be, and that of course was its triumph. And very quickly, the more I saw of Chris Evans, the more I realised it would work. It was so much the antithesis of the Channel 4 Daily, which was exactly right. Not only did you have a liveness and a zaniness, and the Channel 4 Daily was far from live and zany, but you had an inclusiveness. All the Channel 4 Daily had was a man in a broom-cupboard doing voiceovers."

Others remained unconvinced. At the time, veteran commentator Julie Burchill snapped, "The arrival of *The Big Breakfast* sums up the decline of Channel 4; over the years it has developed into a kitsch and camp channel," while writer and comedienne Sandi Toksvig was moved to mutter, "*The Big Breakfast Show* [sic] worries me – in fact it is the most worrying thing I have ever seen on television and if this is an indication of what to expect in the future, then the future looks pretty grim."

Much to such critics' consternation and bemusement, within a matter of weeks, the show's success was unmistakable. A mark of *The Big Breakfast*'s rapid influence was how, only a few months into its life, Channel 4 commissioned a special live edition to see in the New Year on December 31, running from 11.30pm to 1am. All its presenters became very famous, very quickly, but it was Evans who turned into the real hot property. Conscious that offers were already being made to lure the star elsewhere, Channel 4 hastily finalised a new contract that kept him on their station. A three-year deal, supposed to be worth £1.5m, was announced in May 1993 that ensured he stayed at *The Big Breakfast* while also providing scope for Evans to make and present other C4 shows via his own production outfit. This company, ultimately called Ginger Television, was charged with developing a prime time entertainment show for Saturday nights.

Meanwhile, both Channel 4 and Planet 24 sought to safeguard the continuation of *The Big Breakfast* itself and exploit its reputation. A new 'consultant' was engaged to shore-up the programme's content, which turned out to be ex TV-am presenter and producer James Baker. At the same time, *The Big Breakfast*'s format was sold to America, France, Germany and Holland, and in June, C4 brokered a new contract with Planet 24 to keep the British show running at least through to autumn 1995.

On screen, the imaginative, innovative ideas seemed to flow non-stop. 'Invention Corner' found Chris Evans, dressed in a large red wig and white coat, introducing pointless gizmos from amateur inventors hoping for a patent. 'Anorak Of The Week' saw hapless collectors brought in for humiliation and to show off their wares (including bus tickets, sugar sachets, urinals, phone cards, and, inevitably, anoraks) in return for a chance to win the eponymous waterproof. 'The Morning Face' was a periodic feature where viewers could send in photos of people caught asleep in embarrassing, disturbing or amusing positions, while 'Me And My Pet' and 'The People Report' allowed for more audience participation via home videos, with the latter in particular giving students with too much time on their hands a chance to get on TV investigating some trivial sub-*That's Life!* issue.

Computer games were reviewed in 'Master Blaster' with the help of a lucky teenager known simply as Ben The Boffin, and viewers' squabbles were settled in 'Judge The Grudge'. 'The Big Decision' presumed to solve dilemmas from individuals, though the first instalment, "Should I get a dog or a girlfriend?" was abandoned halfway through when Evans declared the subject a ghastly individual who didn't deserve either. A man proposed to his girlfriend on air, and another couple got married in a marquee outside. The garden housed some chickens, and when two were murdered by a visiting fox, an inquest was held and tributes poured in. A runaway chicken was named Lucky, and viewers were invited to decide whether the team should 'Keep it, or eat it?'

Comedian Lenny Henry broke his arm falling off a miniature motorbike he was racing down the canal towpath. Chris Evans went up in a helicopter (where his cameraman threw up over him), sang live with Neil Sedaka, tried to eat some fossilized turds, joined a team of Elvis look-alikes, and fell over his chair. Gaby Roslin was forever being embarrassed: by her past (constantly threatened with clips from *Hippo*); by Chris ("Gaby told me just before, 'I know it, Chris, my boobs are going to fall out by the end of the programme,'"); and by her famous dad, Radio 4 newsreader Clive Roslin.

Another element of the programme that became a real highlight was the 8.30am competition spot. This changed on a monthly basis, mostly involving observational games entitled 'Spot The Sausage', 'Dish Of The Day' or 'More Tea Vicar?' Most spectacular of all was 'One Lump Or Two'. Set around a large outdoor swimming pool made to look like a teacup, callers had to direct a blindfolded guest, perched atop a giant floating inflatable teabag, towards two huge polystyrene sugar lumps, which they had to throw out of the pool to win a prize. During the competition's run in summer 1993, many special guests, presenters and most of the production team ended up soaked, including Sebastian Scott. Chris Evans, naturally, dived into the pool on its very first appearance.

Even when things went wrong on *The Big Breakfast,* it didn't seem to matter, each mistake and gaffe somehow making proceedings all the more endearing and compulsive. On St Patrick's Day 1993, the programme fell off the air for 15 minutes because of a power cut, and when they returned, Evans was seen sticking a plug back into the wall and blaming it on leprechauns. Making light of such occurrences became commonplace – and besides, as Evans regularly intoned, when it all went pear-shaped, "I don't care what they're doing on the other side; it isn't half as good as this!"

In July 1993, after almost 12 months without a break, Sebastian Scott quit his role as *Big Breakfast* editor. Bob Geldof provided a suitably melodramatic tribute, announcing: "Only Einstein has had more influence on popular culture in this century – but he got less money." Scott left behind a programme that had superseded all its founding intentions to become nothing less than a 'brand' and a highly lucrative franchise. *Big Breakfast* spin-offs now included a book, a video and an album, while the profusion of Zig and Zag replica puppets, cuddly toys and tie-in singles recalled the marketing of Roland Rat a decade earlier.

In the very early days of the programme a running joke had involved Chris Evans lying about how many people were watching, reaching a peak when he produced a mock-up copy of *Broadcast* magazine that "scientifically proved" the show was getting 19 million viewers. All the same, come mid-September 1993, the audience had reached an astonishing 2m, making it, at the time, the most watched breakfast programme on British TV.

That was plenty of reason to celebrate *The Big Breakfast*'s first birthday in style. Keith Chegwin, Paul Ross and Mark Lamarr did a joint 'Down Your Doorstep', trying to stage a street party in Rochdale; Bob Geldof joined Zig and Zag in 'The Crunch'; C4 boss Michael Grade turned up to provide a 'Superhint'; and the entire house gathered for a sing-along with Take That, whose lead singer, Gary Barlow, had penned a special birthday ode, 'One Ton Of Fun'. It was a jubilant occasion, and suggested that *The Big Breakfast* was destined to remain at the top of its game.

"With *The Big Breakfast,* everything was got right," recalls David Lloyd. "The hiring was right, the environment was right, and the whole thing was extremely adroitly put together." It also pulled off something of a remarkable coup for breakfast television: "It persuaded an intelligent audience to watch programming that was not necessarily predicated on news," Lloyd continues. "In other words, it showed you can ask an intelligent audience to have some fun in the morning."

Michael Atwell rightly emphasises the significance of *The Big Breakfast*'s unique contrasting of the ordinary and everyday with the totally extraordinary and unexpected. "It all looked anarchic and sprawling, but there was a mad structure to it. It mirrored exactly the households that we were broadcasting to, in the sense that Chris was the dad, Gaby was the mum, Zig and Zag were the children, and the 'Family Of The Week' were the next-door neighbours. I guess Paula on the bed would be the sort of sexy maiden aunt!"

For Michael Grade, the programme was simply, "a huge success, the biggest commercial risk we'd ever taken at Channel 4". Paddy Haycocks adds, "It was just a complete culture shock, because it was so different from what we had tried to do on the Channel 4 Daily. But equally, it was a million miles from the comfortable breakfast television of TV-am. There are moments in TV – turning points – where a culture is changed. When BBC announcers stopped wearing dinner suits. When people stopped smoking cigarettes on screen. Where panel games no longer had to be hosted by someone with received pronunciation. And I think *The Big Breakfast* was a defining moment of change. Sometimes you need somebody to come in with a small creative bomb and blow all the cobwebs off preconceived notions."

Of all *The Big Breakfast*'s achievements during its first 12 months on air, arguably the most substantial was its impact on the medium of broadcasting itself. It revolutionised what was possible and expected on television, while utterly rewriting the rules for what was workable, popular breakfast TV. And such an impact was no greater in evidence than on the fortunes of the new ITV breakfast station, GMTV.

THIRTEEN

"Now breakfast TV is going to be done properly"

"The loss of our licence was the result of one of the most deeply flawed Acts of Parliament ever to reach the statute book," raged former TV-am boss Bruce Gyngell in early 1993. Many within the broadcasting industry were quick to concur with his description of the legislation in question. There was a strong consensus that the Act, through its twin promotion of both increased competition and slacker regulation, had left British television less focused and distinct than before. But as for Gyngell's continual cries of foul in defence of TV-am, a whole 18 months since it failed to renew its franchise, well, this was less convincing. Few could remember witnessing such a long-running case of sour grapes.

All the same, much-publicised events then unfolding at GMTV, TV-am's replacement, seemed uncannily close to bearing out another of Gyngell's maxims: that TV-am's bid for the breakfast television licence had been "the maximum that could sensibly be made". Could the very public and painful distress that overwhelmed a cash-strapped GMTV in the first few months of its life on air be taken as evidence that Gyngell had been right all along? Moreover, was history about to repeat itself and doom the new breakfast service to a crisis identical to that suffered by its predecessor ten years earlier?

GMTV had not exactly been blessed with the most auspicious of starts. It won the breakfast franchise in autumn 1991 under the name of Sunrise Television, but within days was threatened with legal action by BSkyB whose own breakfast programme was also called *Sunrise*. After spending precious time and money coming up with the name GMTV (Good Morning Television), the company had the further distraction of finding someone to buy up its 30% of unsold shares, eventually split between Carlton Television (20%) and existing investors. Then there was the business of persuading each of the other ITV companies to provide regional news summaries to be fed into GMTV every hour, an obligation specified within its contract, and a process that took almost 12 months to finalise.

Charged with overcoming these and other teething troubles were GMTV's chief management duo. Managing Director Christopher Stoddart was a widely respected executive and former General Manager of Tyne Tees Television. Second in command, with the crucial job of Director of Programmes, was Lis Howell. Before joining GMTV, she had enjoyed a long career with ITV before more recently taking the job of a Managing Editor at BSkyB. "I'd been approached by about ten different people who were setting up franchises," she recalls today. "I chose GMTV because I had great admiration for [its founder] Greg Dyke." The thinking behind her appointment was, in her own words, that "as you're a regional ITV person, therefore you'll know the public; you're a Northern woman therefore you look great on paper; and you're working at Sky News, so you know about new media and how do it cheaply."

Both Christopher Stoddart and Lis Howell spent most of 1992 exhaustively banging the drum for GMTV. Stoddart promised, "Unapologetic mainstream TV for middle England. Words like 'innovation', 'experiment' and 'mission agenda setting' are out. Our vision is of cheerful, professional television for ordinary people" (though he declined to specify who these were). Lis Howell admitted to admiring TV-am's "unapologetic downmarket approach", but chose to define its replacement as "warm, cheerful, authoritative and a bit cheeky".

Plans to recruit presenters and reporters proceeded with a similar urgency. After rather casually touting iconic BBC sports host Des Lynam as a potential signing, less costly alternatives were found. Lis Howell looked first to her erstwhile employers BSkyB where she poached sports front man Michael Wilson, "who'd been enormously popular, quite a cult character". Next came ITN newscaster Fiona Armstrong, who took the plunge, supposedly in order to shake off her 'news princess' image. They were both pencilled in to present GMTV's main weekday programme, but only from Monday to Thursday. Fridays, it was decided, needed to have more of a 'weekend' feel, and hence would be fronted by the hosts of the Sunday show, Eamonn Holmes and Anne Davies. Saturdays would be devoted entirely to children's entertainment.

If viewers needed to notice the difference between GMTV and TV-am, then this kind of peculiar division of labour was the right way to go about it. In other respects, however, the new station appeared to ape many aspects of its forerunner. A 'family' of co-hosts and experts were hired, including legal correspondent John Taylor, previously a Conservative Party candidate, and several ex-ITN staff such as former Washington and Moscow correspondent Tim Ewart. Joanna Sheldon, co-host of LWT's *Six O'Clock Show*, was appointed royal correspondent; BSkyB show biz editor, Fiona Phillips, was poached for the role of entertainment reporter; and well-known model Linda Lusardi was confirmed as an in-house fitness instructor.

Behind the scenes, respected journalists Liam Hamilton (editor) and Nigel Hancock (Chief News editor) headed a staff that would eventually total 186, including 76 Visnews personnel responsible for supplying the main news feed. In addition, the small independent company, Waterfront Productions, were lined up to supply their own regular strand entitled *Northern Inserts*, featuring human interest and unusual stories from the north of England hosted by former *That's Life!* and *Hearts Of Gold* presenter Michael Groth.

The BBC's *Crimewatch* editor, Nikki Cheetham, was hired to oversee the quasi-*After Nine* slot *Top Of The Morning* made by the independent company, Bazal Productions, and hosted by TV-am's Lorraine Kelly. Jeremy Beadle, Carol Vorderman and TV-am reporter Michael Hastings were also signed up for the posts of 'special contributor', Science correspondent and Political reporter respectively. When Dr Hilary Jones agreed to come on board, the roll call of ex-TV-am staff threatened to exceed that of those who had never worked in breakfast television before.

Looking back, Lis Howell is careful to explain the nature of GMTV's relationship with its predecessor. "Within the industry, people didn't really like Bruce Gyngell," she argues, "and that was terribly unfair. But he was such an enormous character and so forthright, and the way he ran TV-am was totally unlike the rest of the network. So, within the industry there was quite a lot of goodwill towards GMTV initially, as in, 'Great, now breakfast TV is going to be British and done properly.' In an arrogant sort of way – and I was part of that mistake – the assumption was that anything that anybody did was going to better than what Bruce Gyngell did. Yet some of the nicest people at GMTV came from TV-am."

At the time, she articulated her vision of GMTV as being "a more intimate experience than TV-am", and then added, "If viewers say we look like a major relaunch of TV-am in January [1993] we won't be sorry." After all, there was an established audience for breakfast television on ITV, and it wasn't one that Lis Howell, Christopher Stoddart nor any of GMTV's investors wanted to drive away.

As 1992 ticked by, tempting and mysterious glimpses of life inside the new breakfast TV service were dangled in front of what was hoped would be millions of prospective viewers. "There will be two green rooms," Lis Howell disclosed; "one that looks like the waiting area in one of those fancy Italian restaurants, and another one where the mum with five kids can get on with business. They'll be able to look right into the gallery, and the studio is just a couple of steps along the corridor, so that contributors will actually feel a part of the programme."

She spoke openly about the risks that might lie ahead: "Things may change over the months but we have to keep the faith with the TV-am audience or they'll never forgive us." In fact, it sometimes felt like she preferred to analyse TV-am, for whom she had never worked, rather than GMTV, for whom she did. "If there's one group we think TV-am ignored, it's husbands," she observed. "Blue collar fathers are badly under-represented in the demographics, and we want to get them interested between 6 and 7am as they're getting ready for work."

Christopher Stoddart chose to deploy more mannered terminology. He tried to play up GMTV's place within the fabric of ITV itself, rather than promoting the notion of being an outsider as Bruce Gyngell had been wont to do with TV-am. "We are ITV," he countered. "We're different because we're ITV's breakfast show but we don't compete for audience – we hand it on. Of course, breakfast TV has traditionally got revenue from ITV daytime because TV-am carved out an important medium for certain products. That is not going to change, and there is some competition, but it's an acceptable share."

Away from the steely confidence, glitzy signings and wise words, however, problems had emerged. The construction of new studios was proving to be something of a nightmare. GMTV was to be broadcast from LWT's home on the South Bank of the River Thames, a huge complex complete with a 23-storey tower block recently renamed the London Television Centre. It was to be based in the old *World Of Sport* set and also the adjacent and long-closed down LWT restaurant and bar. But as soon as conversion work had started, both venues were discovered to be suffering from hideous leaks and extensive dry rot. The designs for the ambitious sets specified the inclusion of a genuine log fire. A £15,000 chimney had to be built to ensure that none of the staff would suffocate from its fumes.

The extra cost and effort involved in resolving these and other structural problems ate into GMTV's budget and somewhat undermined the company's carefully calculated financial plan, an aspirational document, which had taken as its basis a desire for GMTV to own nothing at all save for "a few desks and chairs". When the number of weeks until launch day fell into single figures, unease seemed to grow still further and manifested itself in some very public actions. Concluding that GMTV's proposed news content did not rate highly enough, Tim Ewart and a few others returned to their former employer, ITN. Then there was the speed at which *The Big Breakfast* had matched and then exceeded the ratings of the Channel 4 Daily. Talk now was increasingly of how such success, if maintained and improved still further, would impact on GMTV's likely viewing figures. Indeed, advertising agencies were starting to predict that *The Big Breakfast*'s popularity could cost GMTV as much as £4m in lost revenue.

Some safeguards against such an eventuality had been built into GMTV's constitution; the thinking being that any substantial losses would be offset by the low overheads of sharing joint studios and transmission facilities with LWT. Christopher Stoddart tried to raise morale by proclaiming that the company had "tens of millions of pounds of advertising for 1993".

But even if everything went to plan, all targets were hit and maximum monies recouped, the official assessment of the GMTV board was that the company was unlikely to break even at the pre-tax level, before 1996. It would also make a loss of £3.8m in its first year of operation. This was a highly risky, not to say blasé, attitude towards running a breakfast TV service. What if unforeseen factors interposed to turn an anticipated marginal loss into terminal bankruptcy? As Christmas approached, *The Big Breakfast* was pulling in audiences of close to one million. Would all these viewers suddenly switch to GMTV come the New Year?

In public, Lis Howell tried to rally her troops with talk of a new era of ITV breakfast television, and how the launch of GMTV would safely put the entire grisly episode that was TV-am, with all its fancies and foibles, to bed once and for all. In secret, however, she was close to panic.

"*The Big Breakfast* had started," she recalls, "and we'd all waited, thinking their ratings were just a blip. But then their ratings grew and grew, with the press giving them loads of encouragement. I remember in November I wrote a paper for the board, saying we were going to lose 15% of our viewers because of this. But they just said, 'Tough, it's your job to pull them back.' And that's when it started getting nasty. Everybody knew. For a while, you'd been able to boost them up by saying, 'Listen, we are going to beat *The Big Breakfast*.' But by the time it got to within a week of us going on air, we clearly weren't going to beat *The Big Breakfast*. They'd had a three months head start; they'd done fantastically well; and we were changing something that was much loved for something brand new. I look back on it now and think, bloody hell, what a recipe for disaster."

Even though GMTV took over the breakfast franchise on Friday 1 January 1993, management decreed that Monday 4 January would be the station's official launch date. In the words of Lis Howell, any audience watching on New Year's Day would "either be under the influence or under five". Nonetheless, programmes did appear as required from 6am on January 1. An introductory news bulletin was followed by a muted welcome from the new presenting team, a conversation between Lorraine Kelly and Dr Hilary Jones about hangover cures, then a diet of solid cartoons through to 9.25am, including the feature length *Chip'n'Dale Rescue Rangers To The Rescue*.

The following day, a Saturday, saw GMTV's weekend schedules unveiled. It was here that the presence of Disney on the company board could most definitely be felt. Following the unremarkable *Rise And Shine*, a slot for young children, came what was intended to be the big hitter: *Saturday Disney*. This show was crammed full of high profile Disney 'brands', such as *Chip'n'Dale*, *Mickey Mouse*, *Duck Tales* and *Darkwing Duck*, plus a competition to win a trip to Disney World. Holding it all together were newcomer Pippa Ford-Jones and future *Blue Peter* presenter Stuart Miles; both seemed somewhat dwarfed by the comparative prestige of their featured cartoons. The morning ended capably with *Teen Win Lose Or Draw*, a spin-off of the popular ITV daytime quiz, hosted by Darren Day.

Sundays turned out to be rather more awkwardly sequenced, shifting from programmes for adults to kids to adults and then back to kids again. It began with *Timeshift* at 6am, a sort of 'best of'/preview clips show presented by Fiona McDiarmid and including signing for the deaf. Then, ex-Children's BBC host Simon Parkin showed up with his *Posse* from 6.30am, heralded with a title sequence featuring a giant cutout of his face jiggling about to a fanfare. *Sunday Best* followed at 7.20am, a lightweight magazine programme fronted by Eamonn Holmes and Anne Davies. Matters were rounded off with another Disney cartoon.

Then came Monday 4 January: D-Day. Although the whole 6am-9.25am period was billed as GMTV, the first hour resembled almost a separate show entirely. Michael Wilson and Fiona Armstrong hosted a package of features intended for "the early-rising males who work in factories or drive vans". Here was where Linda Lusardi could be found, along with items on holidays, sport and bodybuilding.

From 7am, "Mum and the kids" were the target. Wilson and Armstrong hosted this section as well, but read the news themselves, ostensibly to try to appear more engaging. An abstract Channel 4 Daily-style clock graced the top right of the TV screen, and features included 'Today's The Day' (Beadle's quiz) and the kids' slot *Alarm Alert* (again presented by Simon Parkin). *Top Of The Morning*, from 8.50am, was Lorraine Kelly's domain, along with Dr Hilary Jones hosting his 'Doc Spot' – exactly the same title his feature had on TV-am. Remaining airtime was filled up with other lifestyle magazine fare including viewers' personal appeals in the 'Personal Column' and 'Glossy Gossip' with Richard Barber.

This entire opening gambit was given a verdict, of sorts, in the form of a phone call GMTV reportedly received on January 4 from an elderly woman asking in a distressed voice where Mike Morris had gone. Press response veered from the indifferent to the occasionally caustic. However, as far as the company was concerned, such sniping was irrelevant. GMTV was on the air; the formula was in place, and everything appeared fine. During the first few days in January, GMTV attracted roughly two million viewers – to *The Big Breakfast*'s one million. There was even a minor victory over rival ITN, who had to approach GMTV for footage of Conservative Chancellor Kenneth Clarke discussing Prince Charles' relationship with Camilla Parker Bowles.

Then the unthinkable happened: the ratings collapsed. When added up, the viewing figures across GMTV's first fortnight on screen showed thousands deserting the channel. This became tens of thousands as the month continued. The haemorrhaging was so great that by the end of January, GMTV had fallen back so far as to be on level pegging with *BBC Breakfast News*.

A snap poll of ITV teletext users suggested one explanation: 66% of people claimed to want TV-am back. Perhaps the woman enquiring after Mike Morris' whereabouts wasn't an isolated case. Indeed, a few weeks later the man himself decided to speak on behalf of the nation, claiming to know the

The country is introduced to GMTV's star attraction: a working fireplace. And Fiona Armstrong.

real reason why GMTV was proving such a turn-off: "We miss them and it's rather sad they clearly miss us," he sighed, almost as if TV-am were still a going concern.

Publicity stunts aside, it had become acutely clear that there were pretty stark problems with the service. Overall, the weekend line-up felt solid and important, if rather illogically ordered, and clearly benefited from regular injections of quality children's animation. The same could not be said for the weekday schedules. It was here that all the protracted tough talking and bold thinking from Christopher Stoddart and Lis Howell had to crystallise into a tangible, winning formula for popular and exciting breakfast TV. Instead, viewers were tuning in to find a decidedly hotchpotch and listless effort that had no real sense of coherence or a rapport with audiences.

It wasn't that output was unduly amateurish or accident-prone. The root of the problem lay with GMTV's prevailing tone. The station reeked of taking an audience's loyalty for granted, and of behaving as if viewers were supposed to feel grateful for having such illustrious hosts get out of bed for their benefit.

Behind the scenes, chaos reigned. Lis Howell recalls, "Everyone was so frightened. It's very hard to reconstruct what it felt like at the time. Everything had been so inflated to look so marvellous. When you actually had to do it for real, it was very different from planning it." While the press took to ringing her up in the middle of the night for quotes, her relationship with the ITC was proving to be an even nastier headache. "The ITC was a dreadful organisation, which didn't really know what it wanted except that it wanted to be powerful. It was almost cruel the way it carried on.

"We were desperately trying to pull ourselves around. We'd made a mistake, for example, with our weather forecasts. They were sponsored, so they had to go out at a certain place in the programme. But if they were 30 seconds out, the ITC would ring up and I would be summoned all the way from LWT to their offices on Brompton Road to account for this. I remember going to their offices every day to answer carping points. I had to go myself, and the only time that they were available was 4pm, and I'd been working since 4am. So it was just torture. By the time I'd finished, and then got back to LWT to pick up the car, I'd get home at 8pm, only to have to get up again at 3am. It was ghastly."

A spokesperson for the station somewhat desperately assured all and sundry that: "We have the full support of our board. We are generally happy with the ratings figures but we are constantly monitoring the situation and will make changes we consider will improve the formula." Yet the truth seemed inescapable. Was this TV-am all over again?

Short-term evidence made the comparison seem very tempting. After all, how long had it been, back in 1983, before the presenters started changing? A matter of weeks. Ten years on, and less than a month into GMTV's life on screen, it was announced that Michael Wilson was being "temporarily replaced" as weekday host by Eamonn Holmes. A short while later this became a permanent arrangement, with Wilson confined to the 6-7am slot only.

Fiona Armstrong was supposed to embody the much vaunted but never explained 'F-factor', an epithet with distant echoes of 'sexual chemistry'. Instead, she appeared hassled and uncertain on camera. "I'd worked with Fiona for years at Border Television," Lis Howell remembers, "and now it was just awful, because she's quite a reserved person, she didn't like the limelight. Fiona was really very distressed by it, as was Michael [Wilson]. People react badly under pressure. It's one thing to be on Sky where you're quite comfortable, or on ITN where you're well-protected; but to suddenly be put into that position where everyone's out to get you is very different."

Alterations were also made to the schedule. A newsreader, Jacqui Harper, was employed to better distinguish between different sections of the programme. *Alarm Alert* was replaced with reliable cartoons such as *Super Mario Brothers*. Nigel Baker from Reuters was drafted in to shore up a topical report spot at the peak time of 8.10am. And the 'men only' idea for the weekday 6-7am slot was replaced with a conventional rolling news service.

Then another blow came in the form of the official ratings statistics for the whole of January, published a few weeks into the following month. They showed that GMTV had lost 14.5% of its audience during its first four weeks on air. If this trend went on, by the summer the station could be broadcasting to an audience smaller than that of the Channel 4 Daily. For an ITV company, this was unacceptable, impractical and above all, unaffordable. The shareholders made that very plain. "Obviously one month's figures are too little to judge [GMTV] on," they announced, "but we do expect to see an improvement on what we have seen so far. We will be looking at the situation after three months. The figures aren't as good as they might have been."

That was putting it mildly. The calibre of GMTV's management team, with their legendary track records and infallible pedigrees, would count for absolutely nothing in the long run if the station went bust. So, as the real nature of GMTV's predicament became gruesomely clear, it was the management who became the focus for criticism. And just as had been the case a decade ago, a scapegoat was needed. Lis Howell was asked to resign as Director of Programmes.

"They had to have a fall guy," she contests today, "and it was me. I think they would have liked me to have had a nervous breakdown or have a baby. It sort of pissed them off that I kept going. But it was all to do with confidence, and they were all terrified. And I couldn't handle it very well because I was terrified too."

Her analysis of just where and when things had gone wrong for GMTV centres chiefly on *The Big Breakfast*. "The whole of the GMTV proposal was based on the fact that C4, because of its obligation to the ITC, was going to keep on broadcasting a serious news operation," she argues. "Then the ITC said to C4, you can do anything, you could basically run children's programmes, which is what *The Big Breakfast* was. It completely changed the environment. And I am at fault, because at that stage I was still too much in awe of these people to actually do the sensible thing, which was to go to the ITC and say, 'We cannot go ahead on this basis.' Because everything that we'd planned was going to be threatened by the fact that C4 was being allowed by the ITC to change what it was doing."

It is certainly possible to claim that there was an element of inconsistency on the ITC's part in its contrasting treatment of Channel 4 and GMTV. But then, these were different organisations, with divergent remits and responsibilities, which by law were expected to pursue differing strategies. The ITC had to respond accordingly, acknowledging the wider context of contemporary TV but focusing in the main on individual cases and circumstances. Besides, broadcasting legislation had vastly reduced the interventionist and regulatory powers of the authority. It certainly could not command as much influence as its predecessor, the IBA.

It also seems rather churlish to describe *The Big Breakfast* as simply a children's programme. It was much more than that – it was innovative, alternative and challenging, full-square within Channel 4's obligations under its own ITC licence. "It was difficult for GMTV," concedes Michael Atwell, at the time Commissioning editor for *The Big Breakfast.* "As soon as *The Big Breakfast* started, it overlapped with TV-am for three months, and it immediately took the children off TV-am. GMTV had to struggle because obviously a lot of children and young families it had been expecting to pick up just weren't there."

Yet neither *The Big Breakfast* nor Channel 4 should really be held at fault for seeking to evolve and advance their output, and in the process redefining the landscape of British breakfast TV. It was to promote just such a buccaneering, experimental spirit that Channel 4 had been founded in the first place.

Bearing in mind the problems with the actual fabric of GMTV's output, Lis Howell's criticisms of specific failings within LWT's management have greater resonance. "Despite their enormous experience, the financial people at LWT had no concept of running something that was really difficult and really threatened by competition," she continues. "They had no concept of competition. LWT had never faced competition. Add to this the behaviour of the ITC, being utterly feckless and then lily-livered in carrying out their responsibilities. I actually feel that when we went on air, the ITC were a major part in making GMTV unworkable."

Personal factors must also have played a part, however, and here she is clear. "Maybe I wasn't very good. I somehow thought that with the shareholders we had, they would pull it out of the fire. And of course, I just soldiered on like a stupid idiot, thinking it would come right in the end or I'd pull something out the hat. And I couldn't. I just couldn't."

Lis Howell left GMTV barely two months after the station went on the air. "We did pull in some good guests, like Princess Anne," she adds, "but it didn't do anything for the ratings because everyone was in love with Chris Evans." Even after she'd gone, *The Big Breakfast* continued to haunt her. "On my birthday, a month after I'd been fired, they put a picture of me on their coffee table in front of the cameras and made jokes."

Back at GMTV, there was no time for remorse. The executive board sanctioned the appointment of former TV-am editor, Peter McHugh, as Lis Howell's replacement. McHugh had his own take on where the trouble lay. His initial impressions of the company, as he recalls them today, make for a notable contrast with those of Lis Howell.

"With GMTV, I'd thought you'd get the best of TV-am, plus some other stuff," McHugh explains. "What went wrong was that the audience was told you wouldn't see the joins. Because the audience didn't know that watching TV-am was a bad thing. Nobody had bothered telling them that. But on the day it changed, the day you saw the new programme, you saw the joins. It was different. It made some of the mistakes that were made ten years earlier, sure, but the key thing was there were no stories – there was no substance." In his mind, GMTV's chief faults were rooted in internal factors. "Some people had come from Sky, like Lis Howell," he continues, "while some had come from [daytime magazine show] *This Morning*, and some from TV-am. So in the end, the programme was a bit of Sky News, a bit of TV-am, and a bit of *This Morning*, but nothing else."

Rather than seek to blame everything on *The Big Breakfast*, McHugh realised that a lot of what was turning viewers away from GMTV was GMTV itself. In a sense, Lis Howell and Christopher Stoddart had failed to listen to themselves and heed their own warnings about the importance of not alienating the existing ITV breakfast audience. Instead, they'd come up with a service that, despite boasting several former TV-am faces, had little in the way of content with which to sustain the interest of mainstream breakfast TV viewers. "The key thing was to realise that we had to get stories," McHugh adds. "That was the only way you could get the audience."

McHugh arrived at GMTV exuding drive and commitment, clear in his mind about what he wanted to change. But it was soon evident that he alone could not tackle a problem of this size. After all, GMTV's public reputation was in tatters. Scandalous comparisons with TV-am were being made in all corners of the media. Worse, it had been Bruce Gyngell who in 1991 had predicted that GMTV would go bankrupt within a matter of years. And it was Gyngell who was now back on the scene, issuing those reminders of how TV-am's bid had been "the maximum that could sensibly be made".

Were the old man's preposterous prophecies about to become true? No – McHugh knew that could not be allowed to happen. He could turn the company around, but not by himself. Someone else was needed, with sufficient clout and influence to talk up the business and create a climate where change could happen. Somebody with experience of saving lost causes, and with knowledge of rescuing the laughably stricken and the desperate.

There was only one man who would fit the bill.

FOURTEEN

"Maybe I've already got the F-factor"

"Initially, I had very little to do with setting up GMTV," Greg Dyke recalls; "then it hit trouble early on. Not like TV-am, but it hit trouble, so I went back in."

A pungent sense of *déjà vu* surrounded Dyke's appointment as Chairman of GMTV in March 1993. Here was the man who had 'saved' TV-am, being parachuted in to rescue another floundering ITV breakfast company, proclaiming, as he went, the importance of "good human interest stories" and "a family of presenters on screen who like each other and who are liked by the audience".

If all of this sounded remarkably familiar, Dyke was determined to dispel any notion of history repeating itself. He went to great lengths to play down both the scale of GMTV's troubles and the parameters of his own involvement. "When I joined TV-am, it had 200,000 viewers, two advertisers and no cash," he stressed publicly. "That was a crisis. This isn't. GMTV has a peak audience of two million. It doesn't need saving. I'm not coming in to run the shop; I will just throw in a few ideas." Accordingly, he announced he would only spend two days a week "hands on" at the station, and emphasised how long-term commitment from the company's investors would ensure that GMTV did not go bust. "There is no evidence yet that this is not a viable business," he concluded. To him, the issue was merely a "15% ratings problem".

The fact that Dyke had been approached by the GMTV board in the first place suggested that there was a lot more wrong with the station than just a 15% ratings problem. Having to call in such a high-profile trouble-shooter was tantamount to admitting impending disaster. Indeed, Dyke walked straight into a predicament that seemed to sum up the state of the organisation.

On his arrival, he'd quipped, "I'm not known for the delicacy of my language, so maybe I've already got the F-factor." Just a few days later, the embodiment of the eponymous and much-mocked slogan, Fiona Armstrong, walked out. She'd received a barrage of press criticism for her supposedly clipped and precise manner on-screen; but in truth, her greatest failing was an apparent inability to strike up a rapport with any of her co-hosts or viewers.

Her swift departure made her the station's most notable casualty to date, and prompted Dyke and Director of Programmes Peter McHugh to order a hasty reshuffling of the presenter line-up. Lorraine Kelly was elevated to the status of GMTV's principal female host; with erstwhile *Breakfast Time* face, Fern Britton, enlisted to front *Top Of The Morning*. BSkyB presenter Penny Smith was also signed up to help co-present on weekdays.

This unexpected baptism of fire out of the way, Dyke and McHugh set to work assessing the overall state of GMTV. It was not a pleasant task. They discovered a station caught in the throes of a game of musical slots. Start-up and closing times varied from day to day, while shows of different lengths appeared, disappeared or were combined into one. Sundays were particularly bad: during March, the point at which GMTV ended and ITV's *Disney Club* began was listed in newspapers as changing every single week. The same month, *The Big Breakfast* overtook GMTV in the ratings, the first time Channel 4 had ever beaten ITV at breakfast time.

"We were unlucky in that *The Big Breakfast* had started and was doing very well at the time," concedes Dyke. "But somehow, [GMTV] just didn't gel. So you just had to go back to basics." Dyke and McHugh concluded that the only solution was a complete relaunch. "We had to reassure TV-am viewers that the world hadn't changed," adds McHugh, echoing the comments of the famed telephone caller who'd enquired after the whereabouts of Mike Morris.

Monday 19 April was the date set for a total makeover of the station, including a symbolic overhaul of the studio. The notorious flickering hearth was to go ("The set was horrible, they had that bloody fire," recalls Dyke), and a new sofa was brought in, modelled on the old TV-am showpiece, which was at the time on display in London's Museum Of The Moving Image.

More importantly, in keeping with Dyke's wishes for a "family" of presenters, a stream of recognisable and, crucially, experienced faces were booked. The upshot was the return of several former TV-am stalwarts to reprise their old roles. Both Jimmy Greaves and Paul Gambaccini resumed their TV and film review jobs, while in July, none other than erstwhile complainant and people's champion Mike Morris reappeared to host *Sunday Best*.

The schedules were then given a thorough spring-cleaning. *Parkin's Posse* was dropped for an extended *Sunday Best* and a selection of random cartoons, which for a time included *Valley Of The Dinosaurs*, first shown on the BBC's *Multi-Coloured Swap Shop* a decade and a half earlier. *Top Of The Morning* was streamlined to run from 9am rather than 8.50am, and the weather forecast (which had given Lis Howell so much trouble with the ITC) was moved to a fixed point before each news bulletin. With

Mr Motivator leads Greg Dyke's brazen bid to rescue GMTV

the addition of a daily pop video, a Mad Lizzie replica in the shape of the exuberant Mr Motivator, and lastly, a summer road show (Dyke sending weathergirl Sally Meen round Chris Tarrant's old TV-am haunts), the readjustments were complete.

If any of this appeared shameless or derivative, neither Dyke nor McHugh cared. All that mattered was getting the ratings up. The pair were heartened to see audience levels rally by nearly 30% during April, thanks to the Easter holidays, but this was by no means enough of a turnaround.

Estimates predicted GMTV was on course to lose £10m in its first six months. Accordingly, Managing Director Christopher Stoddart was charged with a mission: to find £5m worth of savings from the station's £38m running costs by the next board meeting on Thursday 20 May or face the consequences.

This rather melodramatic ultimatum left Stoddart no option but to try to get GMTV's various shareholders to renegotiate (with a view to reducing) the cost of their contracts. He had some luck with LWT, who agreed to cuts of up to 20%. The trouble came with Reuters and Disney. Disney argued that it was not in their interests to endorse any reduction, seeing as their weekend slots were the highest ratings winner on GMTV – a situation of which the station's management were all too aware. Reuters would only consent to trimming some peripheral costs while leaving their main £8m supply contract untouched. In the event, Stoddart was only able to deliver £3.5m of cuts, and Dyke himself had personally to persuade Reuters and Disney to make up the remaining £1.5m. The residing impression was that nobody wanted to be loaded with the responsibility of helping to bail out the company.

At the same time, GMTV became cursed with another kind of affliction: plain misfortune, as its senior staff succumbed to muggings (editor Liam Hamilton), burglaries (Hamilton again), or injuries (director Rod Fairweather, who ended up in hospital after gashing his head tripping outside the production gallery). Peter McHugh was desperately trying to revitalise his team, but found his lieutenants engaged in a burlesque of Keystone Cops proportions. He eventually managed to secure an improvement to news coverage by enlarging the features department and handing deputy editor John Scammell, former TV-am programme planner, a brief for overseeing the station's entire planning operation. Drawing breath, McHugh claimed his staff would be "focusing on news stories as told by the people, rather than by experts as they do on BBC1".

Despite all the reorganisation and rescheduling, GMTV was still saddled with an appalling reputation. Its very name had turned into a running joke. Veteran comic Bob Monkhouse referred to it on national television as standing for "Give Me The Valium". Continuing to languish behind *The Big Breakfast* in the ratings, it seemed there was a towering wall of prejudice that the station needed to break down before any of its changes in content and presenters translated into a groundswell of favour amongst viewers.

Looking back, Greg Dyke's assessment of GMTV's initial 12 months on air is characteristically brusque. "It didn't make much of an impression during its first year. I'd say it was all right for London Weekend, because we were getting all these costs paid, and we were making two or three million a year out of it. But it struggled while it was still paying so much."

Changing the exact nature of GMTV's licence obligations, both in terms of programme output and the amount of money it had to hand over to the government for the privilege of broadcasting, was something Lis Howell had come to regret not insisting upon as early as summer 1992. When Dyke and his management team begrudgingly decided upon exactly the same strategy in late 1993, as a means of ensuring GMTV's survival, it was something of a belated vindication for the departed Director of Programmes. It also sent relations between GMTV and the ITC diving to a new low.

While the ITC was legally charged with ensuring that GMTV observed the requirements of its licence, unlike its forerunners, the IBA, it could not actually step in to order any direct changes to the station's output. Nonetheless, it did retain ultimate power over setting the annual cost of the franchise. It was with this in mind that GMTV approached the Commission in winter 1993, to raise the possibility of amending the terms of its contract in the light of current circumstances.

It was a risky tactic. The atmosphere between both parties had been far from cordial for many months. First had come Lis Howell's daily run-ins over programme content, followed by the far more bullish tactics of Dyke and McHugh, and then, most recently, the ITC had warned the station over the non-appearance of its much-vaunted regional output. So it was no surprise that GMTV's bold proposals to more or less tear up the terms and conditions of its contract initially fell upon deaf ears. A secondary plan, to ask other ITV companies to help temporarily subsidise GMTV's running costs, fared even worse – and in addition, won the company universal condemnation from across the ITV network.

The breakthrough GMTV so desperately needed would not come for another six desperate months. There was an official ITC review of all ITV franchises, due out in early 1994. If GMTV were able to anticipate and therefore undermine some of the ITC's likely criticism, it would give them the upper hand.

Consequently, at the start of the year, Reuters were commissioned to take over production of all output between 6 and 7am. The result was the launch of *Newshour* on Monday 21 February. Of course, this was hardly an innovation, being strikingly reminiscent of TV-am's own numerous attempts at opening its service with 60 minutes of straight news, but it did make ratings for GMTV's first hour rise by almost 10% to 1.2m. The programme itself was scarcely groundbreaking material, although as a short-term measure designed to demonstrate that GMTV was serious about its responsibilities, even in dire financial straits, it paid off.

At the start of May 1994, the ITC announced it had decided to revise the terms of GMTV's licence (though not the licence fee itself). The station's statutory weekly minimum quota for news and sports coverage was reduced, and all requirements for factual programmes such as religious, kids' and social action were scrapped. This was, in effect, an admission that the terms under which GMTV's licence had originally been granted were completely impractical. As had been the case with TV-am, what the authorities had desired by way of breakfast television, and what the broadcasters had claimed they were able to provide, both turned out to be hopelessly unworkable in reality. It was a strong indictment of both the ITC and GMTV.

Christopher Stoddart, however, was jubilant. The news marked "a recognition by the ITC that breakfast television has clearly changed since GMTV submitted its licence application in 1991". This was a unique interpretation, especially as he talked about 'breakfast television' almost as if it was something GMTV was fighting against rather than contributing to. But as far as Stoddart was concerned, his company had at long last won some breathing space and the right to respond more flexibly to what its viewers demanded.

Ironically, the one man not around to join in the celebrations was Greg Dyke. Just as his tenure at TV-am had lasted barely a year, so he departed his post as GMTV Chairman 12 months after he arrived, following Granada TV's rather acrimonious purchase of LWT in March 1994. "Greg had led a team of people who'd made it work," recalls Peter McHugh today. "It was made by a team – never made by an individual. The individual's cleverness is recruiting the right team and letting them have their head. I don't know that in the early days of GMTV, people realised that." Carlton TV's Director of Broadcasting Nigel Walmsley was appointed Dyke's replacement – a less high profile figure, if still adept at running a troubled station.

The twin incidents of the franchise revision and Dyke's departure cued in a new phase in GMTV's existence. As Peter McHugh explains: "Then what we had to do was to hang on for the major licence [fee] renegotiations, which we knew were fixed to come six years down the road, and try and minimise our losses. The shareholders then thought we're in for the long haul. We've invested our money. As long as we think they're making a fair fist of what they've got, then we'll back them." The station recognised its limited strengths, and then proceeded to exploit and advance them wherever possible. In time came rising audience levels, an improved reputation, and ultimately a profit. But it proved no easy ride.

A number of factors contributed to the turnaround but they were not always that positive. First and foremost came a now-legitimised leavening of content with more tabloid-orientated fare. This kicked off on an appreciable scale with the recruitment of the outspoken celebrity therapist, Beechy Colclough, and intervention of a different kind in the guise of the Reverend Steve Chalke who seemed qualified to speak on anything from poverty to parenting to the NHS.

Then came more self-consciously ambitious and glossy features, in the shape of expensive outside broadcasts. A trip to France, to mark the 50th anniversary of D-Day, was followed by an extended road show from Spain during the summer of 1994. Here, GMTV stumbled upon another magic ingredient. Enlisted to front the sun-soaked revelries, was former *Blue*

Peter presenter Anthea Turner. At this stage, she had a relatively low media profile, which a series of live transmissions from various Mediterranean resorts did little to change. However, the minute she was invited to assume a place on the GMTV sofa later in the year, she found the limelight and never let go. In a sense, GMTV had been waiting for this kind of attention-seeking, publicity-generating figure all along – someone who, whether they inspired love or hate, still pulled in the viewers. And that's precisely what happened.

Anthea Turner's tenure on GMTV was played out to an epic chorus of press comment and criticism – tackling everything from her appearance, salary and dress sense to her demeanour and ability (or lack of it) to handle heavyweight issues and interviews. The subject that merited the most column inches was her relationship with on-screen co-host Eamonn Holmes. A latent tension was there for all to see, but just how much of it was manufactured in the heat of the moment for the sake of the watching millions – and how much was genuine – puzzled and delighted the media for months.

On occasions, Holmes appeared to make fun of Anthea's dyslexia, deliberately encouraging her to mispronounce people's names, while at other times Anthea seemed almost to play up to her press image of the rather wayward and glib starlet. Documenting this supposed feud in her autobiography, Anthea described how, "I thought [Eamonn] was quite snappy with me some mornings and I felt sure people would begin to notice. For example, if I was working with another presenter, we'd often work out what we were going to say beforehand. When I suggested to Eamonn that we did the same, he'd say, 'I'm not telling you what I'm going to say.' Then when the moment came, he'd throw me a line, which would catch me off guard and make me look stupid. It seemed as if it was almost a sport with him."

There did appear to be a basic clash of personalities here, and over time, Holmes seemed increasingly more relaxed in the presence of other hosts. In summary, this was hardly a recipe for success, and defied all precedent that suggested a strong, good-natured presenting relationship had to be at the core of any popular mainstream breakfast TV programme. But perhaps because GMTV had always utilised a pool of hosts – and Anthea and Holmes were not the station's only front-line presenters – this 'animosity' never threatened to do any terminal damage. After all, it delivered audiences, and therefore advertising revenue. For GMTV, that was enough.

Elsewhere, the station's weekend discussion programme, *Sunday Best,* underwent a gradual evolution from a lightweight magazine into a harder edged current affairs effort. Former Deputy Leader of the Labour Party Roy Hattersley was hired to conduct purposefully heavy-hitting interviews with political figures, while his old boss Neil Kinnock hosted a show together with his wife Glenys in August 1994. However, in October of that year, the show was suddenly dropped and replaced with *The Sunday Programme* hosted by veteran broadcaster Alistair Stewart. The reason for the change was not to do with management decisions but the departure of Mike Morris, who had complained that his show had become so obsessed with politics that it had ended up too indigestible for Sunday mornings.

The Sunday Programme was subsequently launched off the back of a manic press conference, which found Stewart answering questions, eating breakfast and chain smoking all at the same time. This rather raucous occasion was notable for Stewart's vociferous arguing that he didn't think it was right for someone to present something like a game show during the week and then front a serious news programme on a Sunday. 'What – like David Frost does?' a hack instantly snapped back, to Stewart's intense and very visible discomfort.

Tangible evidence that a corner had been turned came in early June 1994 when ratings for the 'peak quarter-hour' of breakfast TV showed *The Big Breakfast* tumbling towards one million while GMTV was holding steady at 1.5m. Ratings remained stable for the rest of the year and as Christmas approached, there were even whispers of the company moving into profit within the next 24 months.

GMTV had, at long last, hit upon a formula that was paying dividends. Its pursuit of both triviality and sensationalism seemed to have rewarded it with a hardcore base of viewers. Peter McHugh recalls, "We never had a strong PR perception. While *The Big Breakfast* was trendy, we were always seen to be untrendy. But the great plus was that people between the ages of 16 and 34 who lived outside of London didn't realise it wasn't trendy to watch us, so they continued to do so."

1995 was the year which confirmed that GMTV was in business and most definitely here to stay. The station began to pursue an expansionist policy that was audacious and determined. "For years Channel 4 was the place show biz stars would go to," continues McHugh, "because the west coast of America had heard that there was this great thing called *The Big Breakfast*, while we were supposed to be fuddy-duddy and middle of the road. Well, we just put our heads down, as we did in the early days of TV-am, and took on the rest of the world."

Entertainment correspondent Fiona Phillips was transferred to a permanent post in LA. Lorraine Kelly had returned to her post-9am slot when Anthea Turner became a regular host. Now Lorraine's daily grab bag of frothy lifestyle fodder was expanded to start at 8.45am. A week of live programming from Sydney brought in still more viewers.

All the while, the company remained careful to cultivate those important additional qualities of grit and respectability. Andrew Neil, swaggering ex-editor of the *Sunday Times*, proved a distinctive choice as stand-in presenter on *The Sunday Programme*. Later in the year, the segment won a new editor in the shape of former *Frost On Sunday* producer Tim Brearley who had also served time on Channel 4's respected series *A Week In Politics*. Brearley had the perfect credentials to satisfy the ITC, but also a flair for the populist to help pull in audiences.

In addition, more new brands were added to GMTV's output, such as the annual 'Get Up And Give' charity drive that first aired in March 1995. This enterprise saw GMTV presenters rattling the tins from a variety of dazzling locations such as Alton Towers, the set of *Coronation Street*, the South Mimms service station on the M25, Heathrow Airport, and the middle of Milton Keynes. The station went live to South Africa for World Cup Rugby, and 'Fun In The Sun' became a regular summer retreat to the resorts.

Liam Hamilton's replacement as editor, David Mannion, introduced further changes to GMTV's profile and structure. Head of News and Executive Producer posts were created, while Lorraine Kelly's magazine was tampered with again from the start of September 1995, when it was shunted back to 9am, renamed *Nine O'Clock Live* and given more of a current affairs agenda. At the same time, GMTV Productions was launched. This was a stand-alone unit intended to develop programmes for the ITV network, C4, the BBC and other broadcasters. The outfit had grown out of the manufacture of a number of home video presentations, such as *Lorraine Kelly's Bringing Up Baby* and *Mr Motivator's BLT Workout*, and the selling of GMTV's 'Holiday Snaps' strand to cable channel Travel.

The chief factor providing the foundation for all of these developments and, for that matter, GMTV's overall success, was the continued appeal of its children's programmes. Indeed, perhaps the company only survived its hazardous early years intact thanks to the reliability of its kids' output. Of course, things hadn't got off to an overwhelmingly propitious start. Simon Parkin was supposed to be the station's main weekday face, but *Parkin's Posse* and its dodgy follow-up, *It's NOT!*, were both pretty ropey efforts.

They had been followed, within a matter of months, by *Parkin's In...*, which found the titular presenter superimposed against a blue screen onto which were projected a variety of locations, and accompanied by an anonymous assistant, completely invisible save for his hands. Each edition revolved around a different theme such as *...Orbit*, *...Hot Water*, or *...Detention*, and was fleshed out with appropriate guests and competitions. In truth, it was a tiresome premise that felt neither interesting nor enjoyable. The closing shot of each show depicted Parkin holding up a tatty piece of paper that read, "A Bazal Production". It seemed somehow fitting.

Eventually, Parkin was palmed off with the unusually entitled *Re:win.d*, a factual show broadcast at the illustrious hour of shortly after 6am. Far better offerings were to be found at weekends where, right from the start, GMTV had rustled up a couple of hits in the shape of *Saturday Disney* and *Disney Club*. The former had seen co-presenter Pippa Ford-Jones disappear within a few weeks, to be replaced by Carmen Ejogo. The original male presenter, Stuart Miles, left in January 1994 (joining *Blue Peter* on 12 September), and a sequence of guest hosts filled his shoes until the actor Matthew Crompton (formerly Darren Murphy in *Brookside*) was signed up in January 1995. But while presenters came and went, the content never varied: dependable Disney cartoons, star guests and ridiculously easy competitions. The same was true of Sunday's *Disney Club*, which went through several line-ups of hosts before settling with sportsman and former model Craig Doyle in November 1995.

Both of these regular shows benefited from the presence of undoubtedly the most successful strand ever aired on GMTV: the series *Mighty Morphin Power Rangers*. This live action fantasy import was first shown as a one-off on Easter Holiday Monday 1994, and such was its immediate popularity that it was quickly stripped across the schedules every day. It was a highly controversial programme – the second series had to be cleared by the ITC before it could be screened due to its supposedly excessive violence. The show also prompted an enormous range of tie-in merchandising, and GMTV were warned twice in one month by the ITC for product placement. Nevertheless, a spin-off series – *VR Troopers* – was eagerly snapped up by the station and proved just as popular with audiences.

Peter McHugh recalls the exact circumstances behind these highly remunerative developments: "We'd still been losing money hand over fist. So I took the best advice, and a guy from Disney said, 'Analyse *The Big Breakfast* audience.' It turned out 60-65% were under 15. He also said, 'Do bear in mind that all kids are fickle – they will go to the next trendy thing as soon as it arrives.' So we bought *Power Rangers*. Channel 4 thought they'd bought it, but we heard they hadn't done the deal, so I flew out to LA, advised by our Head of Research that it would be a good thing. I bought *Power Rangers*; we stuck it on and more or less killed *The Big Breakfast*."

While this is clearly something of an exaggeration, the rise of GMTV's average weekly share throughout 1994 and 1995 was rooted upon the impact of the *Power Rangers* brand. And the investment paid off: after a £10.8m loss in 1993 and a £1.6m loss in 1994, GMTV confirmed it was on course to make its first profit of roughly £1m in 1995.

Amidst the hype and hysteria, occasional incidents suggested that the station had not been able to completely shake off its troubled image. When GMTV tried to renegotiate regional contracts for local news provision, an awkward issue arose that caused Ulster TV to withdraw from the deal. At the last minute, Reuters had to step in and provide a temporary service featuring completely unknown presenters and reporters.

A reprimand from the Broadcasting Standards Council landed on Christopher Stoddart's desk after GMTV inadvertently aired a clip from the American Comedy Awards, showing Jamie Lee Curtis grabbing a comedian's crotch just after he had groped one of her breasts. Most troubling of all, Disney had to reduce its lucrative stake in GMTV from 25% to 20% in advance of the UK launch of the Disney Channel to avoid breaking British media laws.

When yet another complaint arrived from the ITC regarding *Power Rangers,* David Mannion decided to initiate a rethink on the nature of GMTV's dependency on its children's output. He was well aware of the dangers in relying too much on one show – no matter how successful – for keeping up audience share. Besides, competition for younger viewers was on the horizon in the shape of BBC2's new breakfast service of kids' programmes.

As Peter McHugh recalls: "Probably what turned out to be the single biggest change for us was BBC2 deciding to do kids' [shows], because they took away from GMTV the fact that it was a family programme. We used to do things like go abroad; we'd buy things like *Power Rangers*; and we'd run kids' programmes at half term. Then BBC2 launched its children's stuff, and took all the kids away. That changed the dynamic and the financial effect."

The upshot was a scaling back of the amount of children's programming, including *Power Rangers*, from the start of 1996. David Mannion was quick to stress the series hadn't gone for good. "We are going to bring [them] back," he confided, "but it's an opportunity for us to try something fresh and new." This turned out to be more lifestyle, fashion and beauty slots. At the same time it was announced that GMTV's assorted experts and quacks were now to go under the label, 'The A Team', "with the A standing for advice", Mannion explained pedantically.

The fact that the station felt sure enough to try something different and experiment with their output in such a manner summed up the positive mood now pervading its offices. This spirit of buoyancy was capped on Monday 29 January 1996 when the GMTV board met to approve the company's first ever profit figures. An official announcement confirmed a surplus of £1m had been secured, thanks to consistent growth in advertising revenue and resolute cutbacks. Christopher Stoddart beamed: "We are spending more money on programmes. The market is very competitive and we are hoping to hold on to [an] audience share of 39%." He also used the occasion to blame the company's poor start on "trying to change too much too soon", forgetting the fact that radical and near-overnight change had been crucial during the station's opening months to stave off total bankruptcy.

GMTV continued into 1996 with ever-growing confidence. Outside broadcasts headed to Sydney, Switzerland and Dubai. Weekend children's programming was refreshed by swapping *Saturday Disney* for the noisy *Wake Up In The Wild Room* presented by Dave Benson-Phillips, and the Australian children's series *Bananas In Pyjamas*.

The station received its first ever commission to produce programmes for another broadcaster in the shape of a 65-part personality-led therapy series for Sky Television, presented by Beechy Colclough. This was followed by a contract for a networked ITV series, *Liz Earle's Lifestyle*, featuring the eponymous GMTV beauty expert hosting various features from different rooms of her house while entertaining other members of the station's presenting team.

GMTV had come a long way in three years. If its cavalcade of garish items, quarrelling presenters and colour supplement ethos made for some of the most unsubtle television imaginable, it had demonstrated it knew how to pull in audiences and keep them coming back for more day after day. But the station's triumphs weren't entirely of its own doing. GMTV's immediate rival, which had made things so difficult for the company in its early days, was now itself in trouble. *The Big Breakfast*, after making the running in breakfast television for almost two years, had abruptly slipped into a stark and rather undignified decline. All of a sudden, the tables had turned.

FIFTEEN

"Would a giant profit-orientated TV company lie to you?"

The astonishing success of *The Big Breakfast* had taken many, including Channel 4 and the programme's makers Planet 24, by complete shock. "From day one it just did so much better than we'd ever expected," recalls the show's Commissioning editor, Michael Atwell. "Ratings rose very steadily. We didn't know this would happen, as we'd had awful audience research. We'd loved the show, but we really had no idea whether it would work or not." "I think the surprise at the channel was that *The Big Breakfast* got such a wide audience," adds David Lloyd, C4's Head of News and Current Affairs, "because on the face of it, it looked like a youth programme, and you might have thought it was targeted at that audience. But in fact it got a very respectable overall audience, and didn't suffer by comparison even with *BBC Breakfast News*."

Originally pitched into an environment where mainstream breakfast TV had grown too self-obsessed (TV-am) or poker-faced (BBC), *The Big Breakfast*'s deviation from the norm had appeared all the more magnified. An absence of decent competition contrived to suck in more viewers, and when word of mouth took over, the results were incredible.

However, the fact that the show did so well so quickly had a downside. "It set a benchmark," explains Atwell, "which was very hard to ever reproduce." The two million people who tuned in daily towards the end of 1993 would become a yardstick against which *The Big Breakfast* would forever be judged – and increasingly found wanting. Such was the show's dynamism and its ferocious consumption of ideas, talent and energy, that it hit its peak just 12 months after its launch. Yet this peak proved impossible to sustain. And there were another 104 months to come.

The seeds of the problems that would come to undermine *The Big Breakfast* were sown early. The show had entered its second year relatively upbeat. The same mix of engaging humour, participation and self-awareness was present, as were the founding presenting team of Chris Evans, Gaby Roslin and Paula Yates. There were also traces of the programme's flair for pioneering wry features, such as 'The Furthest We've Ever Been' where all the camera leads were extended outside as far as possible purely for the sake of it, and 'Whose Shoes?' which saw a celebrity's footwear paraded on screen for viewers and residents of the studio 'house' to identify. The latter boasted one particularly memorable moment when the owner of the shoes was correctly guessed as Radio One DJ Dave Lee Travis, at which point Evans could be heard announcing that he wouldn't turn up the following week if it meant having to meet the eponymous 'Hairy Cornflake' in person.

At the same time, some items started to bear the marks of slightly unimaginative, jaded thinking. 'An Incredibly Good Looking Man', where a male guest appeared on camera naked, save for a suitable object covering his modesty, seemed more like the sort of stunt that belonged on late night Channel 4 youth television efforts such as *The Word* (also made by Planet 24). Other features bore the hallmarks of mounting a spectacle for outrage alone, or of shameless repetition. It sometimes felt like an element of running on autopilot was creeping into the fabric of the show.

Most significant of all was the change that was detectable within the programme's most emblematic figure. Chris Evans had become a very different person from the one who had fronted *The Big Breakfast* back in September 1992. For a start, he now found his time and attention split between the show and his own company, Ginger Television, which was busy preparing a major new Saturday night entertainment series for Channel 4. This turned out to be the highly successful *Don't Forget Your Toothbrush*, a production that took a huge amount of effort and the filming of no less than three separate pilot editions before making it onto the air.

Then there was the evidence, both on and off screen, that seemed to point towards a worsening in Evans' temperament. His mood swings were allegedly becoming increasingly pronounced and his behaviour more uncompromising. He boasted of how his time on *The Big Breakfast* had prematurely aged him, giving him grey hairs before the age of 30. Tales emerged of Planet 24 staff supposedly reduced to tears on account of his antics, and of the show's growing roster of editors and producers tiring of Evans' irascibility.

All of this came to a head over the issue of how much *The Big Breakfast* 'needed' its star turn and vice versa. Ever since the programme had begun, both Chris Evans and Gaby Roslin had occasionally taken weeks off, replaced by a variety of stand-in hosts who ranged from the impressive (Andrew O'Connor) to the tolerable (Kim Wilde) to the somewhat less than convincing (Dannii Minogue and Mandy Smith). The trouble was that as time had gone on, *The Big Breakfast* had become progressively built upon and around the personalities of Evans and Roslin. The composition and characteristics of the relationship between the pair had come to support the entire programme. As their stature grew, so the show fed off them more and more, elevating the duo's profile even higher – and so on and on in a vicious, apparently unstoppable circle.

Sometimes the stand-ins overcame the legacy of Evans and Roslin to make the format work for themselves. Bob Monkhouse filled masterfully for a week in December 1993, while Radio 1 DJ Danny Baker made a point of declaring on-screen that he regarded his extended shifts during early 1994 as "the best TV job I've ever had". His trademark patter – "Would a giant profit-orientated TV company lie to you?" "They call this post-modern television!" – certainly proved a refreshing alternative to the usual Evans banter, while his brand of features, typified by 'Roll Over Beethoven' where viewers were invited to suggest items they would like to see crushed under the wheels of a large steamroller, were similarly eclectic and distinctive.

All the same, it was to be the matter of stand-ins that would become the most pronounced and the most public running sore for *The Big Breakfast* throughout 1994. The trouble began early in the New Year. Evans took a full week off from January 17, covered by Danny Baker – returning not on the following Monday, but the Tuesday instead. This was part of a new deal hammered out between Planet 24 and Channel 4, which permitted Evans to, in effect, go 'part-time' while working on *Don't Forget Your Toothbrush,* and only present *The Big Breakfast* from Tuesday to Thursday.

A somewhat awkward compromise, this might not have been that bad were it only a temporary measure. However, when *Toothbrush* ended a couple of months later, Evans decided that he rather liked working a three-day week, and expressed his desire to continue missing both Monday and Friday's show. Rather than insist otherwise, Planet 24 agreed to the star's wishes. This was, in hindsight, a major turning point. Through its actions, Planet 24 arguably set a precedent for caving in to Evans' whims and fancies right down the line. The more the company felt it needed Evans to stay on board, so the further it was prepared to go to accommodate his demands.

Planet 24's next mistake was failing to appoint one regular stand-in host to cover each Monday and Friday. Instead, a bewildering medley of people came and went, including former *Neighbours* star and stand-up comic Mark Little, actor Simon O'Brien, and Danny Baker once again. To compound the confusion, Little would sometimes appear on a different day of the week when Evans was off sick, or both male hosts would be on together hosting different features.

This situation reached an extreme one morning when Evans turned up to watch Gaby Roslin and Mark Little presenting the programme while he himself sat off camera amongst the production team. The show on Monday 7 March was the first ever to feature neither Evans nor Roslin – the hosts being Danny Baker and Carol Smillie. Then, when Evans called in sick on Wednesday 13 April (coincidentally the day he was having a new Ferrari delivered), it was Paula Yates who had to rush down to the studios to act as co-host until Little had got out of bed.

It all seemed rather muddled and, worse, never-ending. Mark Little was seconded to 'Down Your Doorstep' from Tuesday 3 May to fill in for a holidaying Keith Chegwin, but was back in the house the following fortnight while Evans had a post-*Toothbrush* vacation. Ominously, when 'Housey Housey', the programme's next big competition, began on Monday 23 May, the game cards distributed to viewers so they could play along at home had pictures of Mark Little and Gaby Roslin on the front but no sign of Evans.

The system of replacements for Roslin was just as patchy, ranging from *Generation Game* co-host Rosemarie Ford to *The Word* presenter Dani Behr. And behind the camera things weren't much better, as the departure of Ruth Wrigley after two years as programme editor robbed the show of its most important surviving link with its heady groundbreaking early days.

The final of 'Housey Housey', on Friday 8 July, involved Gaby Roslin and Keith Chegwin hosting the entire programme from within the star prize, a replica *Big Breakfast* house in Telford, while Mark Little and Paula Yates were based inside the real house in London. Evans was nowhere to be seen. In fact, the procession of alternate and deputy presenters meant that Evans and Roslin did not actually present together for months until the week of Evans' departure from the show.

His farewell on Thursday 29 September 1994, the day after *The Big Breakfast*'s second birthday, was a highly emotional event. The entire studio was shown crying after watching a specially filmed tribute, while the programme's closing sequence, where Evans was stripped of his security pass, his car, bags of clothes and earpiece before walking off into the distance in a cloth cap and coat, hinted at a real relief on the part of some of the production team.

Evans' exit, long-anticipated but still in its own way quite affecting, capped a period of months that had seen *The Big Breakfast*'s trademark vibrancy and creativity increasingly overshadowed by a sense of confusion both on and off camera. That Evans bowed out to such a chorus of mixed emotion was due to the complicated, intensely personal association the star had struck up with the programme.

From the outset, it had been a two-way relationship. *The Big Breakfast* had effectively 'made' Chris Evans, while at the same time, Evans had undoubtedly played the chief role in turning *The Big Breakfast* into a household name and a financial success.

To begin with, both programme and star needed each other. Then, roughly 12 months in, Evans started to give the impression that he had outgrown the show and no longer required or desired its patronage. Tales began to circulate of his alleged mistreatment of fellow cast and crew. His unpredictable absences from the programme suggested he no longer took his responsibilities seriously. When he was on camera, what had once been an impish ill will often looked more like outright malevolence. It was hard to separate myth from reality: Was this the real Chris Evans, or merely a manufactured screen character that played up to the media's depiction of him as a bully and an egotist?

Ultimately, it seemed that Evans no longer respected the format and environment in which he was expected to work. Evidence implied that he no longer respected his colleagues either. For its part, Planet 24 behaved in a manner that made the company appear unduly subservient to the man, prioritising his concerns and events diary above the welfare of the rest of its employees. Given all these circumstances, it is no wonder that by 1994 stories of bad feeling and low morale had so enveloped *The Big Breakfast*.

So there were tears of relief at Chris Evans' departure, but also of confusion and anxiety. Could the programme survive without its principal benefactor? Could it ever hope to match Evans' genius for split second innovation, wit and fancy, never mind overcome the legacy of his tempestuous last few months? Evans had pushed breakfast television to a new level of imagination and excitement, only to get bored with the world he had created, and then challenge it to carry on without him. It was not at all clear how that world, which in effect was the entire *Big Breakfast* brand, could now survive.

The search for someone to take on the daunting task of following in Evans' footsteps had begun back in early August 1994. When news of his departure broke in the press, the *Sunday Mirror* of 7 August promptly ran a bemusing piece, detailing how there was reputedly a chance for anyone at all to become *The Big Breakfast*'s new male host. This 'competition' breathlessly informed readers that the lucky man could be "the bloke down your local pub who has you in stitches with his stories, or the local radio DJ who stands out from the rest".

The publicity stunt did flag up a few contenders, though none of any particularly anonymous background: Grant Stott of BBC kids' programme *Fully Booked*; Greg Scott, warm-up man from *Countdown*; and Albert 'Trix' Thompson, erstwhile host of C4's American Football magazine *Trash Talk* – the presenters of which, appropriately, had been picked in a *Big Breakfast* competition. In the end, Evans' replacement turned out to be someone who had already done time on the programme. This was undoubtedly a sensible strategy. Sadly, the man in question was not Danny Baker.

Paul Ross took over chief presenting duties on *The Big Breakfast* on 10 October 1994 – but only from Monday to Wednesday. For some reason, Mark Little was still contracted to host the programme two days a week, and so continued to turn up on Thursday and Friday. This untidy arrangement somewhat epitomised the prevailing condition of both the show and its producers. Even at this crucial juncture in *The Big Breakfast*'s existence, Planet 24 appeared unable to engineer a smooth transition into any kind of fixed, solid line-up of presenters. Indeed, rather than draw a line under *The Big Breakfast*'s recent problems, Ross's appointment kicked off a convoy of erratic changes, hirings and firings that persisted unchecked for a fatally long period. The result was that on-going elements of inconsistency and instability were introduced to the programme, echoes of which would go on to haunt *The Big Breakfast* until its dying days.

Admittedly, anyone would have had a tough job following Chris Evans, yet circumstances seemed to deny Ross enough of a period in the spotlight to work up a proper relationship with either surviving co-host Gaby Roslin or the programme's viewers. For a start, when Roslin had four weeks off at the beginning of 1995, Ross was saddled with the rather wooden ex-*Word* anchor Amanda De Cadanet as fellow presenter, followed by the frosty Julia Carling. Then from 27 February, Ross's own shift was cut to just Mondays and Tuesdays in the light of tabloid revelations over his private life. Concurrently, Paula Yates and Bob Geldof split up, prompting an even greater frenzy of press publicity, and so Paula also scaled down her involvement in the programme, eventually bowing out shortly after a special *Comic Relief* edition broadcast on Friday 17 March.

In light of this awkward and embarrassing dismemberment, *The Big Breakfast* couldn't help but take on an ever more listless nature. Items and features increasingly suggested only faint traces of former glories, or demonstrated a tendency to go all out for the shock factor. Yet another new competition, 'Beat The Banger', debuted with the theme song, 'Beat the banger, it's bucking up and down', prompting Keith Chegwin to declare on air, "I can't believe that jingle." The following day the lyrics had been quietly changed to "Beat the banger, it's bumping up and down'. Even Zig and Zag failed to escape the encroaching malaise and were saddled with lacklustre and joyless assignments, such as being sent out on the road to, rather appropriately, investigate job hunting.

Developments behind the scenes were also impacting upon the smooth functioning of the programme. The continuing turnover of personnel, ushered in by Ruth Wrigley's departure the previous autumn, was causing more people with long-term experience of working on *The Big Breakfast* to migrate to other positions within Planet 24. Their replacements came both from the lower ranks of the show's existing

*Michael Grade's acupuncture session is interrupted
by another desperate Planet 24 producer*

production team and from outside the company. The biggest change came when Sebastian Scott, having already swapped his role as editor for that of Executive Producer, severed all ties with the programme and was replaced with Bob Massie, previously employed at the Carlton/LWT London News Network.

Massie was seen as a capable pair of hands and, to his credit, did mount one particularly notable edition of *The Big Breakfast* in September, which took the form of a charity drive. A fixed amount of money had to be raised by 9am, but on the morning itself, it quickly became obvious the show was not going to reach its self-appointed target before going off air. Massie had to hastily ring Michael Grade at home to get his permission to continue broadcasting the show beyond 9am, in the process interrupting the C4 boss's acupuncture session.

Even a man capable of brokering a deal with a horizontal Grade appeared incapable of stemming *The Big Breakfast*'s continuing jamboree of presenters. Dani Behr stood in for a fortnight at the end of March 1995, meaning that Gaby Roslin was actually absent for the press-weary Paul

Ross's last show on 4 April. Indeed, April was a particularly bad month for the programme, with Chris Evans' new Radio One breakfast show beginning on Monday 24, further sapping *The Big Breakfast*'s dwindling audience. It is tempting to believe that the exodus of viewers picked up apace with the appointment of the youthful Richard Orford, another of those people you either liked or loathed, as a new host on 10 April. However, thanks to enduring contractual issues from the year before, Orford was only hired to present the show from Monday to Wednesday.

For Mark Little, who on Paul Ross's departure had assumed he would be promoted to the status of proper host, this meant a rather galling relegation to Thursdays and Fridays only. Understandably concluding that his long-term future on the show appeared unlikely, Little booked a month at the Edinburgh Festival later in the year. But within two months, Orford's unconvincing performance in the house had won him a demotion onto 'Down Your Doorstep', and Keith Chegwin was brought back as a replacement.

Confusingly, however, Chegwin was only on screen for Mondays and Tuesdays, while Mark Little was officially appointed 'main presenter' from July 10 1995 to cover the other three days of the week. Yet Little still had his Edinburgh show planned, so ended up taking four weeks off in August, then a further six weeks in October for another stand-up tour. This tumult meant that come the end of 1995, Mark Little had appeared on fewer programmes in total than his nominal 'deputy' Keith Chegwin, despite being officially billed as *The Big Breakfast*'s main presenter.

In the midst of all this came perhaps *The Big Breakfast*'s most misguided venture to date: the 'Eggs On Legs' summer road show. This was not the sort of thing the programme should, or needed to, be doing, not least because it was too much the preserve of TV-am and GMTV – indeed, the tour began on the very same morning as another GMTV 'Fun In The Sun' jaunt (24 July).

'Eggs On Legs' was hosted by Richard Orford and Dannii Minogue, and journeyed to a different town or city each day with a selection of musical guests and half-hearted games entitled 'Cock-A-Doodle-Do-It' and 'Take A Chance On A Chicken'. This painful pilgrimage pottered about for several grim weeks, stopping off at Nantwich, Prestatyn, Nottingham and other glamorous locales.

By now the comedy character Lily Savage, aka female impersonator Paul O'Grady, had taken on Paula Yates' role of *Big Breakfast* celebrity interviewer. However, O'Grady had also prebooked a stint at the Edinburgh Festival and consequently vanished from the scene for four weeks during August 1995 before reappearing in the autumn, but then only on Wednesdays, due to commitments in the West End.

All in all, the non-stop sequence of arrivals, mysterious departures and equally mystifying reappearances seemed to be choking the programme. It is difficult to believe that *The Big Breakfast*'s production team viewed this endless upheaval as insignificant. They certainly cannot have welcomed those instances where presenters disappeared or required reduced working hours because of events beyond Planet 24's control. All the same, it is hard to avoid concluding that by this point, the company was displaying a manifestly poor grasp of the importance of some stability amongst *The Big Breakfast*'s on-screen hosts. "With *The Big Breakfast*, the presenters were terribly important, almost more than the content," reflects former Channel 4 Daily host Paddy Haycocks. "When Chris Evans went, there was a chasm. It was horrible. I don't think it survived his departure for many years."

An ever-changing presenting line-up was a terribly destructive element within a format that required strong consistency amongst its personalities to counterbalance its sprawling features. At heart, *The Big Breakfast* needed a fixed centre around which it could pitch, grow and evolve. Post-Evans this simply never materialised.

Michael Atwell had left Channel 4 at the end of December 1993, but had watched from afar as the programme he had helped to create and sustain gradually declined and then went into freefall. "The best and most successful shows are often the ones that have this complete internal mad logic of their own," he contests today. "They also create their own world. Everything in *The Big Breakfast* made organic sense within the larger-than-life household. However, once you take a central bit of it out, you've destroyed the household and it's really hard to put it back together again. *The Big Breakfast*'s central presenters were very important in all of that – it was a chemistry thing. Once you broke up the chemistry, there was always going to be the problem of trying to replace it and trying to find a formula that works."

Whether through an inability to overcome the legacy of Chris Evans, an impasse at management level, or a widespread sense that the programme could run on forever, *The Big Breakfast* had ended up blessed with an endlessly varying roster of presenters that effectively robbed it of much of its cohesion and profile. It also meant that by the end of 1995, one year on from Evans' departure, it was impossible to give a straight answer to the simple question: Who presents *The Big Breakfast*?

Gaby Roslin, who had battled valiantly on through all the bedlam, now sensed that enough was enough and announced her intention to quit in January 1996. The time was definitely right for her to move on. Her involvement had latterly taken on an increasingly tokenistic and rather unseemly aspect. Being forced to play the now rather lame games and utter the kind of sentiments she'd once carried off with so much imagination and force made for disheartening television. As such, her departure had none of the weight and significance of Chris Evans' exit. If anything, the hype and ceremony mustered during her farewell show seemed almost out of place.

Even so, and in contrast to her former sparring partner, Gaby made it abundantly clear that she would take away nothing but good memories of her time on *The Big Breakfast*. Any regret she experienced was probably due to the burden she'd had to shoulder since her screen partner had disappeared 15 months earlier. In her wake she left a programme whose share of the breakfast time audience had fallen from 25% one year previously to just 16% (compared to GMTV's 38%), whose ratings were now well below the one million mark, and which appeared in every major aspect to have almost totally lost its way.

SIXTEEN

"Obscure words should be kept to a minimum"

Revamping a long-running television programme is a tricky art. It only works if done with confidence and panache, and if the point of the overhaul is immediately and overwhelmingly obvious to viewers. *The Big Breakfast* spent the second half of the 1990s embarking on an accelerating sequence of makeovers, but few were executed with that necessary degree of self-assurance, and only one left the show demonstrably better than it was before. Illustrative of Planet 24's complicated relationship with Channel 4, never mind its viewers, *The Big Breakfast* ended up undergoing one of the longest declines in recent television history – yet time and again, nobody seemed willing or able to pull the plug.

Gaby Roslin's departure on Friday 12 January 1996 could have been the cue for a complete cleaning of the slate and a reworking of the entire *Big Breakfast* brand. What did it stand for? Who was it aimed at? Most importantly of all, how could it best exploit the legacy of its successful early years, so as not to live forever in the shadow of Chris Evans? If it could figure that one out, maybe the programme stood a chance of profitably revisiting former glories, and in the process reinventing the medium of breakfast television. Instead, none of this was to be, and Gaby Roslin's exit ushered in the most unstable period in the show's history so far.

Her much-hyped replacement, from Monday 15 January, was Zoe Ball. Once a *Big Breakfast* researcher herself, Zoe was most well known for her stints on children's programmes *The O Zone* and *Fully Booked*. Viewers were introduced to her during Roslin's last show when Richard Orford rudely disturbed her slumbering in a hotel room.

But fate dictated that even Zoe Ball's opening seconds as *Big Breakfast* presenter were not to go to plan. What was intended to be a dramatic entrance, with her crashing through a stunt door, went horribly wrong when she tripped and fell through the fake entrance, landing on her face. Her co-host Mark Little looked on, nonplussed. It was an unfortunate omen of what was to come.

"Presenters come and go," Ball had exclaimed in the run-up to her first appearance. "I've seen that with my dad [iconic kids' TV presenter Johnny Ball]. But everyone's getting younger. I started working in TV at 19 and people used to go, 'You're so young.' Now you meet pop stars like

Zoe Ball tumbles into the increasingly chaotic and cursed arena of The Big Breakfast

PJ and Duncan, and they're really young. I'm not any more." Zoe certainly seemed aware of how audiences might perceive her new role. But was she sensitive enough to the expectations of her fellow colleagues, or indeed the precise set-up into which she was merrily diving?

Although Zoe Ball and Mark Little were heavily promoted as the new, here-to-stay *Big Breakfast* team, within days of their debut together news began to filter out suggesting that there had been a very palpable and instant deterioration in the relationship between the two hosts. It appeared that there was some fundamental clash of personalities that no one had foreseen and which, no matter how hard the production team tried, could not be disguised.

After just three weeks together on-screen, Little took a week off. In February, Executive Producer Bob Massie was half-jokingly reported as saying he'd like some of the recently disbanded pop group, Take That, to join *The Big Breakfast* as hosts. The following month, when the show won Best ITV/C4 Programme at the TV and Radio Industries Awards, Little took the opportunity to remind the audience, "This is a team award – let's not forget our Gaby Roslin." Feeling slighted, Zoe Ball stormed out.

To be fair, few could have made *The Big Breakfast* work as it stood in its current format, blessed as it was with desultory, self-consciously 'wacky' features such as 'Buddies In The Nuddy' and 'Show Us Your Behind'. Ball's patented catchphrase 'My my!' hardly improved matters, and less than eight weeks into her tenure, Planet 24 was already contriving to counter-schedule both Ball's and Little's holidays to avoid them having to appear in front of the camera together. When the full story of the pair's fall-out broke in the press in March, Little was on a three-week break. His vacation was immediately extended to four weeks, and when he finally returned, Ball instantly began her own holidays. When her break ended up being three weeks rather than two as previously announced, it meant that she and Little had not appeared together on screen for seven weeks.

This clearly could not go on, and with the show's average ratings refusing to rise above 900,000, Little was chosen to be the scapegoat. As was soon to become routine on *The Big Breakfast*, his departure was swift and never officially mentioned on air. He was simply there one day, Friday 12 July, and gone the next. One of the only subsequent references ever made to him on the programme came a week after his exit when a phone interview with The Spice Girls ended with the group shouting "We fancy Mark Little!", at which point they were hurriedly faded out.

Little was removed just ahead of the 1,000th edition of *The Big Breakfast* on Thursday 25 July. It was a hollow celebration. Behind the scenes, Planet 24 had reportedly become engulfed in a huge row that had blown up between its key executives Sebastian Scott, Charlie Parsons and Waheed Alli. It was alleged that Scott had worked for rival company Hat Trick while still being contracted to Planet 24. Another rumour was that Scott had been invited to the party marking the 1,000th show, only for Alli to ring him up demanding that he return the ticket. Scott had supposedly been exiled to a small office down the road from the main Planet 24 premises.

The disastrous fall-out between Zoe Ball and Mark Little and their failure to re-energise the programme's format meant that it was now common to find *The Big Breakfast* being referred to in articles and reviews throughout the media as a byword for one of the most calamitous shows on TV. The 1997 Edinburgh TV Festival book, which reviewed the "triumphs" and "turkeys" of the preceding 12 months, placed it firmly in the latter category, citing Victor Lewis-Smith in the *Evening Standard* fuming, "Anaemic, pallid and bland, that's what *The Big Breakfast* has become, a far cry from the rich and spicy blood pudding dished up two years ago." It also found its way into *Select* magazine's "Top 20 Worst TV Programmes At The Moment", where the snap diagnosis read: "Too many researchers with bob haircuts".

On screen, Zoe Ball soldiered on with Keith Chegwin as an emergency co-host, while off camera another upheaval was underway. Bob Massie decided to quit, and former *Big Breakfast* producer Lisa Clark was brought in as his replacement. She had recently married Dan McGrath, part of Chris Evans' Radio 1 breakfast show team, and during his show on the morning of July 23, Evans promised his audience that McGrath would reveal "exactly what's going on with *The Big Breakfast*". Listeners learned that Clark had decided to appoint yet another "permanent" male host, and also to introduce an entirely new look for the show. Indeed, from Monday 19 August, *The Big Breakfast* was banished to a marquee in the garden while renovations began on the house – and the week after, Zoe Ball and temporary host Simon Gregson were reduced to presenting the programme from a boat following another 'Eggs on Legs' tour around the country.

But if Lisa Clark had factored Zoe Ball into her revamp, she had underestimated the woman's residual anger. Just a few days after Clark confirmed that the presenter was staying on, Ball contradicted her new boss by announcing to the world that she'd had enough. "I was hyped up," she later raged. "I won't allow that again. I was incredibly nervous and they didn't know whether they wanted me to be another Gaby Roslin or a young, sexy thing. Instead of putting my foot down and saying, 'This is me, and this is what I do,' I tried to fit in with what everyone wanted and it totally backfired. I couldn't please anyone – especially myself. I thought I was terrible and that my career in television was dead."

It is somewhat unfortunate that none of this insight appeared to manifest itself during the period when Ball was actually hosting the show. If it had, maybe change would have come sooner rather than later and she might have been persuaded to stay. Instead, she was off, waving goodbye on Friday 30 August. The all-new, totally overhauled and refreshed *Big Breakfast* was then unveiled to the world on the following Monday.

This time two faces with no previous connections to the programme were parachuted into the front line. One was ex-champion swimmer Sharron Davies, reputedly on a £500,000 12-month contract; the other was kids' TV host Rick Adams. This gamble was unsettling enough, but more alarming was what had happened to the framework of the show itself.

Lisa Clark had initiated a total reorientation of *The Big Breakfast*'s style and agenda. It was now to be a family-aimed format, from a house that resembled an upholstered cream sponge, and concerned exclusively with a stodgy diet of lifestyle, glossy-magazine items.

An air of hastiness surrounded the whole enterprise. The refurbishment was completed less than an hour before the relaunched show went on air. Worse, the opening titles hadn't even been finished, and had to be substituted at the last minute with a sprint by a hand-held camera across the garden.

Content-wise, the new *Big Breakfast* made for a mystifying brew. Sharron Davies and Rick Adams were the most unlikely double act on UK breakfast television since Toni Arthur and John Noakes. Both Richard Orford and Vanessa Feltz (Lily Savage's replacement) had been retained, presumably for the sake of continuity, but in reality, they looked terribly out of place in such a changed landscape.

New items included Sharon Stone's sister Kelly reading show biz gossip, Radio 1 DJ Jo Whiley presenting music news, and clothes designer Wayne Hemingway profiling fashions. Karl Crompton, millionaire lottery winner, doled out hints on his success, and Denise Van Outen bellowed weather forecasts from inside a deafeningly loud helicopter. There was even a slot on interior design. This was not a selection of features that the programme should have been running at all. It was pure unashamed GMTV material, precisely the opposite of what *The Big Breakfast* had originally been commissioned to do. Moreover, it was the kind of line-up GMTV did with more bluster, authority and money, and which therefore rendered *The Big Breakfast*'s efforts irrelevant. Why watch at all when there were people doing it better on the other side?

The press hated it ("Dog's Breakfast" "Snap, Crackle And Flop"), ratings barely stirred, and a process of rolling tinkering began. Peter Smith, a solitary link with the show's early days, was replaced with Phil Gayle, and the news bulletins returned to running every 20 minutes, having previously been reformatted to air every half-hour. As soon as it got too dark to see anything in her helicopter during the winter mornings, Denise Van Outen was promoted to a regular daily phone-in feature 'Dial Denise'. In turn, she ended up increasingly co-hosting the whole programme, as Sharron Davies took more and more days off. In fact there appeared to be weeks when the ex-swimmer hardly appeared at all. On one notable occasion she attended the Cheltenham Festival seemingly for her own pleasure rather than to do the show, appearing at 7am to say hello, at 8 am to say hello again, and that was it.

At the start of January 1997, the set was completely changed in an obvious attempt to half-return it to its original style. The showpiece sunken seating area was ripped up and replaced by the old chairs-in-front-of-the-French-windows arrangement, Vanessa Feltz was awarded a bed from which to conduct her interviews, and a 'Family Of The Week' came back in the studio. Yet still nothing seemed to be going right. The morning after the 1997 Oscars, Kelly Stone and Laurie Pike broadcast live from an after-show party, but failed to find anyone to talk to and ended up standing alone in front of the camera for five minutes. C4's children's consumer programme *Wise Up* ran a regular feature where a youngster could meet a celebrity they disliked. Sure enough, one edition found a girl berating Rick Adams: "When are you going to leave *The Big Breakfast?*" Quizzing him over the collapse in viewing figures, Adams squirmed, "Well, ratings are funny things." "He's ruined the programme," the girl stoutly concluded.

All too aware that *The Big Breakfast* had now reached a crisis point in its existence, the Planet 24 management team reviewed their options. After long discussions, they decided that rather than abandon their once all-conquering creation, they would call up one of its founding editors to mount a drastic salvage operation.

"When I came back it was really dire; it was at one of its lowest ebbs," recalls Ruth Wrigley. "Charlie Parsons was over in America, so Waheed Alli said to me, 'Look, it's really bad. Can you reinvent it? If you can, fine; if you can't I'll sell the brand.'"

Lisa Clark, the figure most associated with the last revamp, was replaced with Duncan Gray, a former *Big Breakfast* researcher whom Wrigley had worked with back in the show's early days. Between them, the pair set about overhauling the entire programme, but soon realised it wasn't going to be a quick or easy task. "It was a gradual thing," Wrigley continues. "I started in the spring [of 1997], and people were starting to tune in again by the autumn. We spent the summer getting it right and fixing it. But Duncan and I were given a free hand, which was good. It was quite refreshing. My theory is if something's really bad, you can't make it worse. It's actually very empowering, because you've got nothing to lose. And I always think telly works when you've got nothing to lose, as you can only go one way, and you go with your instincts."

The very first thing the new team did was introduce a plethora of prerecorded material, in order, as Wrigley explains, "to get the links, which Sharron and Rick were doing, down to a minimum." In May, Sharron Davies herself was shown the door, and Denise Van Outen was promoted to take her place. A month later Rick Adams was shunted off onto 'Down Your Doorstep', before being fired and temporarily replaced with Richard Orford. Much attention was paid to the actual content of the show, in order to strip away the superfluous detritus and get the programme "back to core values, back to the house, while keeping everything very short and sharp".

Ruth Wrigley's take on what had gone wrong was clear: "Because *The Big Breakfast* was so cutting edge and so new, it had very soon become a parody of itself and a cliché," she recalls. "So all the stuff that seemed really cool at the beginning – the 'zoo TV', the wackiness and the bright colours – it all got nicked by everybody else. Then it tried to reinvent itself and be serious, and they turned the house into a studio, which was wrong because fundamentally that's why it worked in the first place – it was a real house, and everything grew from that."

Both Wrigley and Duncan Gray spent the best part of the summer searching for a new male host to partner Denise Van Outen. They correctly concluded that establishing strong dynamics between the show's two presenters was vital to securing the stability and consistency of the entire project. But before they could introduce their chosen candidate on-screen, they were suddenly faced with the prospect of covering the news of the death of Diana, Princess of Wales.

One problem *The Big Breakfast* had always struggled with was how to behave on the morning after a major news event, in particular a natural disaster or human tragedy. A classic example was the awkward and unconvincing edition on the morning after the 1996 Dunblane school shooting massacre, where the format was completely the same except that the links into the news were spoken in a solemn voice, and the background music was turned off during the bulletins. C4 also had to apologise for preceding the show with an old *Big Breakfast* trailer showing Mark Little firing a gun at the camera.

Princess Diana's death was handled slightly better through a series of *Big Breakfast News Specials*. As the programme was on the road anyway while more renovation work was done to the house, these *Specials* came from a different place every day, beginning on Monday 1 September with Richard Orford in a suit and Vanessa Feltz in a frock sitting behind a table in The Mall in London reading out faxes and linking into very long news bulletins. Later in the week, Peter Smith was brought back to do self-consciously serious interviews, including one with Planet 24 boss Bob Geldof who indulged in a long, angry rant about the *Sun*.

To have to follow all this was no easy task, but nonetheless, one week later Denise Van Outen and her new on-screen partner appeared together for the first time. The results were instantly impressive. Johnny Vaughan had done stints on *The Big Breakfast* before, but from the moment he was appointed the show's main presenter, he managed to accomplish two things that hardly anyone had done before: make the role his own, and strike up a bond with his co-host.

Vaughan and Van Outen quickly formed a convincing double-act, commanding more influence and respect than any of their immediate predecessors. Moreover, off the back of their success, some engaging features began creeping back into the schedule, such as 'That's Strife', a *That's Life!* parody with Van Outen as Esther Rantzen, Vaughan as sidekick Cyril Fletcher and some shop dummies as the 'team'.

"The show's strengths became Johnny and Denise," observes Ruth Wrigley. "It was a personality thing. Johnny and Denise were good together – funny, quick, they felt very 'now'. Johnny was brilliant; he was very right for the moment. When *The Big Breakfast* first started, we'd aimed at children initially, as they would put the TV on and other people followed. Five years down the line those children were 13, 14, 15, and Johnny was somebody they could key in to and think was cheeky, rude and cool."

Besides its presenters, the programme had also at long last made an attempt to get to grips with its public image. "Channel 4 wasn't interested in *The Big Breakfast* any more; it was a bit of an embarrassment," continues Wrigley. "So, Waheed Alli brought in a woman called Anita Hamilton who'd been responsible for the marketing of Capital Radio. For the first time in its history, *The Big Breakfast* had an in-house Director of Marketing. What she did was work with the channel to market the brand, to make sure it was kept abreast of what was happening, and ensure there was a proper campaign. In a business sense, it was a very canny move. It wasn't just, 'Oh, we've got to make it better,' there were lots of wheels running in tandem. While we were doing our bit, Anita was putting other things in place, so as we editorially got it right, bang, there was a proper campaign in place. It was a proactive strategy."

One offshoot of this was an attempt to sharpen awareness of *The Big Breakfast* as a 'brand'. *The Bigger Breakfast*, a children's holiday programmes strand, began on Monday 21 July 1997. This was designed to provide some continuity between all of Channel 4's shows through to midday, utilising *The Big Breakfast* presenters as hosts. For the initial run, Richard Orford and Denise Van Outen travelled to a different location each day, including Stratford, East Midlands Airport, and the set of C4 youth soap *Hollyoaks*. Subsequent strands were more orientated around *The Big Breakfast* and were based at the house itself.

This, coupled with an exhaustive publicity campaign, helped *The Big Breakfast* to recover some of its previously powerful profile. At the end of the day, much was to do with the celebrity status of its presenters. As GMTV Director of Programmes, Peter McHugh reasons, "While *The Big Breakfast* was not a success commercially, it was a success from a PR point of view. The newspapers couldn't write about Johnny and Denise and say it was a failure, because you can't stick a big photo of Denise in your paper and say it's a failure."

Despite these positive and practical developments, together with demonstrable success in halting the ratings decline, the programme was not entirely born again. A large portion of those unenlightening consumer features persisted, and although viewing figures were not falling any more, neither were they rising or heading anywhere near the levels witnessed in 1993. On hearing that her role was to be scaled down, Vanessa Feltz quit the programme in December, making sure her exit hit the headlines by pouring a plate of baked beans over a Planet 24 editor in the canteen. At the same time, Zig and Zag, who had maintained an occasional presence in the show, were quickly and permanently phased out.

When Duncan Gray moved on in January 1998 another Planet 24 executive, Ed Forsdick, took his place. Having worked for *The Big Breakfast* on and off for the previous six years, Forsdick had a keen grasp of the show's eventful history. "I knew it was a monster that constantly ate ideas and had to be kept stimulated," he recalls. "If you neglected it or didn't try to keep it, its presenters or its viewers amused, it would die."

The biggest challenge he faced was how to sustain *The Big Breakfast*'s refound credibility and spiky attitude into the long term. He was lucky in that, at least to begin with, he inherited a concrete line-up of core presenters. "Johnny Vaughan and Denise Van Outen were at the peak of their popularity," Forsdick emphasises, "and could make anything work. They were also the cornerstone that we built everything around. The great thing about the show was that it could change hugely from day to day and if something didn't work, we'd forget about it and move on."

Big events were staged to drum up attention, including a live link-up from Dublin Castle for St. Patrick's Day in March, plus regular dispatches from the Cannes Film Festival. Richard Orford travelled to Paris for the 1998 World Cup before finally leaving the programme in the autumn. 'Find Me A Model 98' was a nationwide competition to find *The Big Breakfast* 'Face Of 98', while the 'Write On' contest offered budding scriptwriters a chance to pen a short film for screening in July 1999. "The brand was constantly being extended," Forsdick remembers. "It had to be constantly updated – and the Johnny Vaughan/Denise Van Outen brand was very different from the Sharron Davies/Rick Adams brand that preceded them. Presenters had to impose their personalities on the show – that was part of the original premise of it."

Although a defiantly self-confident and energetic programme once again, there was something about *The Big Breakfast* towards the end of the 1990s that failed to inspire quite as much loyalty and excitement amongst viewers, certainly compared to the exhilarating days of 1992 and '93. Its various endeavours and stunts never seemed to grant it enough of a new lease of life to render it unmissable, essential television. When Ruth Wrigley left the show again in 1998 after two years in overall charge, it wasn't long before a worryingly familiar air of listlessness returned, as if a reassuring hand had been taken off the tiller. *The Bigger Breakfast* was summarily scrapped in October 1998 and replaced with Channel 4's in-house service *T4*. The ratings were prone to the occasional wobble, which would always trigger another round of sniping in the press about how the programme was but a shadow of its former self.

While audience levels were clearly down compared to the start of the decade, this kind of comparison ignored the vastly changed context in which *The Big Breakfast* now had to operate. "Whenever the original figures were quoted no-one ever took into account the state of the breakfast marketplace in 1992 and the state x years down the line," contests Ed Forsdick. "We started off without children's programming on BBC2, extremely limited competition from satellite and no real threat from radio – so in a way it was amazing we were getting the numbers we got later on. However, the legacy of Chris and Gaby was never easy to live down and we'd always get it thrown at us."

The criticism levelled at the show towards the end of 1998 was nothing compared to the storm that blew up the following year in the aftermath of Denise Van Outen's departure. Her exit from the house on New Year's Day 1999 had been long-rumoured, and was by and large a good-natured farewell. But when it came to choosing her replacement, the production team made a huge blunder.

Instead of opting for someone they knew would work well with Johnny Vaughan, and more importantly would be able to strike up an instant rapport with viewers, a decision was made based almost wholly upon looks rather than know-how or presenting ability. Passing over a number of viable candidates (including Lisa Tarbuck who had stood in for Van Outen and bonded well with Vaughan), on Friday 9 January 1999 it was announced that the new female host of *The Big Breakfast* was to be teenage fashion model Kelly Brook. A graduate of the famous Italia Conti Stage School, Brook (who'd changed her surname from Parsons to sound "more catchy") was signed up on a salary rumoured to be anywhere between £100,000 and £200,000. She was to make her debut on screen on Monday 1 February.

Kelly Brook was a hugely controversial choice, principally because she had next to no experience in broadcasting. Better known for advertising Lee jeans and modelling Triumph bras, her arrival landed the programme reams of publicity, particularly in the *Daily Star* who rather optimistically proclaimed the advent of the "new queen of morning television" – but not before making her strip down to her underwear for a photo shoot. It was her performance in front of the TV cameras, however, that now mattered. After such a build up, viewers were led to believe that the salvation of *The Big Breakfast* and all that it stood for lay fairly and squarely with an adolescent pin-up. Kelly Brook was on her way: she'll tell us what to do.

With painful inevitability, the whole thing fell apart. Brook proved to be embarrassingly unskilled at even fulfilling a role as Johnny Vaughan's stooge, let alone co-anchor two hours of live television. Just a few weeks after her arrival, the leaking of an internal Planet 24 memo sealed her fate. It detailed how the production team had been instructed when dealing with Brook to avoid using difficult words, and that names in her scripts should be written phonetically and in capital letters. "All intros and links should be kept as simple as possible," the document continued, "with alliteration and obscure words kept to a minimum." The memo concluded by requesting writers to cook up "spontaneous" one-liners that Brook could drop into conversation with Vaughan – to make their relationship look more natural.

In a stroke, all the ground *The Big Breakfast* had recovered during the preceding few years was obliterated. Once more, the show became a national joke. *Heat* magazine instigated a "gaffe-o-meter" to plot Kelly's slip-ups day by day. Articles in both broadsheet and tabloid papers eagerly picked over the programme's very public failings, and noted with relish its willingness to employ disgraced ex-*Blue Peter* presenter Richard Bacon as a new OB reporter.

Unsurprisingly, Kelly Brook did not last long. On July 30, it was announced that she had quit the show, five months before her contract was due for renewal. Ratings seemed to sum up the entire debacle: at an average of 470,000, they were 50,000 lower than 12 months earlier. Four summers ago they'd stood at 870,000.

"One weakness with *The Big Breakfast* was that it was highly dependent on a very particular cast," recalls its original Commissioning editor, Michael Atwell, "but the biggest weakness was that its audience was limited. It was the sort of show that could only ever work for young families with children and young adults and students. It could never work for a mass mainstream, for general, middle-aged, middle class families. So in the end, its peak was 2m and really it could never get beyond that because there was no-one else left." Indeed, where once audiences had fluctuated, now it appeared that ratings were heading remorselessly downwards, doggedly refusing to rally or even flatline.

Throughout 1999 and into 2000, rumours of *The Big Breakfast*'s pending demise were unceasing. Events seemed to betray an absence of vision and the inability of Planet 24 and Channel 4 to formulate a workable strategy for the programme's future. The situation had been muddied in March 1999 by the sale of Planet 24 to Carlton Television for £15m, landing £5m each for its founders Bob Geldof, Charlie Parsons and Waheed Alli. It was doubtful whether a new layer of management would help *The Big Breakfast*'s existence, and also whether Alli was really the right person to represent the company's interests and portfolio at Carlton, having no direct programme-making experience whatsoever.

A modicum of order was restored at the end of August 1999 with the appointment of Liza Tarbuck to replace Kelly Brook. Tarbuck was a familiar face on British TV, being a former star of Granada's popular sitcom *Watching* and Planet 24's BBC1 series *The Weekend Show*. She was also a long-term friend of Johnny Vaughan, and their deep-rooted relationship was evident for all to see on-screen. By this point, however, no amount of repair work could mask the fact that *The Big Breakfast* had become a dangerously soiled brand. During Kelly Brook's time, as had been the case after Chris Evans' departure right up to Johnny Vaughan's arrival, the show had been kicked around, pulled inside out and still no good had come of it.

As if to concede as much, at the start of February 2000, Channel 4 Director of Programmes Tim Gardam circulated a secret performance review amongst his colleagues, calling for ideas on how to refresh some of the channel's best-known staples, including Chris Evans' *TFI Friday*, long-running soap *Brookside*, and above all *The Big Breakfast*. Even at this point, however, Gardam felt moved to stress that just because these respective strands were ageing, no one was suggesting they had to go.

All too soon, Liza Tarbuck got itchy feet, announcing at the end of April 2000 that she wanted to leave to resume her acting career. Denise Van Outen agreed to return to take her place, but on condition that it was only on a temporary basis. Surely now was the time to consider bringing the curtain down for good. Even Johnny Vaughan had lost his flair, and his increasing propensity for rants – against the French, the Germans, or the Millennium Dome – had become a real turn-off. One tirade against travellers had even brought gypsy curses upon Channel 4.

"I think Johnny became very difficult to produce," argues Ruth Wrigley, "because of the cult of personality. A similar thing happened with Chris Evans. Now, I'm a sort of horrible old bossy cow, so I could deal very well with Chris. We had our stand-up rows, and it was the same with Johnny. But with Johnny, when you're a young little producer, which a lot of those people then were, it's very scary. So as a viewer, what I'd be watching was a programme that wasn't controlled or produced, and as a viewer, that's boring. Items would go on and on, with Johnny ranting, and I'd see major movie stars sitting in the house, waiting to be interviewed, but I'd got to go to work."

Where once *The Big Breakfast* had cultivated its cutting edge credentials through a careful choice of presenters and items, it now fought to contrive 'wackiness' through clumsy ideas that almost appeared to parody the very notion of what an obvious *Big Breakfast* 'feature' should comprise. When the programme began, it had spoofed conventions of breakfast television. Now it had become engrossed in an effort almost to spoof the spoof itself, a practice that rarely reaped rewards.

Ratings bumped along at around the 400,000 mark. A few weeks into September 2000 *The Big Breakfast* recorded the lowest early morning viewing figures of all networks, trailing even the fledgling Channel Five. Only the programme's media profile, the fact that it was still well known, and the impression that Channel 4 didn't really know what to replace it with seemed to stop the axe from falling. Indeed, when Johnny Vaughan announced that he intended to quit at the start of 2001, C4 decided to defy all expectations. The show was recommissioned for a further 12 months. Another revamp was ordered, a new executive producer installed, new presenters hired, and the house redesigned for the umpteenth time. Just how much longer could this go on?

SEVENTEEN

"A very happy ship"

The Big Breakfast's woes during the second half of the 1990s were not solely of its own making. Just as GMTV had suffered from the initial success of its Channel 4 rival, so the ITV company was able to capitalise on its own later resurgence to return the favour several years on.

Yet as the new millennium approached, the story of British breakfast television became more than simply the erstwhile vanquished returning to exact revenge on former conquerors. The pace of expansion within non-terrestrial TV had gathered speed during the decade. For those who had access to cable and satellite stations, the number of alternatives open to them at breakfast time had ballooned.

Then there was the impact of Channel Five, launched in March 1997. Its overall effect upon audience share was erratic and inconsistent, but early mornings would prove to be one area where it registered limited but emphatic influence. As the end of the century loomed, providers of breakfast television across the broadcasting spectrum discovered themselves spending increasing amounts of energy and money trying to settle upon a remunerative and workable formula that would help them maintain a distinctive, popular service in an ever more crowded marketplace.

As long as John Birt was calling the shots as Deputy Director-General and later as Director-General itself, BBC breakfast television was certainly no place for fun or frivolity. Throughout the decade, it had remained a starched display of hard news, in-depth reportage and current affairs.

The individual character and personality of all the Corporation's bulletins was submerged under a uniform identity in 1993, rendering *BBC Breakfast News* indistinguishable from any other news programme on the network. At the same time, to better compete with GMTV, *Business Breakfast* was turned into a separate programme starting at 6am and running for a bleak 60 minutes.

Nicholas Witchell relinquished his duties as the chief presenter of *Breakfast News* in 1994, and gave way to ex-BBC Foreign correspondent Justin Webb. Young, enthusiastic and with a patented line in cynicism, Webb made for a rather unusual breakfast anchorman, often appearing alternately too earnest and then too laid back. To help refresh the programme around him, new faces were brought on board including ex-*Newsround* host Juliet Morris. And a new editor was appointed: Tim Orchard, a veteran of *Breakfast Time*.

Meanwhile, BBC management had dictated that a weekday alternative breakfast programme should be introduced on BBC2. Launched in February 1995, *Westminster On-Line* was a hesitant attempt to encourage audiences to use the Internet to contact a live news service. A number of eminent MPs and political commentators made themselves available for questioning from the public, eager to be seen associating with what was then still a largely mysterious and niche form of new technology. However, although ambitious, *Westminster On-Line* never really came alive and tended to get the same people e-mailing every day. It was soon replaced with a far more viewer-friendly proposition: a stream of Children's BBC repeats.

A different approach was tried back on BBC1 from the start of February 1996. *Breakfast News Extra* ran from 9 to 9.20am and was hosted by Juliet Morris. A slightly confusing 'spin-off' strand with consumer reports and guests, the show tackled health, education, technology and entertainment news, besides boasting a daily 'letters page' and a weekly live phone-in. This rather blatant attempt to compete with Lorraine Kelly's enduring slot on GMTV never really settled upon a coherent identity and, as with *Westminster On-Line,* did not last long. It was replaced 18 months later with *Can't Cook Won't Cook*, a show produced, ironically, by the independent company Bazal, which had been responsible for Lorraine's first GMTV venture, *Top Of The Morning*.

In time, Justin Webb moved on from *BBC Breakfast News*, having never quite met those oft-trumpeted high expectations, and was succeeded by another supposed rising star of the Corporation, John Nicholson. The supporting cast of presenters also mutated through numerous line-ups, though while Jon Sopel, Sophie Raworth and Jeremy Bowen were all recognisable BBC faces, none were ever really distinctive enough to grab attention in the way Anthea Turner and Eamonn Holmes did for good or ill on GMTV.

In addition, and rather in contrast to its lofty pretensions, *BBC Breakfast News* gained a somewhat notorious reputation for gaffes. On one occasion sports correspondent Rob Bonnet was thrown by a presenter asking, "Is it a big one?" (She was referring to his birthday.) Another time a guest was captioned "extreme right" only for Justin Webb to hastily point out it was not a description of his political views but merely referred to where he was standing.

The programme managed to maintain a loyal but unchanging audience numbering roughly one million. The statistics indicated that GMTV remained ahead in the ratings, and for a long time this appeared to be simply accepted as an inevitable by-product of the BBC's diligent promotion of an authoritative news service. Then as the end of the decade approached, rumours began to circulate of an impending relaunch, fuelled by the need for budget cuts and the findings of an official Corporation-wide 'news review'. Speculation grew when *Business Breakfast* was scrapped in October 1999, and *BBC Breakfast News* returned to its traditional starting time of 6am.

Sure enough, confirmation of a major shake-up came in March 2000. The entire service was to merge with the concurrent programme on the digital station BBC News 24, and be aired on both channels simultaneously. This was a sensible, if drastic, redeployment of BBC resources. It also bore some rather familiar hallmarks: high profile, no-nonsense, and self-evident. Many were quick to lay the decision for the revamp at the door of the new BBC Director-General, Greg Dyke.

John Birt's departure from the Corporation was welcomed by many as a chance for the BBC to recover its soul from under a smothering of middle management. Dyke arrived to a hugely sympathetic reception, promising radical change, and as 2000 wore on, details quickly emerged about what seemed to be a grand plan for breakfast TV.

Of chief interest was the involvement of veteran broadcaster Moira Stuart who was signed up to front the news bulletins. There was also to be an extra programme on Saturday mornings on BBC2, while airing the same output on both BBC1 and News 24 would save the Corporation £1.5m a year. The show's main hosts were confirmed as existing *BBC Breakfast News* presenters Jeremy Bowen and Sophie Raworth. Job cuts were anticipated, however, thanks to the merging of the previously separate *Breakfast News* and News 24 teams, and there was some time-honoured haggling with technicians over staffing levels.

The programme's new editor, Andrew Thompson, was adamant: "I think GMTV looks a bit old fashioned, lots of plants and shelves, whereas our breakfast programme will look more modern and elegant and stylish. Viewers will have a clear choice." As regards the soon-to-be-late *BBC Breakfast News*, Thompson admitted: "Viewers were never sure when news ended and features began. It felt a bit unstructured. We're doing this [relaunch] in response to the way people now say they want their news."

BBC Breakfast News came to an end just before the 2000 Olympics, and on Monday 2 October the new programme took its place. Enitled simply *Breakfast*, it featured a slick, brightly coloured set, and from the outset tried very hard to appear 21st century. Jeremy Bowen and Sophie Raworth greeted viewers from an elaborate yet uncomfortable looking desk and settee arrangement. Information scrolled conspicuously across the bottom of the screen, and viewers' e-mails were pointedly and somewhat awkwardly squeezed in amongst the reports. A panoply of features was also on display, including the 'Sports Minute' and financial news in the unlikely entitled 'Mutter From The Gutter'.

Moira Stuart postpones retirement plans
in order to steady hearts and minds at a revitalised BBC

While some may have cheered at the disappearance of wall-to-wall desks from BBC breakfast television, there was something about the programme's demeanour that didn't feel right. Bowen looked profoundly uncomfortable trapped in a suit, and veteran broadcaster and writer Ludovic Kennedy caused a media stir when accused him of resembling "an ageing hamster who had just woken up from a long winter's hibernation; in 50 years of viewing I have never seen a presenter more twitchy and ill-at-ease". Sophie Raworth fell foul of the curse that has dogged all female newsreaders and journalists dabbling in breakfast TV: attempting to be relaxed, chatty and amiable, but coming over on screen as clipped and positively glacial.

Changes were soon made at the top, though not specifically because *Breakfast* was seen to be in trouble. In February 2001, Andrew Thompson took a new post in the BBC sports department and was replaced by Richard Porter, BBC News 24's senior editor. Porter saw it as his job to tidy up aspects of the revamp that his predecessor had overlooked. "I'd watched breakfast television for many years," he explains. "I had a very good sense of what it was like and how it had changed over the years, and

197

what breakfast shows were trying to achieve. Just watching the relaunched programme, I could see things that I wanted to do. They were mostly based around changing some of the details of the show – in crude terms, making it stick together a bit better. [I wanted] to change the culture of the place a bit, to make it more of a programme than a news bulletin."

In particular, Porter sought to underline the significance of the programme's new title. "When *Breakfast News* became *Breakfast,* it wasn't just a case of changing the name; the programme had to change intrinsically as a result. I think that was what I was able to develop when I got here."

Porter worked to achieve a far better integration of features than *Breakfast* had primarily displayed, besides altering the presenter line-up by interspersing Bowen and Raworth's shifts with more appearances from other hosts such as Darren Jordan, Bill Turnbull and Sian Williams, and making the studio set more homely. He also exploited the programme's much-vaunted embrace of contemporary technology in order to evolve a far more intensive, two-way relationship with viewers.

"The audience of our programme was particularly happy to communicate with us," he explains, "so we gave them the means through e-mail. And we didn't just do that in the faint hope that somebody might eventually contact us. We did that because every time we tried something new, the response got bigger and bigger. People want to talk to us, and I think it's right that we should give them the means to do so. In practical terms, having that sort of relationship means you have a better understanding of your audience. If you've done an item that strikes a chord, five minutes later you can see because of the response you get. That's a pretty valuable production tool."

In time, *Breakfast* did find a better sense of its own identity, and even though its ratings failed to demonstrate a consistent improvement on its predecessor, the ever-changing broadcasting environment of the late 1990s had increasingly rendered the value of viewing figures open to question. Interpreting breakfast TV ratings had always been a contentious business, given how wildly audiences fluctuated over the whole three hours of programming, plus the relative merits of the 'peak quarter-hour' measurement. Now executives had to deal with the fact that viewing figures for all breakfast television services appeared to be slipping.

Competition was taking many new forms. When Channel Five began, it did not opt for a two- or three-hour weekday breakfast 'show' but went for a strand of programmes including a rather ambitious hour and a half of straight news along with various children's series. Chris Evans also made a short-lived return to early morning TV when his Virgin Radio breakfast show was simultaneously transmitted on satellite station Sky One from October 1998. Undoubtedly a groundbreaking initiative, it did not have quite the impact Sky had hoped for, mostly because of Evans' declining popularity and the way the programme could only feature records that had videos suitable for airing at 8am.

GMTV had not enjoyed a clear run of the field either. A policy of carefully building upon its strengths whilst trying to mask its weaknesses had seen the company attempt to leave the legacy of its disastrous debut behind, but with mixed results. Back in 1996, it had been most concerned with trying to curb its reliance on children's features. Judicious scheduling succeeded in refunnelling such output onto weekends, bolstered by a 25% increase in the budget for kids' programming.

The climax of this was the consolidation of the station's various Disney related offerings into one strand called *Diggit* from March 14 1998. It was very capably hosted by Paul 'Des' Ballard and Fearne Cotton, and ran live for a couple of hours on Saturdays and in a prerecorded version on Sunday. While the familiar mix of cartoons, features, and competitions were present, the idea of having a single coherent identity was new. It was logical, upfront and fresh, and helped strengthen the profile of GMTV as a children's broadcaster.

Elsewhere, tensions had eased once Anthea Turner left the station on Christmas Eve 1996. She was given a typically over-the-top send-off in the shape of a *This Is Your Life* pastiche, delivered in mock-seriousness by Eamonn Holmes, whose relationship with his co-host had not really shown any signs of improvement in the run-up to her departure. Indeed, a few days after her exit, Holmes appeared to come clean about his attitude towards Turner in a newspaper article, labelling her "Princess Tippy Toes" and "Tiny Tears".

"I now felt sick to the stomach," Turner later wrote in response. "It was the ultimate betrayal." It all made for a rather undignified end to this particular chapter in GMTV's history. There had certainly never been this kind of public animosity between presenters in the whole of breakfast television history, and away from the name-calling, there was a sense of a patchy working relationship being elevated to the status of a national tragedy. GMTV had always tried to treat press coverage as a key area for fuelling awareness of the company 'brand'. It was hard to see how any of this particular furore did the station any favours.

Anthea Turner's place on the sofa was filled by existing co-host Fiona Phillips and the ubiquitous Matthew Lorenzo, best known for his hapless presentation of ITV's 1994 World Cup coverage. In an event as regular as the seasons, Lorraine Kelly's segment was overhauled, extended to 8.30am, and given a new name: *Lorraine Live*.

Two former TV-am faces also made a reappearance. In July 1997, Timmy Mallett showed up to front 18 two and a half minute features entitled 'Way To Go' profiling summer holiday locations for kids. Viewers discovered that the man had not changed his routine in the slightest from the one first glimpsed almost 15 years earlier. The following April, John Stapleton returned to his old stamping ground, enlisted after his ITV daytime talk show *The Time... The Place...* was axed. "I went back largely because of Peter [McHugh, Director of Programmes], whom I respected, who'd been my first boss on *The Time... The Place...*, and because it was a good gig," he recalls. "It was a successful programme, and did the sort of journalism and current affairs that I enjoy. It was a very happy ship."

As a veteran of breakfast television virtually since its birth, a return to the scene after several years' absence inevitably proved something of an eye-opener. "It'd changed dramatically, in the sense that so much of it was live. When I started out, hardly ever did we ever do anything live from location. What I found had changed on returning to breakfast television had been a result of ENG, Electronic News Gathering, which meant that for every news story there were reporters, live, topping and tailing the package, or at the scene reporting. But that was what GMTV was all about. And it had mastered it very quickly, which is why I think it ended up really leading the way." Stapleton also pays tribute to the enduring talent of another breakfast TV survivor, Peter McHugh. "Peter's great trick has always been this wonderful knack of picking the story and the issues that people talk about in the pub that night. That's his great skill."

Attempts to expand the GMTV 'brand' had continued apace. A GMTV magazine was launched at the end of April 1997, and the following year Amanda Redington and Lorraine Kelly co-hosted four weeks of outside broadcasts from the 'GMTV villa' in Marbella, including additional shows screened across the ITV network at 1.25pm. This gave the company important exposure at the heart of the daytime schedules, besides plenty of chances to promote its breakfast programme amongst an unfamiliar audience.

A few months later came an event that Managing Director Christopher Stoddart would always cite as his proudest moment while in charge of the company. At the end of November, GMTV secured a renewal of its contract – along with a substantial cut in its annual licence payment to the government. This was a hard-fought and much sought after reduction, but if it implicitly acknowledged Bruce Gyngell's oft-voiced insistence that GMTV had always bid too high for its franchise, Stoddart was not concerned. He was content to point to the most recent ITC programme review, which noted how GMTV was now providing an attractive and generally high-quality service with a greater coverage of senior politicians and more live interviews. The document also sang, "The audience turned to GMTV in their greatest numbers on the days of the biggest news events."

The company was flushed with a sense of vindication and fiscal fortitude. Then, as if on cue, it proceeded to commit a huge mistake. On Friday 11 June 1999, GMTV had to suspend one of its producers, pending a major internal investigation. Evidence had come to light regarding an incident where viewers had been misled into thinking that an employee of a national chain of cosmetic surgery clinics was actually an ordinary customer.

In a recent edition of *Lorraine Live*, the host had interviewed one Anna Cartwright, ostensibly a client of the Transform clinic, in the context of being one of the first women to undergo a new treatment called 'lysonix ultrasonic lipoplasty'. It later transpired that Cartwright actually worked for Transform in its marketing department, a fact known to GMTV staff, but not revealed to viewers or to Lorraine Kelly. The story broke at a time when other consumer and magazine TV programmes were also suffering similar problems with actors and phoney guests impersonating members of the public. GMTV managed to avoid any kind of criminal investigation, but the affair took some sheen off the company's recent run of good luck.

A revelation of a different nature came in July 1999 when it transpired that Prime Minister Tony Blair preferred GMTV to Radio 4's venerated *Today* programme. The news prompted presenter Penny Smith to respond, "Oh, he's said it before. I think we have a similar agenda to the *Today* programme, but we try to cover the stories in a viewer-friendly fashion. I'm sure Tony Blair does watch. Why would he not watch us, given the choice?" *Today* editor Rod Liddle, meanwhile, could only reply, "Of course the Prime Minister must choose for himself what he does in the morning, but I am delighted to say he always seems to be very well informed about what we're doing."

Away from such high-profile incidents, the station increasingly had to pay attention to a new development. GMTV had watched from the sidelines while, following a relaxing of broadcasting ownership legislation in the mid-1990s, ITV companies had embarked on a furious round of takeovers and mergers. However, as the decade drew to a close, the stream of boardroom buy-outs began to impact upon the fortunes of the breakfast station itself, with its respective stakeholders circling each other searching for a big killing.

First to make a move were the Scottish Media Group (SMG) and the *Guardian*, who indicated that they were looking to sell their joint holding in GMTV. In response, Carlton and Granada prepared to make a straight bid for the shares, thought to be worth up to £90 million. Then suddenly SMG changed its mind, decided it wanted to maintain a presence in the

GMTV consortium, secured a deal to buy the *Guardian*'s stake for £20m, and signalled an interest in mounting a bid for the entire company.

A sequence of chequebook battles, bluffs and double bluffs began. At one point it was rumoured that Disney was about to sell its own shareholding. Then the ITC stepped in, warning that any bid to buy the whole station would mean a breach of rules governing advertising revenues. It was only at the start of 2000 that confusion temporarily ceased as SMG, Granada and Carlton divided up the *Guardian*'s stake between them, increasing each of their shares to 25%. The question remained as to what would happen if and when Granada and Carlton, now the two biggest ITV players, decided to merge and GMTV's status as an independent broadcaster would be up for grabs.

Christopher Stoddart and his team resolved to press ahead and assume that their company did indeed have a future – at least in the short term. The closure of two major deals soon followed. First was the acquisition, in association with Children's ITV, of the acclaimed cult Japanese animation series *Pokemon*. This was a major coup and was reflective of how GMTV continued to value providing high quality kids' output early in the morning. Secondly, the company switched its suppliers of news content from Reuters to ITN. It meant that after being kept out in the cold for almost 20 years, the long-established news organisation had finally gained a presence within ITV breakfast television.

GMTV continued to forward an aggressive business agenda. It championed one of its preschool programmes, *Jellikins*, by selling the rights on to broadcasters in 15 countries and licensing 27 companies to produce tie-in merchandise. In March 2000, the company signed its biggest ever international co-production deal with the US firm Itsy Bitsy Entertainment Company. The end result was the successful puppet and animation show *Ni Ni's Treehouse*, featuring tales and adventures from the fantasy Oooberry Land. GMTV even offered to produce *OK!TV*, ITV's first mainstream and very public attempt at masthead television, until negotiations collapsed over the issue of programme rights.

While all this buccaneering and big budget dealing was going on, something unexpected was happening to GMTV's audience. Although it was difficult to draw any substantial conclusions from the figures, the station did not seem to have such a consistent viewing base as before, and on a number of occasions, *Breakfast News* had even come close to challenging the company in terms of the 'peak quarter-hour' rating. So attention shifted back to the main GMTV programme once more. Well-known GMTV Chief Correspondent Martin Frizell had recently been promoted to Executive Producer of weekday output. In March 2000, he was rapidly elevated to the post of editor and charged with halting any major downward trend in viewers.

Five months of hectic planning, research and preparation ensued in order to deliver a major on-screen revamp in the autumn. Information on this mammoth mission was initially withheld from the media, supposedly to ensure maximum impact at a prearranged launch at the Edinburgh Television Festival in August. In the event, this turned out to be a serious error of judgement, as the premiere garnered nothing more than a small mention in the *Daily Star*.

Nonetheless, it transpired that the station had signed five new presenters: Sky TV breakfast anchor Kate Garraway and sport correspondent Andrew Castle, Carlton weather forecaster Clare Nasir, plus existing TV hosts Jenni Falconer and Ben Shepherd. Each was to make his or her debut during what Frizell termed, "A refurbishment, not an overhaul. The autumn schedule is the first step."

Central to this was a new approach towards current affairs. "I'm chasing harder stories," Frizell continued, "which we hope will bring the audience with us. We like to think we're more in tune with our viewers [than the BBC] and we don't have to make lofty decisions about what we think they should be told." The lifestyle content was to remain, however, most prominently in a new Friday strand called *Entertainment Today* fronted by Shepherd and Falconer. Last of all, there was to be another new sofa. "It's been annoying the hell out of me," Frizell moaned of the existing model. "It looked like something from the Queensway autumn warehouse sale 1997. The bold checks distracted viewers from what presenters were trying to put across."

This latest incarnation of GMTV boasted a brighter studio set, extended weather bulletins and the obligatory makeover for Lorraine Kelly's slot, now dubbed *LK Today*. It was no coincidence, of course, that the entire overhaul was timed to overlap with the launch of *Breakfast* on BBC1. Indeed, Martin Frizell was open about aiming to undercut the new BBC effort. "I think our biggest worry is Jeremy Bowen," he contemplated. "At the Edinburgh Festival I kept seeing Jeremy in the bar at the George Hotel with all these young girls coming up and talking to him. I don't think the BBC realise how lethal he could be".

Despite all the hype, Frizell's revamp proved more of a factor in steadying the station's ratings rather than sending them skywards and before the dust had truly settled, news came of further change, this time behind the scenes. In January 2001, Christopher Stoddart announced he was leaving the company. He had been the only Managing Director that GMTV had ever employed, and had also become one of the longest serving executives in ITV history. Now this key figure, who for many was GMTV personified, had decided to move on and take up a new post with the TV horseracing consortium Go Racing.

For all GMTV personnel, indeed throughout the media in general, the thought of GMTV without Stoddart was an uneasy prospect. Who could possibly work up the same kind of reputation and profile within the company from scratch? Moreover, who was best placed to safeguard the station's immediate future? After a brief interregnum, the identity of this salutary individual was revealed to be Paul Corley, former ITV Head of Factual Programming and one time *Nationwide* researcher. He arrived to another chorus of speculation that GMTV's existence was once more in doubt, catalysed by rumours in the press that the organisation was shortly to be absorbed into a new ITV London 'super-franchise'. Corley, however, was upbeat, citing his own appointment as evidence to the contrary: "I think consolidation is a little further down the road than people expect. The reason the GMTV shareholders have appointed me is that they see a future for the franchise."

As if to demonstrate this, a couple of months after his appointment Corley announced plans for GMTV to produce a brand new daytime show. But this was not for a fellow terrestrial station. It was to appear on Sky One, be fronted by Lorraine Kelly, and most contentiously of all would go out directly against ITV's own *This Morning*. Corley was blunt: "One of our biggest shareholders, Carlton, makes *The Big Breakfast* for Channel 4. Commercial television has never restricted its programme divisions from competing on other channels." As far as GMTV was concerned, it seemed the battle for breakfast TV had just opened up a new front: nothing less than the whole of mainstream television itself.

EIGHTEEN

"There is life in the old dog yet"

Away from the campaigning that was enveloping GMTV, a somewhat different yet no less fierce war was unfolding on Channel 4: a war of succession. Although *The Big Breakfast* had been given yet another stave of execution, the jostling of interested parties keen to head a list of notional replacements had reached a new intensity. Given that the mood amongst media circles towards the incumbent's downfall was 'not *if*, but *when*', it was striking to see Channel 4 expend so much confidence and energy on *The Big Breakfast*'s ongoing promotion.

"*The Big Breakfast*'s ratings had gone up and down," recalls its founding Commissioning editor, Michael Atwell, "and then started to go down and down. But they'd managed to arrest it, and it looked for a period that it could keep going. Then once it started its second decline, well, it's very easy in hindsight to say it could never really have recovered. But [the programme's makers Planet 24 had] demonstrated that it could arrest a decline. [The thinking went] 'If you can do that once, maybe you can do it a second and third time.'"

To oversee *The Big Breakfast*'s next revamp, a new Executive Producer was appointed. Richard Hopkins had worked on the programme during its early days before leaving to help make *Hotel Babylon*, *Gaytime TV* (both Planet 24 shows) and the first series of *Big Brother*. Hopkins had previously also edited C4's attempt at a regular late-night satire slot, *The 11 O'Clock Show*, and so, as a few of the more acerbic commentators noted at the time, knew something about having to flog a format that had run out of steam a long time ago. January 2001 was fixed as the month for the changeover, and after Johnny Vaughan and Denise Van Outen had said their goodbyes on Friday 12 there was a week's hiatus before the remodelled *Big Breakfast* debuted on Monday 22.

The show had the misfortune to relaunch in an environment where, such was its reputation, many throughout the TV industry were actively agitating for its failure. They were not to be disappointed. Hopkins had assembled a ragbag line-up of hosts comprising comedian Paul Tonkinson, Irish TV presenter Amanda Byram, plus previous co-presenters Donna Air, Melanie Sykes and Richard Bacon. With all these personalities fighting for attention, the programme gave the immediate impression of being rooted not around a solid, double-handed core of presenters but a confusing melee of contrasting and conflicting characters.

The makeover was supposed to reorientate *The Big Breakfast* more towards older teenagers rather than 14-15 year olds, but – as is often the case with programmes that consciously try to cultivate a 'trendy' following – the results backfired. A garish new logo resembled an unsubtle pastiche of 1960s pop art, while the brash opening credits were reminiscent of the maligned C4 youth effort *The Girlie Show*. Tonkinson felt out of place from the off, appearing constricted by the format and unable to deploy his comic traits to good effect. Worst of all, the show was just as unexciting and staid as its previous incarnation, and consequently the revamp seemed to have no point whatsoever.

Hopkins left within two months, and his duties were assumed by the programme's Managing Editor, Ben Rigden. A mere three days after taking over, Rigden sacked Paul Tonkinson and pretty soon elements of the old set began reappearing, including the two presenters' chairs in front of the French windows. By this stage, the ratings for the programme were close to 200,000, the figure that had brought the axe down on the Channel 4 Daily – a service that, compared to the current incarnation of *The Big Breakfast*, seemed positively radiant.

Careful diagnosis revealed a mixture of problems, both specific and precise, but also deep-rooted and more general. Of the former, numerous aspects of *The Big Breakfast*'s presentation, format and delivery seemed at fault. Where once there was a tight, ordered schedule to support each programme, now features were rarely at the same time two days in a row, ran late and or were endlessly repeated. The crucial post-8am peak-audience slot would often be frittered away on in-jokes or semi-regular appearances from obscure experts. The paper review might appear twice in the same hour, while some days there could be up to half a dozen guests and on other days, none at all.

Thanks to a lack of rapport between the presenters and viewers, it was almost impossible to feel involved with the show and consequently to take much interest in what was happening on screen. The intense, pressurised and fast-paced format did not do the surviving hosts many favours. Mike McLean, the stand-in presenter promoted to fill Tonkinson's shoes, came over as a rather self-centred individual with a tendency to dominate proceedings, while Amanda Byram seemed incapable of responding to any sort of unscripted remark, sometimes clinging to her clipboard in terror ("Right now, here is a break", was one of her particularly notorious cues). Richard Bacon sounded forever as if he were trying desperately to be post-modern, ultra-ironic, and deliver every line as if it was in inverted commas, but only succeeded in appearing rather patronising and flippant. None of the team seemed able to command the same respect or make as much impact as their immediate predecessors.

In general, the tone of *The Big Breakfast* was now acutely exclusive and not a little arrogant. The programme had always featured smutty jokes and innuendos, but now they showed up by the bucketful and seemed unimaginative and lazy. At heart, it felt that so much was being taken for granted, and that the production team and presenters just did not deem it necessary to deliver.

In April, Channel 4's latest boss Michael Jackson argued, "There is life in the old dog yet. *The Big Breakfast* is a very important show for us; it is also a unique show. The intrinsic idea is a good one and we and the production team are working hard to make it as good as it can possibly be." Two months later, however, the channel grudgingly announced it was inviting submissions for potential replacements. It tried to avoid much fanfare, and was careful to emphasise that it was not signalling an immediate end to the show. All the same, this was the first sign that C4 were willing to consider giving *The Big Breakfast* the chop. A deadline of 9 July was set for the receipt of proposals.

The somewhat vague and hesitant character of this landmark news was a lot to do with the nature of Channel 4's contract with Planet 24. The production company had been careful to insist on a clause that stated that the channel had to provide it with a year's notice before any termination of *The Big Breakfast*'s contract. Any changeover, therefore, was always going to be a drawn-out process, with negotiations likely to drag out over many months. Planet 24 had also won the right to be guaranteed the chance to make a pilot for any potential replacement show. This touched upon something of even more fundamental concern: the question of just what could be put in the place of *The Big Breakfast*. Should the new programme be, for instance, a solely news-based service, or straightforward entertainment?

Channel 4 still had a statutory obligation to innovate and cater for minority tastes not being provided for elsewhere, but a lot had changed since 1992 when *The Big Breakfast* was launched, and the days were long gone when the country had only four TV channels to choose from. The 1990s had been a decade where Channel 4 had been forced to reposition and redefine itself, behave far more commercially, and to try to hold onto its audience share in the face of a multitude of other stations.

It all meant that come 2001, *The Big Breakfast* was in essence a relic from another age. This was not because it embodied a time when TV was more edgy, risky and innovative, however. It was more to do with the fact that the programme used to represent something that really was 'different', but which was now hardly distinctive and original at all. What did *The Big Breakfast* of 2001 do that other channels did not? Almost nothing. Many of its features were duplicates of those you could find more slickly and comprehensively delivered on, say, GMTV or Sky's breakfast service, especially the ubiquitous lifestyle, fashion and travel items.

So the manner in which Channel 4 went about flagging up the notion of replacing *The Big Breakfast*, and then actually doing so, was by design tentative in the extreme.

A few weeks after the June announcement, a little more information emerged. The new show was to be aimed at 16- to 34-year-olds, and would be entertainment-based. Various production companies and programme makers began to signal their interest and draw up proposals. MTV announced that it intended to submit a bid under the helm of its Director of Programmes and Scheduling, erstwhile C4 youth presenter Murray Boland (son of former Planet 24 executive Tony Boland). Also throwing their hats into the ring were Chris Evans' company Ginger Television, Talkback Productions (responsible for *They Think It's All Over* and numerous other comedy series), Endemol Entertainment UK (the company behind *Big Brother*) and Princess Productions (co-run by original *Big Breakfast* editor Sebastian Scott).

Producers had only to send in a three-page submission at this stage, which perhaps accounted for the reason why C4 ended up receiving 51 proposals in total. But again, what was supposed to happen next was frustratingly unclear.

To start with, the channel had maintained that it would declare its initial findings on or close to Monday 23 July, and ask a shortlist of companies to put together a more detailed bid by August 10. Nothing more was heard until the end of July, however, when C4 suddenly extended its original deadline and asked everyone concerned for another three-page proposal by Thursday 2 August. Confusingly, the channel was now expressing a desire to see pitches aimed more at the upper end of that key 16- to 34-year-old target range, and for a greater topical element.

The significance of this uncertainty is summed up by former *Big Breakfast* editor Ruth Wrigley who was now based at Endemol and playing a key role in developing ideas for the new breakfast programme. "I think the channel hadn't quite worked out what it wanted to do," she argues. "When you read the detailed document about what it wanted, it was *The Big Breakfast*. There was nothing new; there wasn't a radical new thing at all."

Even so, producers had to do their best to grapple with the channel's ambiguous requests, and submit the information required as best they could. After a few more weeks, a proper shortlist of eight companies was drawn up. Endemol, Talkback and Planet 24 all won a place, as did MTV who had teamed up with the independent company, At It (makers of C4's *Jo Whiley* show); RDF Media (*Scrapheap Challenge* and *Shipwrecked*); Monkey Kingdom (comprising former Ginger Television staff David Granger and Will MacDonald); a joint bid from Princess Productions and BSkyB; and The Liam Hamilton Consortium (headed by the eponymous former editor of GMTV). Everyone then sat back to play the waiting game.

On screen, *The Big Breakfast* carried on as if nothing was happening, and made little attempt to present itself as a genuine contender for maintaining its slot. The running order was still awry, Richard Bacon was busy cultivating a snippy relationship with newsreader Jasmine Lowson, and Roland Rat of all people was hired to 'co-host' for a week, prompting inevitable 'Rat Joins Sinking Ship' tabloid comparisons with TV-am.

An unexpected diversion came in the shape of the terrorist attacks on the United States on 11 September. *The Big Breakfast* was immediately dropped and a temporary early-morning edition of *Channel 4 News*, hosted by one of its regular anchors Krishnan Guru-Murthy, installed in its place. This proved to be so effective, both in terms of presentation and ratings, that Channel 4 started wondering whether it had been wrong about its initial specifications regarding the new show, and if it should actually be aiming for a more news-based service instead. Guru-Murthy was so convincing as a breakfast host that one executive was moved to declare, "He could just as easily interview Kylie Minogue as Colin Powell."

With C4 still refusing to categorically state that *The Big Breakfast* had been axed, the indecision was compounded further by the way the field of contenders kept changing. Endemol pulled out in September, declaring it could not effectively realise its pitch within the budget set by Channel 4. The whole process was then held up to allow C4's new Controller of Entertainment, Danielle Lux, to make a proper contribution. Finally it was announced that the decision over which two or three short-listed companies were to make pilots would be revealed in the week beginning October 8, and that the completed pilots were to be delivered by November 7.

One consequence of these endless delays was that C4's schedules became increasingly tarnished by the lingering presence of *The Big Breakfast*, which continued to haemorrhage viewers. It began to look like whoever ultimately did take over might inherit close to no audience at all. It was not until October 11 that it was confirmed that Talkback and Planet 24 had been asked to make pilots, and only at the end of the month did news come of a similar invitation being extended to RDF and BSkyB/Princess. The intervening period had been filled with rumours. At one stage, Princess was supposed to have bagged Krishnan Guru-Murthy, and RDF had pitched a show that mixed the spirit of off-the-wall game show *Banzai* with topical news. Talkback then insisted that it had signed up Guru-Murthy, to which Planet 24 retorted that it had lined up Radio 1 DJ Chris Moyles as host.

If C4 hoped that naming the quartet of lucky bids would help clear up proceedings, it was wrong. Matters became still more complicated on November 6 when Endemol was abruptly allowed back into the race on condition that it paid for its own pilot. Danielle Lux had to struggle to placate an angry Peter Fincham (from Talkback), Stephen Lambert (RDF) and Henrietta Conrad (Princess) at a drinks party for outgoing C4 boss Michael Jackson. When the delivery date for pilots was put back to Monday November 12, more hysterical speculation ensued. RDF let slip that it was hoping to bag BBC Choice presenter Christopher Price and *Girlie Show*-host Claire Gorham as their front-line team. Talkback retorted by claiming that it had recruited BBC *Working Lunch* front man Adrian Chiles.

Just when it started to look as if it would not even be over by the end of the year, Channel 4 came to a decision. On December 20, it declared that the joint BSkyB/Princess Productions bid had been victorious. It capped a memorable week for the satellite broadcaster, as just a few days earlier the company had won another terrestrial contract to produce an early morning bulletin for Channel Five. And though the news was somewhat buried in the festivities of the season, there was still a sense of relief, if not jubilation, across the media that an era was at last being brought to an end.

As had been the case with TV-am a decade earlier, once *The Big Breakfast*'s fate was sealed, its last few months were seen out to a chorus of endless hand-wringing and a highly unbecoming bitterness.

No attempt was made to disguise the way that the programme's production was being wound down. Presenters held up phone cards with out of date fax numbers on, before adding flippantly, "If you've got a fax don't send one, cos we haven't had a machine for six months." On Monday 18 February, Zig and Zag returned for what was billed as "the next six weeks", or to be more precise the last ever six weeks, but even they could not quite live up to their former glories, and were not helped by appearing at a different time every single morning.

The general air of incompetence also seemed to increase. On Monday 25 February, the news bulletin at 7am had to be scrapped and a stand-in found to read the subsequent updates because no one in the office had remembered that Jasmine Lowson had booked the day off. Richard Bacon took to beginning each programme appearing self-consciously scruffy or talking to someone else rather than paying attention to the camera. When a few choice clips from the previous ten years were aired, even footage from the patchy late 1990s appeared of a high standard compared with the current effort.

A diligent Keith Chegwin consigns all traces of The Big Breakfast to deep underground

Friday 29 March 2002 was the last ever show. It was an occasion sorely lacking in dignity. There was no sign of a much-speculated appearance from Chris Evans or of the house exploding, but there was plenty of grisly self-aggrandisement. The programme was extended by an extra hour, and the house packed with cheering folk of no particular identity, plus a guest band who seemed out of place on account of being talented. Vanessa Feltz was present, conveniently forgetting how she had previously quit the show over principles and a plate of baked beans; while out on location, Keith Chegwin took great pleasure in symbolically planting a *Big Breakfast* 'time capsule' in someone's front garden in Stevenage.

Perhaps the lowest point of all came in another live OB with Mike McLean. Having earlier made great play of transporting the giant gnome that usually sat in the programme's garden to a mystery venue, the address in question turned out to be a suspiciously familiar location. "For the first time ever," McLean confusingly began, "I'm going to reveal its new spiritual home." It was C4's headquarters at 124 Horseferry Road, London. "This is the home of the powers-that-be," McLean continued, and in a wholly unbecoming and bitter gesture the camera pulled back to show that the gnome had been deposited directly opposite the entrance to the Channel 4 HQ and was giving a two-fingered salute to newly appointed Chief Executive Mark Thompson. "It's the very least we can do after all the sh...stuff they've given us over the last nine and a half years," McLean concluded.

During the last hour of *The Big Breakfast*'s life, a mini-documentary was shown, filled with former presenters speaking about their time on the series. Here, finally, the real significance of the whole occasion hit home, especially on glimpsing clips and anecdotes from the early years and hearing former presenters testify to the programme's founding strengths. Then it was back to the house for a raucous sing-along before the hosts danced away over the canal bridge. No one seemed that emotional, and there certainly weren't any tears. In fact, nobody seemed bothered at all. It was easy to feel the same.

Even the absolute end was a botched job. After a welcome burst of the original theme tune, a highly evocative montage of sound clips was played while a camera depicted the interiors of the now deserted house. The mood was then promptly shattered by a crass and very cheap computer graphic of the property being blown up.

Just where had it all gone wrong? The answer has to lie with *The Big Breakfast*'s early ratings success, which had so taken both Planet 24 and Channel 4 by surprise. It fundamentally altered expectations of the show, and meant that *The Big Breakfast* changed from being perceived as a rather unpredictable outsider to a mainstream player in the breakfast TV market. This reached its zenith in 1993 when the programme was attracting audiences of around two million. But such an achievement set a benchmark against which the show's future performance would always be judged. Anything less than a maximum audience of two million would be regarded as evidence of a decline, and ultimately a failure – as proved to be the case. So the show was effectively disabled by its own triumphs, and ratings inevitably fell as it aged and lost its early distinctiveness.

The problem then became one of finding a way to constructively draw upon and revisit *The Big Breakfast*'s initial accomplishments in a way that did not simply involve bringing back all the original and increasingly tired features. But almost every sequential relaunch seemed to only make things worse, prolonging the confusion still further. *The Big Breakfast*'s decline could and should have been far better managed. Ideally, the programme should have ended long before 2002, but for various reasons (legal, contractual, and indecision on the part of C4) it remained on air long past the point where it had lost all novelty value and potential to be exciting, entertaining television.

Accordingly, to try to generate a reason for its existence in the schedules, Planet 24 kept desperately revamping the show in the hope that it would one day get it right. But this merely looked like vacillation and, when the makeovers kept going wrong, incompetence. It all led to perhaps *The Big Breakfast*'s biggest blunder of all, the relaunch of January 2001. Because this was such a public event, when it did backfire, the fall-out was all the more of a disaster.

"I guess the truth is that the novelty had worn off and it was never going to be possible to recreate it," concludes Michael Atwell. "The channel probably should have killed it off a few years earlier, but on the other hand, you can't kill something off without replacing it with something, and until you know what you've got to replace it with, you're better limping along with what you've got and try and make it work." Stifling pressure meant that *The Big Breakfast* was unable to bow out when tradition dictates all successful creations should take their leave: at the peak of their game. Instead, it had to settle for a ponderous descent into tedium and pointlessness, an affliction that did little for the overall health of British breakfast television.

NINETEEN

"No puppets, dancing girls or whooping crew members"

While *The Big Breakfast* had been heading towards its raucous demise, an illustrious band of TV executives were grappling with the task of realising the show's replacement. The team behind what would become Channel 4's third breakfast television service ignored the possibility that they were being handed a particularly toxic chalice, and instead approached their task brimming with self-confidence and a certainty that their undertaking would be a great success.

At the heart of the BSkyB/Princess Productions operation was a trio of accomplished and experienced media figures. There was renowned 'safe pair of hands' BSkyB Director of Broadcasting and Production Mark Sharman. Alongside him was James Baker, ex-TV-am presenter and producer, *Big Breakfast* consultant, GMTV producer and now Sky Head of Content and Creative Affairs. Then there was perhaps the most important person of all: Princess Productions' joint Managing Director, Sebastian Scott.

Back in 1992, Scott had proved vital in helping to turn *The Big Breakfast* format into workable, popular and remunerative television. Now it was Princess who had come to be perceived by Channel 4 as the key ingredient to the foundation and viability of *The Big Breakfast*'s successor. Certainly, the channel argued, Sky may be providing facilities and financial security as well as a solid production base, but Princess would supply the all-important personality and attitude.

Scott and fellow ex-*Big Breakfast* executive Henrietta Conrad had formed Princess in 1996. A consistent and impressive track record of output – including daily entertainment series *Light Lunch*, wry business quiz *Show Me The Money,* and most recently a makeover for Channel Five's topical talk show *The Wright Stuff* – suggested that more good things lay ahead. The fact that Scott's name was now once more attached to breakfast television meant that from the outset, press interest in the company's latest effort was unwavering.

A few sketchy details about the new show had emerged in the immediate wake of C4 announcing Sky and Princess's victory. Sky Sports presenter Kirsty Gallacher was definitely on board as a host. The programme was to be broadcast from BSkyB's existing HQ in SW London, a 75-strong production team would be employed, and Scott was to be Executive Producer. News bulletins would come from Sky News, augmented by footage from Sky Sports, CBS, Fox, and Reuters – and the show's initial contract would run for an entire 12 months.

Beyond that, however, information on what the programme would actually be about was noticeably scarce. Indeed, it would prove a frustratingly long time before specifics concerning the shape and tone of *The Big Breakfast*'s replacement became common knowledge.

To begin with, aspirations were spoken of in the broadest of terms, or simply not at all. Mark Sharman regularly waxed lyrical on the brave new dawn approaching, trumpeting, "The success of this bid is a resounding endorsement of Sky's pool of production talent and Princess's leading role as a producer of live daily programmes."

It was not until late February, exactly one month before *The Big Breakfast* was due to end, that the sophistry was swapped for substance. Concrete plans for the show were announced by its newly appointed editor, Mark Killick, another figure with an impressive track record. Killick had come straight from the BBC, where he had held the post of Creative Director for Consumer Programmes and had previously helped to expose the notorious Robert Maxwell pension scandal. Outlining his latest project, Killick struck a familiar tone of eloquence mixed with bravado. C4's new breakfast programme would be: "The TV equivalent of the *Sun*. We think of *BBC Breakfast* as a broadsheet like the *Times*, while GMTV is mid-market – the *Daily Mail*... This is going to be a very aggressive pursuit of audiences and we will aggressively seek out new viewers. What we are looking for is news with a twist. We will have news in an entertainment wrapper."

But with this outburst came the first signs that all was not well amongst the new generation breakfast telly dream team. Killick's remarks were pointedly and hastily dismissed by C4, for fear of provoking cries of 'dumbing down'. His exposition also sat somewhat at odds with the line being peddled by BSkyB, who continued to refer to the new programme exclusively in generalisations.

It was clear that communications between the various parties – Channel 4, BSkyB and Princess – were not as well organised as they had seemed. The conflicting pronouncements also suggested both confusion and indecision over the character of the new programme. If a tangible identity for the show had been decided, why couldn't and shouldn't it be articulated?

With confirmation that there would be an interregnum between the end of *The Big Breakfast* and the start of its successor – but no precise details as to how long it would be – an air of listlessness descended upon proceedings. Channel 4 announced that it wanted to see the new programme getting 500,000 regular viewers by Christmas, but would it even be on the air by then? Aside from the announcement in mid-February that existing Sky News presenter Chris Rogers had been confirmed as a second host, nothing else was known. Word came that Henrietta Conrad had even flown out to New York to inspect current US breakfast output for inspiration.

The key problem was proving to be the composition of the presenting team. In order to honour the format of the pilot, which had involved no less than five people cramped behind one desk, all facing the camera, Scott and Conrad needed at least another two hosts. The amount of time it was taking to find them implied either a surfeit of potential contenders or a dearth of anyone suitable at all.

Their ominously protracted search was not concluded until Monday 25 March, the week of *The Big Breakfast*'s farewell, when the lucky pair were named as Capital Radio DJ Edith Bowman and Sky Sports rugby front man Mark Durden-Smith. At the same time, it was announced that the show would go under the name *Rise*, intended to emulate other contemporaneous popular one-word products such as the magazine *Heat*. The word *Rise* was to be pedantically written on-screen as *RI:SE* with the intention that the letters would look like, and be substituted with, the hours and minutes of a digital clock. This curious affectation confirmed the programme makers had one eye on style. Details on the whereabouts of any content were still in short supply.

As the launch date neared, the presenting team swelled still further. RTE host Liz Bonnin was recruited to front entertainment news, while the vague-sounding 'features' were to be covered by Radio One DJ Colin Murray together with journalist and BBC local radio broadcaster Henry Bonsu. This phalanx of presenters, it was confirmed, would appear on-screen all together or in groups of two or three, but never alone. Clues also emerged concerning the look of the show. Immediacy and functionality were the keywords here: there were to be no sofas or fussy sets, no opening or closing credits, no cameras getting into shot, and certainly no banter with the production team. Instead, emphasis was placed on all things hi-tech. *Rise* would boast ultra-modern graphics, a 'six-pack' of news every half-hour, a 'ticker' scrolling across the screen, and hand-held e-mail devices called 'blackberries' given to all the presenters, allowing viewers to contact them directly.

It all sounded very glossy and modern, but as for what *Rise* would actually be about, all viewers had to go on was Sebastian Scott's bombastic pre-debut eulogy that the show would be "for people who want to know about Bin Laden, Beckham and Britney Spears".

The first ever edition began at 6.55am on Monday 29 April 2002. Though nothing actually went wrong, the much-vaunted "no-nonsense" approach and all out effort to downplay the significance of the occasion made for a

*Mark Durden-Smith and a plethora of producers
breeze in – and out – of Channel 4*

distinctly clinical event lacking in both sparkle and energy. With no grand gestures to occupy attention, the viewer could not help but focus in on the minutiae of the programme – and it was here that *Rise* could be found wanting.

Ever since 1983, breakfast TV launches had been ceremonial affairs that demanded to be watched. This one was quite different. The presenters were even talking amongst themselves when the cameras went live. It was also telling that it had been deemed important to begin with a list of what *Rise* was not, rather than what it was. "There are no puppets, dancing girls or whooping crew members", announced a rather foppish Mark Durden-Smith, his shirt unbuttoned almost to his navel. Only then came the "*Rise* promise": "We'll give you all you need to know about everyone you care about, in just 30 minutes."

The show did indeed unfold in half-hour chunks, each virtually identical in content. Priority was given to high-profile show biz gossip, celebrity appearances and scandals. The 'six-pack' turned out to be a two-minute dash through half a dozen stories spliced with melodramatic sounds and images. They were delivered by a slightly ill at ease Chris Rogers, who had to contend with the news 'ticker' inching distractingly beneath his nose and rather undermining his entire role.

It seemed something of an oversight not to have booked a big-name guest for the debut show. Instead, viewers had to make do with US comic Denis Leary, who looked unsure of quite what he had stumbled into. Most alarming of all was the behaviour of the presenting team, who consistently gave an impression of ignoring the TV audience completely. Throughout the programme, they interrupted and talked over each other, swapped mumbled in-jokes, and bickered about who was to make the coffee. It was almost as if they wanted viewers to feel unwelcome.

Perhaps inevitably, ratings for the first show were not good. An average of 200,000 viewers – just 5% of the audience share – tuned in, lower than GMTV, *BBC Breakfast* and BBC2. Channel 4 bravely argued that this was not a cause for concern, and that *Rise* was for "a totally different market. It's absolutely not in the business of attracting viewers from GMTV or *Breakfast*." Yet this did beg the question as to where exactly its audience, which was supposed to improve upon *The Big Breakfast*'s tiny rump of erstwhile devotees, was going to come from.

Press response to the debut edition was more tepid and 'so what?' than exceptionally negative. What really hit the headlines happened just four days later: the sudden departure of editor Mark Killick. This surprise exit was something of a record, not just in breakfast television, but the TV industry as a whole. Few could believe that before *Rise* had even completed its first week on air, one of its chief mentors had walked. All the man left behind was a brief parting memo: "Hi everyone. You probably noticed that Princess Productions and I have had a series of differences of opinion over the past few weeks. Anyway, suffice to say that we have come to the end of our road together and I am leaving the show. Good luck with it."

As a news story, Killick's exodus compounded the fact that *Rise*'s ratings had refused to move off the 200,000 mark throughout its first five days, and created the unfortunate perception of a programme already in freefall. Attempts to dampen down the hysteria were not aided by the inevitable round of recriminations. "Sources" claimed that the pilot edition of *Rise* had been "completely different" to the version now on screen and had a much "edgier news content". Another testament ran, "He just didn't get it. Mark Killick going is not about anything that's gone on in the last four days... he was out of kilter with the rest of the production team and in particular with Sebastian Scott." C4 chipped in with typically loaded remarks: "It had become obvious for some time that Mark's interpretation of the show was at odds with the rest of the production team. We wish him well in the future."

Away from the name-calling, the whole affair confirmed the extent of the problems underpinning the entire project. This was the kind of crisis that should have been resolved long before *Rise* hit the air; the fact that it had not been was an indictment of the whole operation, and one that did not bode well for the future.

Killick was hurriedly replaced with Deborah Turness, deputy editor of Channel Five News. She inherited a programme that already commanded little or no positive press or publicity, a miniscule portion of viewers, a confusing format and flawed presentation. Within a few weeks, she also faced the first rumours of a change in the presenting line-up.

At the start of June, the *Sunday Mirror*, which had already predicted the show's demise the previous month, reported that Colin Murray was about to quit, unhappy with plans to scale down his studio presence and revamp the output. Of all the *Rise* team, Murray had arguably proved least convincing on screen, a combination of his rather diffident personality and his exact function being never properly defined to viewers. If anyone were to go, in order to thin the numbers, he seemed to be the most obvious candidate.

A spokesperson quickly denied all such rumours, claiming that the presenting team was safe and everyone was here to stay. Nonetheless, talk of plans to tinker with the format proved to be well founded. Sebastian Scott went on record to confirm that changes were already in the pipeline. *Rise* would now be switching to more "conventional" means of telling stories, more reporters would be assigned to outside broadcasts, and more on-screen trailing of upcoming items would be used to make the show "easier to navigate". Scott summed up the strategy by acknowledging that viewers had simply not embraced the programme's initial approach to newscasting. "Audiences want familiarity," he admitted. "Telling everything in 30 minutes is not what they want."

Confidence that they knew exactly what viewers wanted had formed the basis of BSkyB/Princess's original pitch for the breakfast contract. Scott's remarks seemed to imply that audiences were now at fault for desiring something different to that which *Rise* was providing. All the same, changes duly followed. The number of presenters on the main desk dropped to three, helped by the quiet and unpublicised exit of Henry Bonsu. The 'six-pack' was ditched, but only in name, so Chris Rogers still read half a dozen stories in each bulletin, a practice which now made even less sense than before. A newspaper review and more guests were also added.

Yet ratings remained embarrassingly low. Though audiences had climbed a little during June, thanks to interest in the World Cup, and peaked at 400,000 after some unsubtle endorsement of *Big Brother,* when the reality game show ended, the figures instantly dropped and by late August were back to 200,000.

Little by little, the precepts intoned by Mark Durden-Smith at the start of the very first programme fell apart. The hi-tech elements vanished. The 'news ticker' and the 'blackberry' e-mail devices were scrapped. Presenters started running and whooping around the studio. Cameras and crew members began to get into shot. Semi-regular performances were introduced at the end of each show from a selection of musical guests, and Durden-Smith, along with other presenters, would join in with them, 'dancing' alongside the featured artists in an embarrassingly self-conscious manner.

Meanwhile, the one issue that had so maligned *The Big Breakfast* a few years into its existence took root on *Rise* after just a matter of weeks. This was the otherwise simple matter of keeping the same faces on screen every day. Due to the presenting team numbering almost half a dozen and the main desk only being large enough to realistically accommodate three at a time, different combinations of hosts kept showing up without warning. This made the programme seem at best tending towards the anonymous, and at worst downright disorganised. Neither had any thought apparently been given as to who could best deputise for the person who had been promoted as the chief presenter, Mark Durden-Smith. Whenever he was absent, an entirely new individual was brought in, seemingly at random, such as jobbing Channel 4 faces Al Convy or Richard Blackwood.

On Monday 30 September, it was announced that Deborah Turness had quit. A spokeswoman for *Rise* claimed that she had left on good terms ("She did a great job, we enjoyed working with her and wish her well"), but her departure spoke volumes about the climate behind the scenes. How could any of its on-screen problems be corrected if editorially *Rise* remained prey to senior staff coming and going every few months?

Sampling the show in its present state was like seeing history spooling backwards before your eyes, and the fabric of breakfast TV unravelling in gruesome, close-up detail. The arrival of a studio sofa suggested that proceedings were turning into a poor copy of GMTV. Then some noisy, slapstick games were introduced and summoned up memories of *The Big Breakfast* in its twilight years. Colin Murray went on his way in October. Shortly afterwards came news that the old *Big Breakfast* house had been destroyed by fire, reputedly the work of arsonists. It was somewhat ironic that, having been 'blown up' by computer at the end of the final show, the residence now lay in actual ruins.

As the 20th anniversary of British breakfast television loomed, it all seemed rather depressing and sad. It was hard to believe that things had gone so off the rails. Talk increasingly turned to the prospect of *Rise* receiving yet another revamp, this time on an unprecedented scale. It was speculated that, on the appointment of the show's third editor in six months, the entire programme would have to be completely remodelled. It would even be moved from its present rather isolated location to somewhere nearer central London where guests would be more inclined to travel.

Against news that ratings had slid to a miniscule 155,000, a full relaunch for the show was confirmed. From January 2003, *Rise* was to be based inside Whiteley's shopping centre in Bayswater – a setting recalling one of the proposals that Michael Grade had received and rejected as a replacement for the Channel 4 Daily. The new editor was Justin Gorman, a producer with a background in entertainment programming including the talent shows *Popstars* and *Model Behaviour*. Charged with revamping *Rise* from top to bottom, he immediately sacked Liz Bonnin and Chris Rogers and took the entire show off the air for a month to give everyone time to take stock and regroup.

This was a bold and much needed display of commitment and action. Sebastian Scott was careful to give Gorman his full support, underlining how, "The show will return with a fresh look and feel. Currently all aspects of the show are under review and these changes will be honed when off air." Indeed, while off air, the scale of the "review" became larger by the day. Kirsty Gallacher chose to jump before she was pushed and then Mark Durden-Smith announced that he too had decided to leave.

A period of mayhem followed as all sides blamed each other for failing to secure a workable role for Durden-Smith within the programme's new format. His exit also forced Gorman to bring forward news of a brand new presenter whose appointment had only just been finalised. Iain Lee was to have hosted *Rise* alongside Durden-Smith and Edith Bowman. The erstwhile front man of the beleaguered satirical effort, *The 11 O'Clock Show,* now found himself as the show's only male presenter. In addition, it meant that Edith Bowman became the only remaining member of *Rise*'s original line-up.

Finally, just days before the revamped programme was due back on air, it was revealed that the final half-hour of each edition would be independently presented by comediennes Mel Giedroyc and Sue Perkins. The pair had found success several years earlier with the Princess production *Light Lunch*. It was clearly hoped that they could recreate the same magic all over again.

The new model *Rise* debuted on Monday 20 January 2003, almost 20 years to the day since *Breakfast Time* began. Whiteley's shopping centre instantly presented itself as a decidedly unconvincing location for a breakfast programme. An outside shot revealed the building to be remote, grimy, and shrouded in the darkness of the pre-dawn: quite the last thing you wanted to see on a TV screen first thing in the morning.

Edith Bowman made a point of displaying the half-finished set, as if viewers were supposed to be impressed with the fact that the programme's shower facilities hadn't yet been built. With its cavernous interiors, wooden floors and angular furniture, the new studio had an air of icy functionality. There was precious little sense of warmth flowing out to encourage an audience to feel welcome. An artificial and incredibly noisy breakfast bar peopled by ordinary members of the public added to the off-putting ambience.

Content-wise, the programme had been reformatted to resemble a chat show with topical guests and more of those *Big Breakfast*-style games. But saddled with a front man who had something of a reputation for being cynical and unsympathetic on camera, the reworked *Rise* demonstrated more than ever the dangers of misreading the medium of early morning telly, where talking *to* rather than *at* viewers is vital, and large doses of humility, sincerity and infectious enthusiasm are essential. Instead, Iain Lee dominated proceedings, demanding that viewers experience the programme on his terms while upstaging his co-host in the process.

There was also nothing in the new format that other shows and channels had not already done, which was not in itself unusual, except that *Rise* failed to do any of them better, or in a way that encouraged viewers to tune in day after day. The news bulletins were now completely isolated from the rest of the programme, marginalized so as to somewhat lose significance. Mel Giedroyc's and Sue Perkins' self-conscious patter, endless courting of the frivolous, plus their melodramatic matronly turns of phrase exhibited their well-honed professionalism, but also served to highlight the fact they were doing exactly the same act they had five years ago, only less convincingly and without the same poise.

Within a few days, the familiar pattern of events began again. News came that viewing figures had dropped to 100,000. A few weeks later, audiences were so low that the first section of the programme regularly scored a zero rating. Edith Bowman announced she was leaving as soon as her contract ended in March.

Then war broke out in Iraq, and from Thursday 20 March ITN launched a temporary emergency news bulletin to run every weekday from 7 to 8.10am. Wisdom suggested that here at last was a convenient exit strategy for Channel 4 – but it was not to be the case. *Rise* continued to air from 8.10 to 9.30am, looking more unnecessary and undignified than ever before. When the war concluded in April, moreover, it reverted to its previous length and introduced *Big Brother* 2003 winner Kate Lawler as a new presenter. The appointment reflected *Rise*'s growing preoccupation with anything to do with reality TV; indeed, by the summer barely a day was passing without a grinning troupe of faces from the latest reality effort (be it BBC, ITV or C4) turning up to bask in the show's dubious patronage. The programme appeared desperate to associate itself with anything resembling the current talk of the tabloids, readily surrendering hours of airtime to dozens of celebrity wannabes. At the heart of it all, Lawler played the role of unquestioning, often-lifeless spectator to Iain Lee's relentless court jester and often crude interrogations.

As the year rolled on, the press repeatedly intimated that the plug was about to be pulled. For a time it seemed that C4 boss Mark Thompson and his staff were too busy attending to other facets of their station to work out what to do with their resident breakfast albatross. Finally, however, *Rise*'s stubborn failure to generate convincing ratings, let alone talked-about television, demanded action.

"Everyone involved in the show has worked very hard," announced Tim Gardam, C4 Director of Programmes, on Friday 19 September, "and there is no doubt it has improved in quality and content and is now a confident programme. But we have to reluctantly concede that *Rise* is not going to grow a sufficient audience to justify it continuing into a third year." As such, the programme would come off air for good in December 2003.

This long-expected news might have been the cue for an outbreak of rejoicing throughout the media. Instead, perhaps because speculation had dragged on for so long, word of *Rise*'s cancellation was greeted with rather muted, weary relief. The programme was coming to an end at last, but its passing represented the failure of yet another breakfast service. And while Channel 4 had at last found the nerve to deal with the one persistently weak point in its schedules, it now had an equally troublesome problem on its hands: thinking up something to put in *Rise*'s place.

TWENTY

"Like nitro-glycerine in a spin dryer"

January 2003 was a particularly significant month for seasoned players of the breakfast television game. It was exactly 20 years since Britain's TV screens had first played host to daily breakfast programmes, and one decade since TV-am had made way for GMTV. At a number of high-profile social events and parties, various figures from past and present gathered to review all that had taken place since that wintry Monday morning when Frank Bough had first welcomed viewers to the warm furnishings and red sofas of Lime Grove.

It was a time for fond nostalgic reminiscence, but also for sober reflection. Breakfast TV had come a long way in its 20 years. It had evolved from a quaint experiment regarded with suspicion and scepticism into a medium that had become a mainstay of the television landscape.

Now, however, all those working within breakfast TV knew that they faced substantial and pressing questions over maintaining remunerative relations with viewers, investors and broadcasters into the future. Such an illustrious anniversary afforded a useful opportunity to survey the condition of this most influential of TV genre. What had it accomplished? What lessons could be drawn from its history? And what chance did it have in a world of ever-growing competition for television audiences and multiplying channels?

A spirit of endless reinvention had manifested itself throughout GMTV's existence, but it became noticeably more pronounced as the company notched up its first decade. A self-conscious flirtation with 'reality television' had inspired the feature 'Inchloss Island' in 2001, where five strangers were abandoned on a remote outcrop off the south coast of England and monitored while they tried to lose weight. The following year, the station dabbled in another prevalent TV trend, talent shows, in the shape of 'Tot Stars' which featured children between the age of five and 11 singing famous songs.

Both projects had won GMTV decent sized audiences and a healthy portion of publicity, yet these and other forays into different programming styles seemed indicative of the number of choices the station now faced. Should GMTV seek to integrate closer in spirit and ethos to ITV as a whole, concentrate on promoting its own brands and personalities, or simply reject all talk of expansion and focus solely on preserving its core service?

The dilemma was compounded by the lengthening shadow of behind-the-scenes chicanery. For all its various streamlining tactics and development strategies, Managing Director Paul Corley had to lead GMTV's 10th birthday celebrations against the murmur of rumoured takeovers. More than ever, it seemed that the future of ITV's breakfast service would not be decided on screen, but off camera, around boardroom tables and behind locked doors. Every week came new tales of supposed infighting amongst ITV's top players, or the likely consequences of a merger between the two giant companies Carlton and Granada. Just as a handful of suits had dispatched TV-am to oblivion, so the existence of GMTV appeared to rest solely in the hands of a dozen or so faceless executives.

As if this was not enough, there continued the vexing matter of just how to interpret the station's recent ratings performance. The figures made for a confusing picture, as the total proportion of breakfast viewers was not getting any larger, but it seemed that audience preferences had become more fluid and changeable.

One beneficiary appeared to be Channel Five, who now regularly beat Channel 4 in terms of early morning ratings, mainly off the back of its kids' output. Channel Five had by now also introduced a live feed from the Sky News breakfast show *Sunrise*, which had made its debut on terrestrial screens on 7 January 2002. Long-serving GMTV executives were unable to suppress a wry smile when remembering this was the show that had forced its own name change back in 1992.

Nonetheless, the very fact that GMTV had even made it to its 10th birthday, and in relatively rude financial health, was a considerable achievement. Such had been the tide of critical adversity coupled with economic obligations that washed over the company on its launch in 1993 that it had been tempting on more than one occasion to ascribe it a future of never-ending mayhem and mediocrity.

Instead, the GMTV of 2003 boasted an assured and confident on-screen personality and an extremely precise grasp of who its audience was and what it wanted to see. It may not have possessed a line-up of presenters or features as instantly resonant or inclusive as *Breakfast Time* or TV-am, but through a combination of accident and design, it had evolved into an undeniably popular exponent of mainstream breakfast television.

Its founder, Greg Dyke, now reflects, "When GMTV won its licence, it banked on a number of things: that Channel 4 would never produce a popular television breakfast show, which it [then] did, and that the BBC would never play children's [programmes] on BBC2, which it did. But if you look at GMTV over the period of time, in the end it's not a bad business. I think it's lost about £100m over the first ten years. But it's now making ten million a year. It's not a terrible investment."

"I've felt that it's only in the last three or four years we've been seen to have arrived," contests GMTV Director of Programmes Peter McHugh. "When we started generating news in our own right, which other papers and other organisations picked up, then people had to take notice of us. It's also [thanks to] the self-confidence of those who make the programme who, when they get outside of London, realise that breakfast television, whether it's us or the rest, is watched by a lot of people – and some of them have O Levels."

John Stapleton agrees that one of GMTV's lasting strengths is its often-unreported popularity across all parts of the United Kingdom. "The relationship with viewers has got cosier and cosier. Particularly in the provinces. I come from Manchester, and when I go to watch Manchester City FC I get loads of people saying, 'Ah, I love the show.' Certainly there's no question that it's watched by a hell of a lot of people." Stapleton has his own take on the reasons for this enduring success: "I think it's because there's a bit in it for everybody. If you want the part with the news, you watch the *Newshour*; if you want the show biz, you watch a bit later on; if you want the makeover and fashion stuff, you watch Lorraine. A bit like a national newspaper."

GMTV faces a future where its relationship with the rest of the ITV network is drawn far closer than ever before, but at the same time is becoming all the more complex. The company has necessarily ended up increasingly absorbed in trying to develop its identity as a stand-alone broadcaster, while struggling to establish a place within an ITV plagued by falling viewing figures, the costly collapse of its digital service, and ongoing moves towards greater consolidation.

In the face of all this, Peter McHugh remains resolute. "The breakfast television franchise has always been an anomaly from the day it was invented. Will it be subsumed into ITV? Logic suggests yes. Will that be a good thing? I would say, no. I think there's a financial premium to be got from running it as a separate organisation. I think the journalistic ethos of GMTV – and TV-am – has been based on the fact that it's been a separate franchise, bidding and running against the rest of the world. And therefore, if it is subsumed, will that disappear? Probably. If it doesn't happen, it will be because we've made the case that the added financial value of being separately run could be a plus. If we can't prove that, then the 20 years of breakfast television will become just a footnote in history."

Speaking with experience of working across all the mainstream breakfast TV services throughout those 20 years, John Stapleton is similarly robust: "Obviously GMTV will change, things will evolve – they've got to. But it's held up very well against all kinds of competition. GMTV will hold its own well. I don't have much doubt that it will."

Since 1983, TV executives have monitored the fluctuating ratings of breakfast television programmes with feverish attention, reacting to perceived trends and patterns with wild extremes of jubilation and despair. Searching for tangible reasons why viewers choose certain shows over others has proved an equally exhaustive and contentious affair – no more so than when seeking to confront and justify one of the most drawn-out events in breakfast TV's history: the decline of *The Big Breakfast*.

Increased competition undoubtedly played a part. When the series began in 1992, there were really only two other TV breakfast programmes: TV-am and *BBC Breakfast News*. When it ended ten years later, it was up against *BBC Breakfast*, GMTV, kids' shows on BBC2 and Channel Five, plus a whole range of satellite and cable channels.

But *The Big Breakfast* also suffered because it lost the ability to hook increasing numbers of viewers. In the main, people tend to watch breakfast television for brief periods in-between doing other things, such as getting ready to go to school or work. By necessity, therefore, breakfast TV shows have always had to pitch themselves to audiences that will be constantly shifting and channel hopping. And to do this well they need a very obvious, immediate on-screen profile so it is instantly clear from the moment you switch on that, for instance, you are watching the BBC and will be getting a mostly news-based service, or GMTV where it will be features and chat.

For several years after its launch, *The Big Breakfast* had a very strong identity, a well-sequenced format of items and an inclusive feel, all of which meant it could capture and retain viewers. Over its last few years, however, there were so many changes to the show, its presenters and the whole ethos of the programme that it simply became impossible to fathom what exactly '*The Big Breakfast*' as a concept stood for. It was no longer an obvious brand.

Even when the series regained some of its core strengths through the tight and effective relationship between Johnny Vaughan and Denise Van Outen, those qualities proved difficult to sustain once both presenters had moved on. "After Chris Evans and Gaby Roslin, *The Big Breakfast* didn't ever really settle down again until Johnny and Denise," recounts the programme's original Commissioning editor, Michael Atwell. "They stabilised the decline in the ratings, but in a way it didn't solve the problem, because the audience had still disappeared."

"I think *The Big Breakfast* was probably on too long," adds C4 Head of News and Current Affairs David Lloyd, "because it was a programme that was great when it was working, and was a bit cheesy when it stopped working. But there was a constant debate inside the channel as to whether its day was done. And I think maybe a bit of inertia intervened.

After all, it's the only success the channel has ever had at breakfast, so it's not surprising that people clung on to it perhaps a little too long."

One of its first editors, Ruth Wrigley, asserts the significance of *The Big Breakfast*'s basic inability to cope with the passing of time and the need to maintain a vibrant attitude. "Things evolve," she states. "A lot of the success of *The Big Breakfast* was due to Chris and his relationship with Gaby. Mark Little and Zoe Ball were brilliant in their own right, but it just didn't work between them. A similar thing happened when Denise Van Outen went and Johnny Vaughan was left with Kelly Brook. So part of it was down to losing that on-screen relationship, and part of it was the pressure, when you're so cutting edge, to reinvent yourself. You're forced down that line of having to rethink yourself: 'the ratings are slipping, so why don't we repaint the studio a different colour?'" In short, she concludes, "*The Big Breakfast* stopped being must-see TV. It happens to lots of things – you are a victim of your own success. When Johnny Vaughan started to talk for 13, 14 minutes, lo and behold, the ratings started to slip. Viewers just went, 'what?' They didn't have the time."

With British breakfast television remaining as turbulent and competitive as it has always been, the need for a programme to have a clear, enduring persona is paramount. So the fact that *The Big Breakfast*'s replacement, *Rise,* enjoyed a lifespan of precisely 20 months landed Channel 4 with a daunting problem.

Current Chief Executive Mark Thompson has made a point of speaking on several occasions of his desire to see C4 reclaim more of a reputation for niche-based, experimental and groundbreaking output. The presence of *Rise* in the schedules did not help his station cultivate an image of pushing the envelope. Channel 4 was the only place you would ever be likely to see a breakfast show made by Princess Productions, but it did not follow that C4 was right to hand them the franchise, or should have treated the commission as a logical application of its remit. Instead, its decision appeared rooted in a no-risk strategy, with *Rise* perceived as a bankable, solid effort to shore up the station's battered standing in the aftermath of *The Big Breakfast*. Except the whole thing backfired.

For Ruth Wrigley, the blame lay with Channel 4 management: "They weren't clear about what they wanted. Their brief was all a bit of a mishmash, which was what *Rise* was. It tried to please too many people." "The big problem with *Rise* was, who was it aimed at?" contests Michael Atwell. "We were very lucky on *The Big Breakfast* because we got the young families and children, but we also picked up the student and young adult audience, which we weren't expecting to get. When you looked at *Rise,* it was a young adult early morning programme, so maybe they were trying to get the students because they didn't think there was anyone else to get. But the problem is that there are not that many of them – and

*A smug Iain Lee threatens the fall and Rise
of 21st century British breakfast television*

probably not enough in terms of the advertising to pay for an expensive early morning show."

David Lloyd is more precise in his analysis. "I think the problem with *Rise* was simply one of basic design. The presenters were all very well but they didn't have enough to feed on. There was just not enough content. And what I think is now clear [is that] people need *content* in the morning, something that will get them up. It doesn't have to be sombre, or po-faced, but it does have to be content." The programme's persistent vacuum of substance is emphasised by Peter McHugh. "What did you take from [*Rise*] to say to friends? Did you get the news from it? No. The weather? No. Did you get information from it? No. What did you get from it? You got what *The Big Breakfast* had at the end, which was not very much. What was *Rise* proof of? It was proof that, thank God, people keep getting it wrong on telly because if we all got it right we'd be out of a job."

Former *Big Breakfast* Executive Producer Ed Forsdick takes a more philosophical view. "*Rise* appeared to have homogenised the whole genre. I did watch it, and it did give me some of what I want in the morning – but it didn't make me laugh and very rarely surprised me. But perhaps people don't want that any more."

Reflecting on *Rise*'s unhappy birth, brief life and prolonged death, it's useful to recall just how poor *The Big Breakfast* had become on the point of its execution, and how tempting it was at times to acknowledge that virtually any kind of replacement would have been an improvement.

That replacement needed to be something that instantly blew away all memory of its predecessor's unfortunate decline. *Rise* needed to sum up everything about Channel 4 in the 21st century, just as *The Big Breakfast* – at its inception – did about the end of the 20th. Instead, it merely featured people of little substance saying nothing of consequence, and who delivered hardly anything in the way of engaging, inclusive television that encouraged you to repeatedly tune in. From start to finish, its twin chief concerns of topical news and entertainment were catered for more comprehensively and professionally on the BBC and GMTV.

"I hoped it would work for them," asserts erstwhile Channel 4 Daily host Paddy Haycocks, "but I think it was a much more flawed concept than the original Channel 4 Daily. And I think to make the same mistake twice, and for the channel to end up getting 200,000 viewers all over again, I just think it's such an indictment." If breakfast TV on C4 is to survive, innovate and entertain at the same time, it needs to be bold, obviously different from its rivals, treat an audience with respect and promise viewers a return on their investment. A show that actually generated a few memorable moments would be a start.

"There was a great opportunity there that hasn't been exploited," concludes Haycocks. "That younger market, the articulate, opinion-formers, they're important as benchmarks of what's around. They're quite an important opinion-forming lobby. I think that's why *The Big Breakfast* was very successful. That market pushed it. They talked about it, they watched it, they emulated it. *Rise* was a bizarre way of solving that equation. It was a bit like saying 2+2=13. I don't understand how they came up with a number, a balancing number, on the other side."

The BBC notched up 20 years of breakfast television with a programme that possessed far more dynamism and colour than did any of its recent early morning incarnations. *Breakfast* had come to enjoy a competent diet of both hard news and lighter magazine-type features, and, thanks to an overhaul of the presenting line-up, a more engaging tone.

Autumn 2002 had seen a changing of the guard with the rather testy Sophie Raworth and the avuncular Jeremy Bowen replaced by Sky News' Natasha Kaplinsky and, returning to breakfast television after a gap of almost a decade, Dermot Murnaghan. The new pair immediately bonded well, giving the show a major shot in the arm. Ratings also began to creep up on GMTV, until the outbreak of war in Iraq in March 2003 when *Breakfast*'s audiences rocketed. The programme benefited from a clear sense of identity, pace and authority, handled coverage of hostilities far better than did its rivals, and seemed to manage a transition back to 'peacetime' without too much of a jolt. In all, *Breakfast* has gone some way to revitalising the Corporation's early morning output after years of inertia.

"The chief aims [of *Breakfast*] are based on two things," outlines its current editor, Richard Porter. "One, clearly you want to produce a programme that gets as large an audience as possible; but also, working for a BBC programme, you have to do that in a way that upholds your public service responsibilities. And in crude terms that means the BBC will sometimes do things that won't get you the biggest audience. But I do think that you should expect to watch my programme and see the values of BBC1. We are one eighth of BBC1, and there are times where it's obvious when we're connected to them. For example, they did a couple of themed days [in 2002], the NHS Day and the Crime Day, and in both cases they were launched by us with quite extensive coverage."

It can certainly have been no hindrance to have one of breakfast television's most iconic figures in charge of the whole Corporation, even though Greg Dyke insists he had no direct input into *Breakfast*: "I sent in my suggestions and no-one took any notice of them," he observes waspishly.

Despite *Breakfast*'s semi-informal format and relaxed air, there is no disguising the fact that it is at heart a news programme and more in the tradition of *Breakfast News* than its illustrious antecedent *Breakfast Time*. Yet memories of sofas, coffee tables and Weather Windows retain their piquancy, and it is still hard not to feel regret that the BBC once thought it necessary to swap their pioneering breakfast format for what was a very conventional and, as it turned out, depressingly long-running deskbound model. Could – and should – the sofa have lasted longer than it did?

"I felt it could have done," reflects David Lloyd. "I thought it was actually a very intelligent mix. But that wasn't the view of BBC management. And I suppose time has proved them right, because there was no point in tussling it out with TV-am and everybody trying to have a battle of the sofas. What was built in the aftermath of my departure [1986] is how it's been ever since. The idea of making it newsier still has served the BBC well, because it's given them very clear territory which nobody else can really match."

Peter McHugh strongly maintains that whatever good *Breakfast Time* did came about in spite of rather than because of its parent corporation: "*Breakfast Time* was inhabited by three groups of people: those at the top who were going places, a few people coming in at the bottom starting off in television, and the rest, who'd been sent there as punishment and who didn't want to be there. At the BBC you took a job at *Breakfast Time* so you could hopefully bump into somebody important from current affairs in the bar and move on."

Such testimony suggests that it is amazing the original *Breakfast Time* survived for as long as it did. Richard Porter, however, is very conscious, not only of the BBC's eventful history of producing breakfast television, but also of more traditional perceptions of the network. From what he implies, the days of suffering dreary indigestible tracts of financial analysis over tea and toast are a thing of yesteryear. "It's true of BBC news programmes in the past that we've been seen as being remote and a bit authoritarian," he observes, "and not perhaps in tune enough with the real concerns of our audiences. Just by understanding our audience a bit better, and producing items that are still perfectly within the range of what the BBC should be doing, [we can remain] better in tune with what people want to hear and the way they want to hear it."

"I think now it's very much run by the BBC news division, and they don't have producers who are comfortable with feature material," observes *Breakfast Time*'s first editor, Ron Neil. "That was the *Nationwide* legacy – back then people were comfortable with feature production material. Yet we talk about *Breakfast* being much more newsy, but they don't present from behind desks now. So these things are swings and roundabouts."

All the same, the occasion of breakfast television's 20th anniversary was an instructive reminder that the one programme that started it all off and really set a standard for everything that followed only survived in its original form for three years. Nick Ross, one of the first faces of breakfast TV, speculates: "Had the BBC not lost its nerve, some form of the *Breakfast Time* news-and-show biz mix could still survive today. *Breakfast Time* helped set the tone for dozens of daytime shows like GMTV. It strengthened the trend for broadcasters to speak to their viewers as equals. But in one thing it didn't succeed: it didn't survive. Its legacy is therefore fragmented at best."

There is undoubtedly something special about British breakfast television which ensures that those who have had spent time working on any of its incarnations forever retain very strong opinions about it – either hugely positive, or extremely negative, but never anywhere in-between. Peter McHugh remembers how, "That insular feeling at TV-am bound us together, stayed for all time, and was as true then as it is now." GMTV's first Director of Programmes Lis Howell, on the other hand, has a very different attitude. After being forced to resign, she has "never watched GMTV from that day to this. To be perfectly honest, it's not my sort of station. I'm interested in news. The BBC news, the way it looks now, is how I wanted GMTV to be."

Ron Neil outlines how his period on *Breakfast Time* was, "the most bonding experience; you became a very close knit team. I still have extremely close friends as a result of breakfast television. You become very close when you're trying to start something new against the odds. We had a party every Friday morning! Looking back, to start a completely new service, it was pretty exciting. I was very lucky."

Veteran TV-am host Nick Owen speaks warmly of how his old employer inspired great loyalty amongst its staff and bequeathed a legacy that was: "The secure establishment of the genre of breakfast TV. Half the people who work at GMTV were at TV-am, and their format is still very similar to ours." Channel 4 Daily newsreader Carol Barnes, however, sums up the legacy of her programme as simply, "How not to do breakfast TV." And as for her view on contemporary breakfast television, the answer is similarly blunt: "Don't watch it. Enough's enough."

Even after more than 20 years, breakfast television retains a potential for generating a degree of controversy and celebrity beyond that of most other television formats. The reasons lie with a cocktail of factors. Paddy Haycocks identifies the significance of its permanence on TV screens day in day out, year after year: "It's carved out a far more insular space for itself than the rest of daytime and evening programmes. It's almost more clearly defined than anywhere else in the schedule. And that's why everything that happens to it earns a place in copy, in print, in news analysis. There's actually a disproportionate amount of notoriety and interest in what essentially is a comparatively low yielding product within the whole of British TV."

Breakfast television's permanence on the small screen has, over time, resulted in it taking on other facets of a more functional, even psychological, nature. "The thing about breakfast television, as with breakfast radio, is that people switch on almost to be reassured that nothing has happened in the world, and that everything is where it should be," observes former TV-am Director of Programmes Mike Hollingsworth. "One of those reinforcing factors is that you see the same people day after day. If you see a different face, it's slightly jarring. So you switch on to see a friendly face in the corner of the room or at the end of the breakfast table, smiling back at you."

Being the primary source of information as well as reassurance for people waking up in the morning has often handed breakfast television another important obligation: that of being first to brief the country on major events which have transpired while most of the population have been asleep. As Peter McHugh stresses, "There's a whole host of things you need to know. You need to know what's happened overnight. And unlike radio, what [we're] saying to people is, do you want to see the pictures?" Richard Porter chooses to cite something that Ron Neil professed on the launch of *Breakfast Time*. "He said you have to produce a programme that understands what people are doing at that time of day. You have to do things that work in short bursts, because that might be the only time you've got for your audience to concentrate. You have to use simple, straightforward language. You can't have the same approach as *Newsnight*, because you don't have the same relationship with your audience."

Debates and disagreements over just how that relationship should be realised, and how information and entertainment should be presented, have prompted just as much innovation within breakfast television as boardroom showdowns, industrial disputes and sackings. "There's a particular problem with breakfast TV where you employ people for several hours a day at that time of the morning, who have not slept very long," notes Paddy Haycocks. "Those egos can bristle like mad and the psyche can get out of proportion. It's like nitro-glycerine in a spin dryer."

Peter McHugh takes a slightly different line. "When GMTV started rather badly, someone said to me, what's wrong with GMTV [compared to TV-am]? I said, 'The presenters are no better and no worse than any of the previous presenters, the sets are no better and no worse; it's that there are no stories.' And that's been true throughout the 20 years. You don't watch it for the presenters – you watch it for what they're telling you."

Surveying the entire breakfast TV landscape in 2004 in light of all these testimonies produces a picture that, while hedged about with apprehension, expectation and a lot of bravado, is far from dull or predictable. The fortunes of both ITV and the BBC's services seem prey, more than ever, to forces beyond the control of those working at the coalface. Major upheaval may come when GMTV is perceived to have become too uneconomical or unworkable within a single ITV network, or if the BBC is forced into a programme of harsh internal reform in the wake of the Hutton Report and the desperately regrettable resignations in January 2004 of Chairman Gavyn Davies and Director-General Greg Dyke.

The fact that it took so long to scrap *Rise*, however, portends ill for the chances of breakfast TV becoming an arena for new, intelligent, exciting and fun programmes sooner rather than later. The programme's baleful drawn-out presence in the schedules smacked of a parent channel that was both unwilling and unable to come up with a positive, constructive strategy for early morning television. When Mark Thompson spoke in September 2003 of C4's plans for *Rise*'s replacement, he could only rather hazily conclude: "There are advantages in having a live element in the morning. But we don't think Channel 4 has to offer a single live programme. It is not going out to tender: the problem is that no new ideas came through three years ago when this was tried." Sure enough, after *Rise* bowed out in typically crass and clumsy fashion on Friday 19 December 2003, its place in the schedules was taken by a bunch of repeats and US imports – one in particular, *Bewitched*, was 40 years old, while another, *The Salon*, came straight from the channel's forever-bulging portfolio of reality TV shows. C4 have confirmed that they have no plans to launch any kind of new, stand-alone breakfast service in the near future. It seems that viewers seeking a little elucidation and wit over their cereal will, for the moment at least, have to reconcile themselves with one of the big two, the BBC or GMTV – or chance their luck on one of the legion of obscure satellite stations.

Even after over 21 years, however, breakfast television has still not been able to completely overturn generations of prejudice against the idea of sharing your early mornings with a TV set. "It has developed a relationship with viewers," contests Ron Neil, "but it's never had a huge audience on television. The one thing it's never done, which American television did, is become the dominant broadcaster in the morning. To this day radio is still the dominant broadcaster in this country. 20 years ago there was a slight feeling – I remember this quite distinctly – that it was almost immoral to watch television in the morning, that it was rather disgusting. There was a bit of snobbishness about it, and that probably still exists. I think also at that time in Britain it was still very much a one television set society. That one television would be in the sitting room, whereas in America the telly was in the kitchen. So while you were getting the cornflakes, the telly would be on."

"It's never really become as profound in our society as American breakfast television has in the States," Greg Dyke adds. "I suspect it's to do with the strength of national radio. If you go to the States, breakfast television is the biggest thing in show business, and it's never become that big here and I don't think it will. It's probably to do with allocation of resources. I think it's legitimate, but I think a lot of people still don't watch television in the mornings."

If on balance this concluding prognosis appears more gloomy than upbeat, it is worth remembering that history shows how life can pull surprises. Precedent can be just as much ignored as followed. The Channel 4 Daily survived for over three years. Many thought TV-am doomed after just three months. GMTV's launch seemed to represent a macabre case of history repeating itself. Hardly anyone was prepared to accept that *Breakfast Time* would vanquish its rival from day one, let alone set a template for mainstream breakfast TV that continues to this day.

Indeed, one hugely significant motif that resonates throughout the entire history of breakfast television is the contention over just what exactly qualifies as 'success' and 'failure'. Definitions have changed with the seasons to suit whatever agenda is currently at large within the relevant broadcasting authority or TV executive suite. What were accepted as adequate viewing figures for the Channel 4 Daily one month were slammed as derisory the next. *Breakfast Time*'s sofas were reassuring and iconic emblems in 1985, but cumbersome and outdated antiques in 1986.

All long-running programmes are subject to upheaval triggered by a change in top-level management. For breakfast TV, though, the results have always been more dramatic and sweeping, thanks to its unusually prominent public profile. From its birth, breakfast television has attracted attention, speculation and intrigue quite unlike that of any other small screen genre. Its novelty and its celebrity have and probably always will render it unique within the broadcasting landscape.

So while acknowledging the current climate of uncertainty, it is also possible to view it as a potential crucible for something unexpected and, who knows, quite extraordinary. After all, there is one other resounding theme that emerges from a study of breakfast TV: that the struggle to find out exactly what its purpose is, who watches it, what works and what doesn't, can throw up utterly unique and revolutionary creations.

Certainly, the consensus amongst breakfast TV veterans past and present is that the era of originality and experimentation is far from over. "I wouldn't have thought the period of innovation has passed," reflects David Lloyd. "There's no reason why something shouldn't have the same freshness and vitality and originality as *The Big Breakfast* had. Absolutely none." But as Ruth Wrigley argues, "You can't predict these things." For her, the next big leap forward in breakfast TV will "be by accident, and it'll be something that we won't expect".

"I think it's a genre that's still open to innovation," confirms Michael Atwell. "We know that a relatively small proportion of the total audience watches in the morning, but we also know that in other countries, like America, they can get huge numbers of them. So I think it must be possible. And that's where the potential lies. The great thing about television is that it's always reinventing itself, and that'll carry on." Richard Porter strikes a similarly self-assured note when reflecting on the condition of breakfast TV as a whole. "I think the future's pretty secure at the moment. Everybody is mindful of the way the audience is fragmenting; that there are very many more means of getting your news beamed into your house. But I'm pretty confident at the moment. I do think you can get growth by having a better programme. I think it's as straightforward as that."

There are, however, a couple of notable voices that echo a slightly more cautionary air. "I don't see how it's going to evolve," reasons Ron Neil. "I can't see what the next development is. They'll be tweaking; one editor will come in and put in desks, another will take desks out." "It's difficult to know what will happen to [breakfast television] now," adds Greg Dyke; "whether it'll just plod on or whether it's got another jump. You need to look at the behaviour of kids. Little kids clearly are watching satellite television – if not, then BBC2 – but mostly satellite. I suspect it will just fragment like the rest of television."

Their concerns hint at something else that continues to undermine the creation and production of breakfast television: the ongoing struggle of programme-makers and presenters to come to terms with what has already been and gone, and face up to the triumphs and tragedies of breakfast television shows of the past.

The successes and failures of yesteryear become weapons in the armoury of those battling to shape breakfast TV's future. Repeated attempts are made to fashion a programme that emulates times gone by, yet all efforts to recreate a 'golden age' of breakfast television are usually doomed to fail simply because no one can agree on exactly what was 'golden' in the first place. One group of people spent the best part of a decade trying to reconstitute just what it was that made *The Big Breakfast* a hit. Another strived for many years to come up with a formula that effectively combined the substance of *Breakfast News* with the élan of *Breakfast Time*. GMTV, as with TV-am before it, can never afford to rest on its laurels for fear of being outpaced and outflanked by a TV industry constantly in flux.

The longer these – and all shows like them – continue, the harder it is for them to deal with their own past. The upshot is that ideas, schemes and scams, as wildly ambitious as they are blatantly short-sighted, blow up from out of nowhere. They wreak total havoc, complete triumph, or both, and then suddenly pass in a blaze of glory or total embarrassment, leaving a trail of wrecked egos, budgets and reputations in their wakes. That is the essence of breakfast television, and that is why you can guarantee that it is a form of television that will never be anything less than controversial and surprising.

As Michael Grade noted when explaining his decision to replace the Channel 4 Daily with a new programme: "Now that the toothpaste was out of the tube, there was no way of squeezing it back and reverting to blank screens in the morning." There will always be something on television to start the day. So best clear a space for your TV set on the kitchen table, pop some bread in the toaster and start warming the teapot, because in a few moments it'll be...breakfast time.

238

Breakfast Television Principal Personnel

Names are organised in chronological order of appointment
Dates refer to first and last appearance in role
Asterisk denotes still in job as of February 2004

BREAKFAST TIME (BBC1)   1983-1989

BBC Management

George Howard	Chairman (1980-1983)
Ian Trethowan	Director-General (1977-1982)
Alasdair Milne	Managing Director of Television (1977-1982) Director-General (1982-1987)
Aubrey Singer	Managing Director of Radio (1978-1982) Managing Director of Television (1982-1984)
Bill Cotton	Managing Director of Television (1984-1988)
Michael Grade	Controller, BBC1 / Director of Programmes (1984-1987)
Michael Checkland	Director of Resources (1982-1985) Director-General (1987-1993)
John Birt	Deputy Director-General (1987-1993)

Production Team

Ron Neil	Editor (1983-1984)
Tam Fry	Technical Co-ordinator
Mike Hollingsworth	Producer (1983-1984)
David Lloyd	Editor (1984-1986)
Peter McHugh	Producer (1985)
Dave Stanford	Editor (1986-1989)
Bob Wheaton	Editor (1989)

Presenters

Frank Bough	(1983-1987)
Selina Scott	(1983-1986)
Nick Ross	(1983-1986)
Mike Smith	(1983-1986)
Sue Cook	(1983-1986)
Debbie Rix	Newsreader (1983-1985)
Francis Wilson	Weatherman (1983-1989)
David Icke	Sports Correspondent (1983-1985)
Russell Grant	Astrologist (1983-1986)
Diana Moran	Fitness Guru (1983-1986)
Fern Britton	Newsreader / Co-presenter (1983-1984)
Andrew Harvey	Newsreader / Co-presenter (1983-1986)
Guy Mitchelmore	Newsreader / Co-presenter (1983-1986)
Bob Wilson	Sports Correspondent (1984-1989)

Lynn Faulds Wood	Consumer Correspondent (1984-1986)
Steve Blacknell	Entertainment Correspondent (1984-1986)
Zoe Brown	Teenage Correspondent (1985)
Sue Carpenter	Newsreader (1985-1986)
Debbie Greenwood	(1985-1986)
Sally Magnusson	(1985-1989)
Sally Jones	Sports Correspondent (1986-1989)
Jeremy Paxman	(1986-1989)
John Stapleton	(1988-1989)
Kirsty Wark	(1988-1989)
Jill Dando	(1988-1989)
Laurie Mayer	(1989)

TV-AM (ITV)   1983-1992
Management

Peter Jay	Chief Executive and Chairman (1983)
Dick Marsh	Vice-Chairman / Chairman (1983-1984)
Michael Deakin	Director of Programmes (1983-1984)
Jonathan Aitken	Acting Chief Executive (1983)
Timothy Aitken	Chief Executive (1983) Chairman (1984-1988)
Clive Jones	Managing Editor (1983-1984)
Greg Dyke	Editor-in-chief (1983-1984)
Anne Wood	Head of Children's Output (1983-1984)
Peter McHugh	News Editor / Editor (1983-1985)
Roger Frye	Director of Finance (1983-1984)
Tony Vickers	Director of Sales / Managing Director (1983-1992)
Adrian Moore	General Manager (1984-1988)
Kerry Packer	Investor
Bruce Gyngell	Managing Director / Chairman (1984-1993)
Mike Hollingsworth	Programme Controller / Director of Programmes (1984-1985)
Bill Ludford	Controller, News and Current Affairs (1984-1989) Director of Programmes (1989-1992)
Nick Wilson	Producer / Controller, Children's Output (1984-1991)
John McColgan	Weekend Editor / Programme Controller (1984-1986)
Jeff Berliner	News Editor / Controller, News and Current Affairs (1987-1992)
Ian Irvine	Chairman (1988-1992)
Stephen Barden	Managing Editor (1988-1992)

Presenters

David Frost	(1983-1992)
Michael Parkinson	(1983-1984)
Anna Ford	(1983)
Angela Rippon	(1983)
Robert Kee	(1983)
Nick Owen	(1983-1986)
Anne Diamond	(1983-1990)
Lynda Berry	Newsreader / Co-presenter (1983-1984)
Mike Morris	(1983-1992)
Henry Kelly	(1983-1986)
John Stapleton	(1983-1984)
David Philpott	Weatherman (1983-1987)
Wincey Willis	Weather Forecaster (1983-1986)
Lynn Faulds Wood	Consumer Correspondent (1983-1984)
Lizzie Webb	Fitness Expert (1983-1989)
Roland Rat	Superstar (1983-1985)
Timmy Mallett	Children's Presenter (1983-1992)
Chris Tarrant	Contributor (1983)
Gyles Brandreth	Contributor (1983-1990)
Gordon Honeycombe	Newsreader (1984-1989)
Jayne Irving	(1984-1988)
Richard Keys	(1984-1990)
Tommy Boyd	Children's Presenter (1984-1990)
Jonathan Dimbleby	(1985-1986)
Michaela Strachan	Children's Presenter (1985-1992)
Adrian Brown	(1986)
Caroline Righton	(1987)
Alvin Stardust	Children's Presenter (1987-1990)
Kathy Rochford	(1988-1989)
Kathryn Holloway	(1988-1990)
Kathy Tayler	(1989-1992)
Lorraine Kelly	(1989-1992)
Lisa Aziz	Newsreader (1989-1992)
Ulrika Jonsson	Weather Forecaster (1989-1992)
Mike Brosnan	Children's Presenter (1990-1992)
Dr Hilary Jones	Contributor (1990-1992)
Chris Evans	Children's Presenter (1991)

Other

Terry Farrell	Architect
Tim Wight	Shop Steward (ACTT)

BBC BREAKFAST NEWS (BBC1)   **1989-2000**

BBC Management

John Birt	Deputy Director-General (1987-1993) Director-General (1993-2000)
Tony Hall	Head of News and Current Affairs / Director, News (1989-2001)

Production Team

Bob Wheaton	Editor (1989-1994)
Andrew Thompson	Editor (1998-2000)

Presenters

Nicholas Witchell	(1989-1994)
Laurie Mayer	(1989-1991)
Kirsty Wark	(1989-1990)
Sally Magnusson	(1989-1998)
Jill Dando	(1989-1994)
Justin Webb	(1993-1998)
Juliet Morris	(1994-1997)
John Nicholson	(1998-2000)

CHANNEL 4 DAILY (C4)   **1989-1992**

Channel 4 Management

Michael Grade	Chief Executive (1988-1997)
Liz Forgan	Director of Programmes (1988-1993)
David Lloyd	Commissioning Editor, News and Current Affairs (1987-2003)
Michael Atwell	Commissioning Editor (1988-1993)

Presenters

Carol Barnes	Newsreader (1989-1990)
Paddy Haycocks	*Streetwise* (1989-1990)
Debbie Greenwood	*Streetwise* (1989-1990)
Garry Rice	*Box Office* (1989-1990)
Dermot Murnaghan	*Business Daily* / Newsreader (1989-1992)
Richard Whiteley	*Countdown Masters* (1989-1991)
David Roper	*Box Office* (1990-1992)
Caroline Righton	Newsreader (1991-1992)

THE BIG BREAKFAST (C4)   **1992-2002**

Channel 4 Management

Michael Grade	Chief Executive (1988-1997)
Michael Jackson	Chief Executive (1997-2001)
Mark Thompson	Chief Executive (2002-2004)*

Liz Forgan	Director of Programmes (1988-1993)
Tim Gardam	Director of Programmes (1998-2003)
Stuart Butterfield	Director of Sales and Marketing (1993-1997)
David Lloyd	Commissioning Editor, News and Current Affairs (1987-2003)
Michael Atwell	Commissioning Editor (1988-1993)
Danielle Lux	Controller of Entertainment (2001-2003)

Production Team

Bob Geldof	Co-founder, Planet 24 / Co-presenter (1992-1993)
Waheed Alli	Co-founder, Planet 24
Charlie Parsons	Co-founder, Planet 24 / Executive Producer (1992-2002)
Sebastian Scott	Editor (1992-1993) Executive Producer (1993-1995)
Ruth Wrigley	Editor (1992-1994) Executive Producer (1997-1998)
Ed Forsdick	Researcher, Producer (1992-1996) Executive Producer (1998-2000)
Bob Massie	Executive Producer (1995-1996)
Lisa Clark	Executive Producer (1996-1997)
Duncan Gray	Executive Producer (1997-1998)
Richard Hopkins	Executive Producer (2000-2001)
Ben Rigden	Executive Producer (2001-2002)

Presenters

Chris Evans	(1992-1994)
Gaby Roslin	(1992-1996)
Paula Yates	(1992-1995)
Mark Lamarr	(1992-1993)
Zig and Zag	(1992-1997)
Paul Ross	(1993-1995)
Keith Chegwin	(1993-1996)
Danny Baker	(1994)
Mark Little	(1994-1996)
Richard Orford	(1995-1998)
Lily Savage	(1995-1996)
Zoe Ball	(1996)
Sharron Davies	(1996-1997)
Rick Adams	(1996-1997)
Denise Van Outen	(1996-2001)
Vanessa Feltz	(1996-1997)
Johnny Vaughan	(1997-2001)
Kelly Brook	(1999)
Richard Bacon	(1999-2002)
Lisa Tarbuck	(1999-2000)
Paul Tonkinson	(2001)
Amanda Byram	(2001-2002)
Mike McLean	(2001-2002)

GMTV (ITV)   1993-

Management

Christopher Stoddart	Managing Director (1993-2001)
Lis Howell	Director of Programmes (1993)
Peter McHugh	Director of Programmes (1993-2004)*
Liam Hamilton	Editor (1993-1995)
Greg Dyke	Chairman (1993-1994)
David Mannion	Editor (1995-1996)
Martin Frizell	Editor (2000-2004)*
Paul Corley	Managing Director (2001-2004)*

Presenters

Michael Wilson	(1993-1994)
Fiona Armstrong	(1993)
Eamonn Holmes	(1993-2004)*
Anne Davies	(1993-2001)
Fiona Phillips	(1993-2004)*
Lorraine Kelly	(1993-2004)*
Mike Morris	(1993-1994)
Penny Smith	(1993-2004)*
Dr Hilary Jones	Contributor (1993-2004)*
Simon Parkin	Children's Presenter (1993-1996)
Mr Motivator	Fitness Expert (1993-1998)
Carmen Ejogo	Children's Presenter (1993-1996)
Anthea Turner	(1994-1996)
Alistair Stewart	(1994-2001)
Craig Doyle	Children's Presenter (1995-1997)
John Stapleton	(1998-2004)*
Kate Garraway	(2000-2004)*
Andrew Castle	(2000-2004)*

Other

Mike Hollingsworth	Founder, Daybreak TV
Christopher Bland	Chairman, LWT

BBC BREAKFAST (BBC1)   2000-

BBC Management

Greg Dyke	BBC Director-General (2000-2004)

Production Team

Andrew Thompson	Editor (2000-2001)
Richard Porter	Editor (2001-2004)*

Presenters

Jeremy Bowen	(2000-2002)
Sophie Raworth	(2000-2002)
Moira Stuart	Newsreader (2000-2004)*
Dermot Murnaghan	(2002-2004)*
Natasha Kaplinsky	(2002-2004)*

RISE (C4)   2002-2003

Channel 4 Management

Michael Jackson	Chief Executive (1997-2001)
Mark Thompson	Chief Executive (2002-2004)*
David Lloyd	Commissioning Editor, News and Current Affairs (1987-2003)
Tim Gardam	Director of Programmes (1998-2003)
Danielle Lux	Controller of Entertainment (2001-2003)

Production Team

Mark Sharman	BSkyB Director of Broadcasting and Production / Deputy Managing Director (2000-2003)
James Baker	BSkyB Head of Content and Creative Affairs (2000-2003) Controller, Sky One (2004)*
Sebastian Scott	Managing Director, Princess Productions* / Executive Producer (2002-2003)
Henrietta Conrad	Managing Director, Princess Productions (2002-2004)*
Mark Killick	Editor (2002)
Deborah Turness	Editor (2002)
Justin Gorman	Editor (2002-2003)

Presenters

Mark Durden-Smith	(2002)
Kirsty Gallacher	(2002)
Chris Rogers	(2002)
Edith Bowman	(2002-2003)
Liz Bonnin	(2002)
Colin Murray	(2002)
Henry Bonsu	(2002)
Iain Lee	(2003)
Mel Giedroyc	(2003)
Sue Perkins	(2003)
Kate Lawler	(2003)

IBA / ITC

Lady Plowden	Chairwoman (1975-1980)
Lord Thompson	Chairman (1981-1988)
George Russell	Chairman (1989-1996)

BIBLIOGRAPHY

Bough (Frank) *Frank Bough's Breakfast Book* (1984, Weidenfeld & Nicolson, London)

Briggs (Asa) & Joanna Spicer *The Franchise Affair* (1986, Century Press, London)

Cotton (Bill) *Double Bill: 80 Years Of Entertainment* (2000, Fourth Estate, London)

Davidson (Andrew) *Under The Hammer: The ITV Franchise Battle* (1992, Heinemann, London)

Day-Lewis (Sean) ed. *One Day In The Life Of Television* (1989, Grafton Books, London)

Donnelley (Paul) *TV Babylon* (1997, Vista Books, London)

Grade (Michael) *It Seemed Like A Good Idea At The Time* (2000, Pan Books, London)

Horrie (Chris) & Steve Clarke *Citizen Greg: The Extraordinary Story Of Greg Dyke And How He Captured The BBC* (2000, Simon & Schuster UK Ltd., London)

Leapman (Michael) *Treachery: The Power Struggle At TV-am* (1984, Allen & Unwin, London)

Leapman (Michael) *The Last Days Of The Beeb* (1986, Allen & Unwin, London)

Milne (Alasdair) *DG: The Memoirs Of A British Broadcaster* (1988, Hodder & Stoughton, London)

Rosenthal (Ruth) ed. *Inside BBC Television: A Year Behind The Camera* (1983, Webb & Bower, Exeter)

Turner (Anthea) *Fools Rush In* (2000, Little Brown And Company, London)

Broadcast
Daily Express
Daily Mirror
Daily Telegraph
Evening Standard
Guardian
Independent On Sunday
Listener

NME (New Musical Express)
Observer
Radio Times
Star
Sunday Express
Sunday Times
Televisual
TV Times

REFERENCES

All quotations are taken from interviews conducted specially for this book by the author, except:

CHAPTER ONE

"It's the last new thing in television..." *Inside BBC Television: A Year Behind The Camera*, ed. Ruth Rosenthal, 1983, Webb & Bower, p.141   11

"Your enemies will use it against you..." *The Last Days Of The Beeb*, Michael Leapman, 1986, Allen & Unwin, p.132   16

"We had a number of options..." *DG: The Memoirs Of A British Broadcaster*, Alasdair Milne, 1988, Hodder & Stoughton, p.68-69   17

"Put aside any preconceptions..."; *TV Times*, 29/1-4/2/83   21

"Breakfast TV will certainly get..."; ibid   21

"All the presenters have some say..." ibid   21

INDEX

IAN JONES writes on television for the acclaimed websites *Off The Telly* (*http://www.offthetelly.co.uk*) and *TV Cream* (*http://tv.cream.org*). His work has covered topics as diverse as *Nationwide*, *The Simpsons*, TV theme composers, the *Seven Up* series, *Treasure Hunt*, youth TV, Alan Bleasdale, *I, Claudius* and the history of Channel 4, and has received recommendations from, amongst others, the British Film Institute and the *Observer* newspaper. In 2000, he conceived and edited *Off The Telly*'s self-published project *TV24: British Television On March 9, 2000*, documenting and analysing an entire 24 hours of output on UK terrestrial television. In addition to being the editor of *TV Cream*'s weekly e-mail guide to digital television and radio, Ian has also contributed articles to *Scriptwriter* magazine and has participated in programmes on TV history for Granada Television and Channel 4.